3rd Workshop on South and Southeast Asian Natural Language Processing 2012

(SANLP)

Held at the 24th International Conference on Computational Linguistics (COLING 2012)

Mumbai, India
8 December 2012

Editors:

Virach Sornlertamvanich
Abbas Malik

ISBN: 978-1-62748-351-3

Printed from e-media with permission by:

Curran Associates, Inc.
57 Morehouse Lane
Red Hook, NY 12571

Some format issues inherent in the e-media version may also appear in this print version.

Printed by Curran Associates, Inc. (2013)

For permission requests, please contact the Association for Computational Linguistics at the address below.

Association for Computational Linguistics
209 N. Eighth Street
Stroudsburg, Pennsylvania 18360

Phone: 1-570-476-8006
Fax: 1-570-476-0860

acl@aclweb.org

Additional copies of this publication are available from:

Curran Associates, Inc.
57 Morehouse Lane
Red Hook, NY 12571 USA
Phone: 845-758-0400
Fax: 845-758-2634
Email: curran@proceedings.com
Web: www.proceedings.com

COLING 2012

24th International Conference on Computational Linguistics

Proceedings of the 3rd Workshop on South and Southeast Asian Natural Language Processing (SANLP)

Workshop chairs:
Virach Sornlertlamvanich and Abbas Malik

08 December 2012
Mumbai, India

Diamond sponsors

Tata Consultancy Services
Linguistic Data Consortium for Indian Languages (LDC-IL)

Gold Sponsors

Microsoft Research
Beijing Baidu Netcon Science Technology Co. Ltd.

Silver sponsors

IBM, India Private Limited
Crimson Interactive Pvt. Ltd.
Yahoo
Easy Transcription & Software Pvt. Ltd.

Introduction

Welcome to the 3rd Workshop on South and Southeast Asian Natural Language Processing (WSSANLP - 2012), a collocated event at COLING 2012, 8 - 15 December, 2012. South Asia comprises of the countries, Afghanistan, Bangladesh, Bhutan, India, Maldives, Nepal, Pakistan and Sri Lanka. Southeast Asia, on the other hand, consists of Brunei, Burma, Cambodia, East Timor, Indonesia, Laos, Malaysia, Philippines, Singapore, Thailand and Vietnam.

This area is the home to thousands of languages that belong to different language families like Indo-Aryan, Indo-Iranian, Dravidian, Sino-Tibetan, Austro-Asiatic, Kradai, Hmong-Mien, etc. In terms of population, South Asian and Southeast Asia represent 35 percent of the total population of the world which means as much as 2.5 billion speakers. Some of the languages of these regions have a large number of native speakers: Hindi (5th largest according to number of its native speakers), Bengali (6th), Punjabi (12th), Tamil(18th), Urdu (20th), etc.

As internet and electronic devices including PCs and hand held devices including mobile phones have spread far and wide in the region, it has become imperative to develop language technology for these languages. It is important for economic development as well as for social and individual progress.

A characteristic of these languages is that they are under-resourced. The words of these languages show rich variations in morphology. Moreover they are often heavily agglutinated and synthetic, making segmentation an important issue. The intellectual motivation for this workshop comes from the need to explore ways of harnessing the morphology of these languages for higher level processing. The task of morphology, however, in South and Southeast Asian Languages is intimately linked with segmentation for these languages.

The goal of WSSANLP is:

- Providing a platform to linguistic and NLP communities for sharing and discussing ideas and work on South and Southeast Asian languages and combining efforts.

- Development of useful and high quality computational resources for under resourced South and Southeast Asian languages.

We are delighted to present to you this volume of proceedings of the 3rd Workshop on South and Southeast Asian Natural Language Processing. We have received total 39 submission in the categories of long paper, short paper and demonstration. On the basis of our review process, we have competitively selected 9 long papers for oral presentations, 12 short papers for poster presentations and 2 demonstrations.

We look forward to an invigorating workshop.

Virach Sornlertlamvanich (Chair WSSANLP),
National Electronics and Computer Technology Center (NECTEC), Thailand

M.G. Abbas Malik (Chair of Organizing Committee WSSANLP),
Faculty of Computing and Information Technology (North Branch),
King Abdulaziz University, Saudi Arabia

Workshop Chair:

Virach Sornlertlamvanich (National Electronics and Computer Technology Center (NECTEC), Thailand

Workshop Organization Co-chair:

M. G. Abbas Malik (Faculty of Computing and Information Technology (North Branch), King Abdulaziz University, Saudi Arabia

Invited Speaker:

Christian Boitet (GETALP - LIG, University of Grenoble, France)

Organizers:

Aasim Ali (Punjab University College of Information Technology, University of the Punjab, Pakistan)
Amitava Das (Jadavpur Univeristy, India)
Smriti Singh (Indian Institute of Technology Bombay (IITB), India)

Program Committee:

Naveed Afzal (King Abdulaziz University, Saudi Arabia)
M. Waqas Anwar (COMSATS Institute of Information Technology, Pakistan)
Sivaji Bandyopadhyay (Jadavpur University, India)
Vincent Berment (GETALP-LIG / INALCO, France)
Laurent Besacier (GETALP-LIG, Université de Grenoble, France)
Pushpak Bhattacharyya (IIT Bombay, India)
Hervé Blanchon (GETALP-LIG, Université de Grenoble, France)
Christian Boitet (GETALP-LIG, Université de Grenoble, France)
Miriam Butt (University of Konstanz, Germany)
Eric Castelli (International Research Center MICA, Vietnam)
Amitava Das (Norwegian University of Science and Technology, Norway)
Choochart Haruechaiyasak (NECTEC, Thailand)
Sarmad Hussain
(Al-Khawarizmi Institute of Computer Science, University of Engineering and Technology, Pakistan)
Aravind K. Joshi (University of Pennsylvania, USA)
Abid Khan (University of Peshawar, Pakistan)
A. Kumaran (Microsoft Research, India)
Haizhou Liv (Institute for Infocomm Research, Singapore)
M. G. Abbas Malik (King Abdulaziz University - North Jeddah Branch, Saudi Arabia)
Bali Ranaivo-Malançon (Universiti Malaysia Sarawak, Malaysia)
Hammam Riza (Agency for the Assessment and Application of Technology (BPPT), Indonesia)
Rajeev Sangal (IIIT Hyderabad, India)
L. Sobha (AU-KBC Research Centre, Chennai, India)
Virach Sornlertlamvanich (National Electronics and Computer Technology Center (NECTEC), Thailand)
Sriram Venkatapathy (Xerox Research Center Europe, France)

Table of Contents

3rd Workshop on South and Southeast Asian Natural Language Processing (SANLP)

Program

Saturday, December 8, 2012

	WSSANLP Session I
9:30–9:50	Opening Remarks
9:50–10:50	Invited Talk by Christian Boitet
10:50–11:15	*Computational evidence that Hindi and Urdu share a grammar but not the lexicon* K.V.S Prasad and Shafqat Mumtaz Virk
11:30–12:00	**Tea Break**
	WSSANLP Session II
12:00–12:25	*Semantic Relation Extraction from a Cultural Database* Canasai Kruengkrai, Virach Sornlertlamvanich, Watchira Buranasing and Thatsanee Charoenporn
12:25–12:50	*Bengali Question Classification: Towards Developing QA System* Somnath Banerjee and Sivaji Bandyopadhyay
12:50–13:15	*Morphological Analyzer for Kokborok* Khumbar Debbarma, Braja Gopal Patra, Dipankar Das and Sivaji Bandyopadhyay
12:15–13:40	*Comparing Different Criteria for Vietnamese Word Segmentation* Quy T. Nguyen, Ngan L.T. Nguyen and Yusuke Miyao
13:40–14:30	**Lunch Break**

Saturday, December 8, 2012 (continued)

	WSSANLP Session III
14:30–16:30	**Posters and Demonstrations**
	Using English Acoustic Models for Hindi Automatic Speech Recognition Anik Dey, Li Ying and Pascale Fung *Tagger Voting for Urdu* Bushra Jawaid and Ondřej Bojar *BIS Annotation Standards With Reference to Konkani Language* Madhavi Sardesai, Jyoti Pawar, Shantaram Walawalikar and Edna Vaz *Automatic Extraction of Compound Verbs from Bangla Corpora* Sibanshu Mukhopadhayay, Tirthankar Dasgupta, Manjira Sinha and Anupam Basu *Influences of particles on Vietnamese tonal Co-articulation* Thi Lan Nguyen and Do Dat Tran *Toward an amazigh language processing* Fatima Zahra Nejme, Siham Boulaknadel and Driss Aboutajdine *Bidirectional Bengali Script and Meetei Mayek Transliteration of Web Based Manipuri News Corpus* Thoudam Doren Singh *Rule-based Machine Translation between Indonesian and Malaysian* Raymond Hendy Susanto, Septina Dian Larasati and Francis M. Tyers *Building Multilingual Search Index using open source framework* Arjun Atreya, Swapnil Chaudhari, Ganesh Ramakrishnan and Pushpak Bhattacharyya *Automatic Searching for English-Vietnamese Documents on the Internet* Quoc Hung Ngo *Error tracking in search engine development* Swapnil Chaudhari, Arjun Atreya, Ganesh Ramakrishnan and Pushpak Bhattacharyya *An Efficient Database Design for IndoWordNet Development Using Hybrid Approach* Venkatesh Prabhu, Shilpa Desai, Hanumant Redkar, Neha Prabhugaonkar, Apurva Nagvenkar and Ramdas Karmali *IndoWordNet Application Programming Interfaces* Neha Prabhugaonkar, Apurva Nagvenkar and Ramdas Karmali
16:30–17:00	**Tea Break**
	WSSANLP Session IV
17:00–17:25	*A Light Weight Stemmer for Urdu Language: A Scarce Resourced Language* Sajjad Ahmad Khan, Waqas Anwar, Usama Ijaz Bajwa and Xuan Wang
17:25–17:50	*Morpheme Segmentation for Kannada Standing on the Shoulder of Giants* Suma Bhat
17:50–18:15	*Manipuri Morpheme Identification* Kishorjit Nongmeikapam, Vidya Raj RK, Nirmal Y and Sivaji B
18:15–18:40	*Domain Based Classification of Punjabi Text Documents using Ontology and Hybrid Based Approach* Nidhi Krail, Vishal Gupta
18:40–19:00	Closing Remarks

Computational evidence that Hindi and Urdu share a grammar but not the lexicon

K. V. S. Prasad[1] and Shafqat Mumtaz Virk[2]
(1) Department of Computer Science, Chalmers University, Sweden
(2) Department of Computer Science and Engineering,University of Gothenburg, Sweden
and Department of Computer Science and Engineering UET, Lahore
prasad@chalmers.se, virk.shafqat@gmail.com

Abstract

Hindi and Urdu share a grammar and a basic vocabulary, but are often mutually unintelligible because they use different words in higher registers and sometimes even in quite ordinary situations. We report computational translation evidence of this unusual relationship (it differs from the usual pattern, that related languages share the advanced vocabulary and differ in the basics). We took a GF resource grammar for Urdu and adapted it mechanically for Hindi, changing essentially only the script (Urdu is written in Perso-Arabic, and Hindi in Devanagari) and the lexicon where needed. In evaluation, the Urdu grammar and its Hindi twin either both correctly translated an English sentence, or failed in exactly the same grammatical way, thus confirming computationally that Hindi andUrdu share a grammar. But the evaluation also found that the Hindi and Urdu lexicons differed in 18% of the basic words, in 31% of tourist phrases, and in 92% of school mathematics terms.

Keywords: Grammatical Framework, Resource Grammars, Application Grammars.

1 Background facts about Hindi and Urdu

Hindi is the national language of India and Urdu that of Pakistan, though neither is the native language of a majority in its country.

'Hindi' is a very loose term covering widely varying dialects. In this wide sense, Hindi has 422 million speakers according to (Census-India, 2001). This census also gives the number of native speakers of 'Standard Hindi' as 258 million. Official Hindi now tends to be Sanskritised, but Hindi has borrowed from both Sanskrit and Perso-Arabic, giving it multiple forms, and making Standard Hindi hard to define. To complete the 'national language' picture, note that Hindi is not understood in several parts of India (Agnihotri, 2007), and that it competes with English as lingua franca.

It is easier, for several reasons, to talk of standard Urdu, given as the native language of 51 million in India by (Census-India, 2001), and as that of 10 million in Pakistan by (Census-Pakistan, 1998). Urdu has always drawn its advanced vocabulary only from Perso-Arabic, and does not have the same form problem as Hindi. It is the official language and lingua franca of Pakistan, a nation now of 180 million, though we note that Urdu's domination too is contested, indeed resented in parts of the country (Sarwat, 2006).

Hindi and Urdu 'share the same grammar and most of the basic vocabulary of everyday speech' (Flagship, 2012). This common base is recognized, and known variously as 'Hindustani' or 'Bazaar language' (Chand, 1944; Naim, 1999). But, 'for attitudinal reasons, it has not been given any status in Indian or Pakistani society' (Kachru 2006). Hindi-Urdu is the fourth or fifth largest language in the world (after English, Mandarin, Spanish and perhaps Arabic), and is widely spoken by the South Asian diaspora in North America, Europe and South Africa.

1.1 History: Hindustani, Urdu, Hindi

From the 14th century on, a language known as Hindustani developed by assimilating into Khari Boli, a dialect of the Delhi region, some of the Perso-Arabic vocabulary of invaders. Urdu evolved from Hindustani by further copious borrowing from Persian and some Arabic, and is written using the Perso-Arabic alphabet. It dates from the late 18th century. Hindi, from the late 19th century, also evolved from Hindustani, but by borrowing from Sanskrit. It is written in a variant of the Devanagari script used for Sanskrit.

But the Hindi/Urdu has base retained its character: 'the common spoken variety of both Hindi and Urdu is close to Hindustani, i.e., devoid of heavy borrowings from either Sanskrit or Perso-Arabic' (Kachru, 2006).

1.2 One language or two?

Hindi and Urdu are 'one language, two scripts', according to a slogan over the newspaper article (Joshi, 2012). The lexicons show that neither Hindi nor Urdu satisfies that slogan. Hindustani does, by definition, but is limited to the shared part of the divergent lexicons of Hindi and Urdu.

(Flagship, 2012) recognizes greater divergence: it says Hindi and Urdu 'have developed as two separate languages in terms of script, higher vocabulary, and cultural ambiance'. Gopi Chand Narang, in his preface to (Schmidt, 2004) stresses the lexical aspect: 'both

Hindi and Urdu share the same Indic base ... but at the lexical level they have borrowed so extensively from different sources (Urdu from Arabic and Persian, and Hindi from Sanskrit) that in actual practice and usage each has developed into an individual language'.

But lexical differences are not quite the whole story. (Naim, 1999) lists several subtle morphological differences between Hindi and Urdu, and some quite marked phonological ones. Most Hindi speakers cannot pronounce the Urdu sounds that occur in Perso-Arabic loan words: `q` (unvoiced uvular plosive), `x` (unvoiced velar fricative), `G` (voiced velar fricative), and some final consonant clusters, while Urdu speakers replace the ṇ (retroflex nasal) of Hindi by `n`, and have trouble with many Hindi consonant clusters.

Naim does not think it helps learners to begin with Hindi and Urdu together. Those who seek a command of the written language, he says, might as well learn the conventions exclusive to Urdu from the beginning.

Thus there are many learned and differing views on whether Hindi and Urdu are one or two languages, but nothing has been computationally proved, to the best of our knowledge. Our work demonstrates computationally that Hindi and Urdu share a grammar, but that the lexicons diverge hugely beyond the basic and general registers. Our as yet first experiments already give preliminary estimates to questions like 'How much do Hindi and Urdu differ in the lexicons?'.

Overview Section 2 describes Grammatical Framework, the tool used in this experiment, and Section 3 lists what we report. Section 4 describes the Hindi and Urdu resource grammars, some differences between them, and how we cope with these differences. Section 5 presents the general and domain-specific lexicons used in this experiment. Evaluation results are given at the ends of Sections 4 and 5. Section 6 provides context and wraps up.

This paper uses an IPA style alphabet, with the usual values and conventions. Retroflexed sounds are written with a dot under the letter; ṭ, ḍ, and ṛ (a flap) are common to Hindi and Urdu, while ṇ and ṣ occur in Sanskritised Hindi (though many dialects pronounce them `n` and š). The palatalised spirant š and aspirated stops, shown thus: k^h, are common to Hindi and Urdu. A macron over a vowel denotes a long vowel, and ˜, nasalisation. In Hindi and Urdu, `e` and `o` are always long, so the macron is dropped. Finally, we use ñ to mean the nasal homorganic with the following consonant.

2 Background: Grammatical Framework (GF)

GF (Ranta, 2004) is a grammar formalisim tool based on Martin Löf's (Martin-Löf, 1982) type theory. It has been used to develop multilingual grammars that can be used for translation. These translations are not usually for arbitrary sentences, but for those restricted to a specific domain, such as tourist phrases or school mathematics.

2.1 Resource and Application Grammars in GF

The sublanguages of English or Hindi, say, that deal with these specific domains are described respectively by the (English or Hindi) *application grammars* Phrasebook (Caprotti et al 2010, (Ranta et al., 2012) and MGL (Saludes and Xambó, 2010). But the English Phrasebook and English MGL share the underlying English (similarly for Hindi). The underlying English (or Hindi) syntax, morphology, predication, modification, quantification, etc., are captured in a common general-purpose module called a *resource grammar*.

Resource grammars are therefore provided as software libraries, and there are currently resource grammars for more than twenty five languages in the GF resource grammar library (Ranta, 2009). Developing a resource grammar requires both GF expertise and knowledge of the language. Application grammars require domain expertise, but are free of the general complexities of formulating things in English or Hindi. One might say that the resource grammar describes how to speak the language, while the application grammar describes what there is to say in the particular application domain.

2.2 Abstract and Concrete Syntax

Every GF grammar has two levels: abstract syntax and concrete syntax. Here is an example from Phrasebook.

1. Abstract sentence:
   `PQuestion (HowFarFrom (ThePlace Station)(ThePlace Airport))`
2. `Concrete English sentence: How far is the airport from the station?`
3. `Concrete Hindustani sentence: sṭešan se havāī aḍḍā kitnī dūr hæ?`
   (स्टेशन से हवाई अड्डा कितनी दूर है? , اسٹیشن سے ہوائی اڈا کتنی دور ہے؟)
4. `Hindustani word order: station from air port how-much far is?`

The abstract sentence is a tree built using functions applied to elements. These elements are built from categories such as questions, places, and distances. The concrete syntax for Hindi, say, defines a mapping from the abstract syntax to the textual representation in Hindi. That is, a concrete syntax gives rules to linearize the trees of the abstract syntax.

Examples from MGL would have different abstract functions and elements. In general, the abstract syntax specifies what categories and functions are available, thus giving language independent semantic constructions.

Separating the tree building rules (abstract syntax) from the linearization rules (concrete syntax) makes it possible to have multiple concrete syntaxes for one abstract. This makes it possible to parse text in one language and output it in any of the other languages.

Compare the above tree with the resource grammar abstract tree for "How far is the airport from the station?" to see the difference between resource and application grammars:

```
PhrUtt NoPConj (UttQS (UseQCl (TTAnt TPres ASimul) PPos (QuestIComp (CompIAdv
(AdvIAdv how_IAdv far_Adv))(DetCN (DetQuant DefArt NumSg) (AdvCN (UseN
airport_N)(PrepNP from_Prep (DetCN(DetQuant DefArt NumSg)(UseNstation_N))
)))))NoVoc
```

3 What we did: build a Hindi GF grammar, compare Hindi/Urdu

We first developed a new grammar for Hindi in the Grammatical Framework (GF) (Ranta, 2011) using an already existing Urdu resource grammar (Virk et al., 2010). This new Hindi resource grammar is thus the first thing we report, though it is not in itself the focus of this paper.

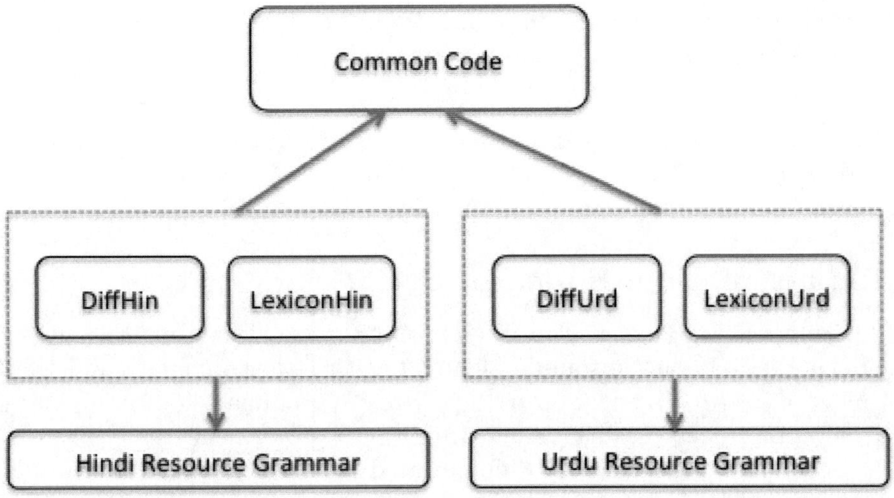

Figure 1: Hindi/Urdu Functor.

We used a functor style implementation to develop Hindi and Urdu resource grammars, which makes it possible to share commonalities between two grammars. Figure 1 gives a picture of this implementation style. Most of the syntactic code resides in the 'common code box', and the minor syntactical differences (discussed in Section 4) are placed in each of the 'DiffLang box'. Each resource grammar has its own lexicon. This mechanically proves that Hindi and Urdu share a grammar and differ almost only in the lexicons.

We evaluated our claim by (1) porting two application grammars to Hindi and Urdu: a Phrasebook of tourist sentences (Ranta et al., 2012), and MGL, a mathematical grammar library for school mathematics (Caprotti and Saludes, 2012), (2) randomly producing 80 abstract trees (40 from each of the Phrasebook, and MGL), (3) linearizing them to both Hindi and Urdu, and finally checking them either for correctness, or badness (see Section 6 for results).

4 Differences between Hindi and Urdu in the Resource Grammars

We started from the script based GF resource grammar for Urdu, and adapted it for Hindi almost entirely just by re-coding from Urdu to Hindi script. A basic test vocabulary accompanies the resource grammars, and this was changed as needed: it turned out that Hindi and Urdu differ up to 18% even in this basic vocabulary. Section 5 deals with the application lexicons.

We do not give any implementation details of these resource grammars in this paper, as the interesting bits have already been explained in (Virk et al., 2010). But we describe below resource level differences between Hindi/Urdu, and strategies to deal with them.

4.1 Morphology

Every GF resource grammar provides a basic test lexicon of 450 words, for which the morphology is programmed by special functions called lexical paradigms. Our Hindi morphology simply takes the existing Urdu morphology and re-codes it for the Devanagari script. Lexical differences mean that the morphologies are not identical; e.g., Hindi sometimes uses a simple word where Urdu has a compound word, or vice-versa. But there are no patterns that occur in only one of the languages, so the test lexicon for Hindi works with few problems.

We could in principle implement the subtle morphological differences noted in (Naim, 1999), but we ignored them. That these differences are minor is shown by the fact that our informants find the resulting Hindi entirely normal.

4.2 Internal Representation: Sound or Script?

The translation of "How far is the airport from the station?" was written in IPA, representing the sound of the Hindi/Urdu. It sounds identical in the two languages, and thus we could label it 'Hindustani'. An obvious approach to writing grammars for Hindi/Urdu from scratch would be to represent the languages internally by sound, so that we would get just one grammar, one shared lexicon, and differentiated lexicons only for those words that sound different in Hindi and Urdu. For output, we would then map the IPA to the Hindi or Urdu script.

But we were starting from (Virk et al., 2010), which uses an internal representation based on written Urdu. It would be a fair sized task to re-do this in terms of speech, though the result would then be immediately re-usable for Hindi and might also help capture similarities to other South Asian languages. We reserve this re-modelling for future work.

So, in the present work, we changed the Urdu grammar to a Hindi grammar merely by replacing written Urdu by written Hindi. This script change was also done for the basic lexicon, though here some words were indeed different even spoken. Our parallel grammars therefore give no indication that Hindi and Urdu often sound identical.

One compensating advantage is that script-based representations avoid spelling problems. Hindi-Urdu collapses several sound distinctions in Persian, Arabic and Sanskrit. A phonetic transcription would not show these collapsed distinctions, but the orthography does, because Urdu faithfully retains the spelling of the original Perso-Arabic words while representing Sanskrit words phonetically, while Hindi does the reverse. Each language is faithful to the sources that use the same script. We see that it will not be entirely trivial to mechanically go from a phonetic representation to a written one.

Obviously, the more the Hindi and Urdu lexicons overlap, the more the wasted effort in the parallel method. But as we shall see, the lexicons deviate from each other quite a bit. We have designed an augmented phonetic representation that keeps track of spelling, for use in a remodelled grammar.

4.3 Idiomatic, Gender and Orthographic Differences

In addition to spelling, Hindi and Urdu also have orthographic differences, not often remarked. Indeed some apparently grammatical differences result from in fact idiomatic, gender or orthographic differences.

For example, the lexicon might translate the verb "to add" as "`joṛnā`" in Hindi, and as "`jame karnā`" in Urdu. The imperative sentence "add 2 to 3" would then be rendered "`do ko tīn se joṛo`" in Hindi, and "`do ko tīn mẽ jame karo`" in Urdu. But the choice between the post-positions "`se`" and "`mẽ`" is determined not by different grammars for Hindi and Urdu, but by the post-positional idiom of the chosen verb, "`joṛnā`" or "`jame karnā`", as can be seen because either sentence works in either language.

A gender difference appears with "war", rendered in Urdu as "`laṛāī`" (fem.). This word works in Hindi as well, but has more a connotation of "battle", so we chose instead "`sañgʰarṣ`" (masc.). The shift from feminine to masculine is driven by the choice of word, not language.

Orthographic differences next. "He will go" is "`vo jāegā`" in both languages; in writing, (वह जाएगा, وہ جائے گا), the final "`gā`" (गा, گا) is written as a separate word in Urdu but not in Hindi. Similarly, "we drank tea" is "`hamne cāy pī`" in both languages, but in writing, (हमने चाय पी, ہم نے چائے پی), the particle "`ne`" (ने, نے) is written as a separate word in Urdu but not in Hindi.

These differences were handled by a small variant in the code, shown below. To generate the future tense for Urdu, the predicate is broken into two parts: finite (fin) and infinite (inf). The inf part stores the actual verb phrase (here "`jāe`"), and the fin part stores the copula "`gā`" as shown below.

```
VPFut=>fin=(vp.s!  VPTense VPFutr agr).fin; inf=(vp.s!  VPTense
VPFutr agr).inf
```

For Hindi, these two parts are glued to each other to make them one word. This word is then stored in the inf part of the predicate and the fin part is left blank as shown below.

```
VPFut=>fin=[]; inf=Prelude.glue ((vp.s! VPTense VPFutr agr).inf)
((vp.s! VPTense VPFutr agr).fin)
```

Similarly in the ergative "`hamne cāy pī`" ("we drank tea"), Urdu treats "`ham`" and "`ne`" as separate words, while Hindi makes them one. We used for Urdu, `NPErg => ppf ! Obl ++ "ne"` and for Hindi, `NPErg => glue (ppf ! Obl) "ne"`.

4.4 Evaluation and Results

With external informants

As described earlier, we randomly generated 80 abstract trees (40 from each of the Phrasebook, and MGL), linearized them to both Hindi and Urdu. These linearizations were then given to three independent informants.

They evaluated the Hindi and Urdu translations generated by our grammars. The informants found 45 sentences to be correct in both Hindi and Urdu. The other sentences were found understandable but failed grammatically - in exactly the same way in both Hindi and Urdu: nothing the informants reported could be traced to a grammatical difference between Hindi and Urdu. For this paper, the point is that all 80 sentences, the badly translated as well as the correctly translated, offer mechanical confirmation that Hindi and Urdu share a grammar.

We note for the record that the 35 grammatical failures give a wrong impression that the grammar is only "45/80" correct. In fact the grammar is much better: there are only a handful of distinct known constructs that need to be fixed, such as placement of negation and question words, but these turn up repeatedly in the evaluation sentences.

A result that has not been the focus of this paper is that we greatly improved the Urdu grammar of (Virk et al., 2010) while developing the Hindi variant. Errors remain, as noted above.

With internal informants

The second author is a native Urdu speaker, while the first speaks Hindi, though not as a native. With ourselves as internal informants, we could rapidly conduct several more extensive informal evaluations. We looked at 300 Phrasebook sentences, 100 MGL sentences, and 100 sentences generated directly from the resource grammars. We can confirm that for all of these 500 English sentences, the corresponding Urdu and Hindi translations were understandable and in conformance with Urdu and Hindi grammar (barring the known errors noted by the external informants).

We note particularly that randomly generated MGL sentences can be extremely involuted, and that the Hindi and Urdu translations had the same structure in every case.

5 The Lexicons

As we noted in Section 1, Urdu has a standard form, but Hindi does not, though official Hindi increasingly tends to a Sanskritised form. Hindustani itself counts as 'Hindi', and is a neutral form, but has only basic vocabulary, a complaint already made in (Chand, 1944). So to go beyond this, Hindi speakers have to choose between one of the higher forms. Elementary mathematics, for example, can be done in Hindustani or in Sanskritised Hindi, attested by the NCERT books (NCERT, 2012), or in English-ised Hindi, which can be heard at any high school or university in the Hindi speaking regions.

We arbitrated the choice of Hindi words thus: when we had sources, such as the NCERT mathematics books or a government phrase book, we used those. Otherwise, we used (Snell and Weightman, 2003) and (Hindi-WordNet, 2012) to pick the most popular choices.

5.1 The general lexicon

Out of 350 entries, our Hindi and Urdu lexicons use the same word in 287 entries, a fraction of 6/7 which can easily be changed by accepting more Urdu words as Hindi' or by avoiding them. We note in passing that the general lexicon is any case often tricky to translate to Hindi-Urdu, as the cultural ambience is different from the European one where GF started, and which the test lexicon reflects. Many words ("cousin", "wine", etc.) have no satisfactory single equivalents, but these lexical items still help to check that the grammars work.

5.2 The Phrasebook lexicon

This lexicon has 134 entries, split into 112 words and 22 greetings. For 92 of the words, the Hindi and Urdu entries are the same; these include 42 borrowings from English for names for currencies, (European) countries and nationalities,and words like "tram" and "bus". So Hindi and Urdu share 50 of 70 native words, but differ on 20, including days of the week (except Monday, "`somvār`" in both Hindi and Urdu). The greetings lexicon has 22 entries, most of which are hard to translate. “Good morning” etc. can be translated though they are often just “hello” and “bye”. Greetings are clearly more culture dependent: Hindi and Urdu differ in 17 places.

An example not in the Phrasebook drives home the point about greetings: airport announcements beginning “Passengers are requested ...” are rendered in Hindi as “`yātriyõ se nivedan hæ` ...” (यात्रियों से निवेदान है) and in Urdu as “`musāfirõ se guza:riš kī jātī hæ` ...” (مسافروں سے گزارش کی جاتی ہے), which suggests that Hindi and Urdu have diverged even in situations almost tailored for ‘Bazaar Hindustani’!

5.3 The Mathematics lexicon

Our MGL lexicon, for use with high school mathematics, has 260 entries. Hindi and Urdu differ on 245 of these. The overlapping 15 include function words used in a technical mathematical sense, “such that”, “where”, and so on.

As examples of the others, here are some English words with their Hindi and Urdu equivalents in parentheses: perpendicular (`lañb` लंब, `amūd` عمود), right-angled (`samkoṇ` समकोण, `qāyam zāvī` قائم زاوی), triangle (`trib`^{h}`uj` त्रिभुज, `mašallaš` مثلث), hypotenuse (`karṇ` कर्ण , `vitar` وتر), vertex (`šīrṣ` शीर्ष, `rās` راس).

This total divergence comes about because Urdu borrows mathematical terms only from Perso-Arabic, and Hindi, only from Sanskrit. There would be more overlap in primary school, where Hindi uses more Hindustani words, but the divergence is already complete by Class 6. The parallel English, Hindi and Urdu texts (NCERT, 2012), from which we got the list above, show that the grammar of the Hindi and Urdu sentences continue to be identical modulo lexical changes, even when the lexicons themselves diverge totally.

Since it often happens in mathematics that every Hindi content word is different from its Urdu counterpart, the languages are mutually unintelligible. Even function words can differ. Either “`yadi`” or “`agar`” can mean “if” in Hindi, but the Sanskrit “`yadi`” is often chosen for reasons of stylistic unity with the Sanskrit vocabulary. Urdu never uses “`yadi`”.

5.3.1 More on Hindi mathematical terms

Our Hindi words were taken mostly from the NCERT books, which particularly in the later classes use Sanskritised Hindi. They make good use of the regular word-building capacity of Sanskrit. For example, “to add” is “`joṛnā`” in the lower classes, but “addition” becomes “`yog`” in the higher classes. This allows constructs like (`yogātmak`, additive), which is like (`guṇātmak`, multiplicative), (`b`^{h}`āgātmak`, divisive) and so on.

One might think the NCERT books overly Sanskritised, but it is hard to find other solutions, short of massive code switching between English and Hindi. NCERT books are widely used all over India. We have no sales figures for the NCERT mathematics books in Hindi, but there are not many widely available alternatives. If Hindi is to become a language for mathematics, these books might be a major lexical source.

5.4 Contrast: the converging lexicons of Telugu/Kannada

Hindi and Urdu make a very unusual pair, agreeing so completely at the base and diverging so much immediately after. Related languages usually go the other way. An example is the pair Telugu/Kannada, two South Indian languages.

Telugu/Kannada do not share a base lexicon, and so are mutually unintelligible for everyday use, unlike Hindi/Urdu.

But at higher registers, where Hindi/Urdu diverge, Telugu/Kannada converge. So where a Hindi speaker listening to technical Urdu would understand the grammar but not the content words, the Telugu speaker listening to technical Kannada would recognise all the content words but not the grammar.

For mathematics, Telugu/Kannada use a Sanskrit-based lexicon essentially identical to that of Hindi. We do not list the exact Telugu and Kannada versions, but do note that the convergence Hindi-Telugu-Kannada would be improved by deliberate coordination. For completeness, we mention that a smaller part of the higher vocabulary, mostly administrative terms, is shared with Urdu.

Further,Telugu/Kannada are in fact grammatically close, so a Telugu speaker who knows no Kannada would need only a brief reminder of grammar and a basic lexicon to read mathematics in Kannada—the mathematical terms would be familiar. A hypothetical "Scientific Kannada for Telugu Speakers" need only be a slim volume. It is the general reading in Kannada that would need a bigger lexicon. This parallels the situation of an English speaking scientist trying to read French—the scientific reading is easier!

But for a Hindi-speaking scientist trying to read Urdu, it is the everyday texts that are easier, not the scientific ones.

5.5 Summary of lexical study

Our figures suggest that everyday Hindi and Urdu share 82% of their vocabulary, but this number drops if we move to a specific domain: for tourist phrases, to 69%, and for very technical domains, such as mathematics, to a striking 8%.

An English speaker who knows no mathematics might hear mathematics in English as built of nonsense words that function recognizably as nouns, adjectives, verbs and so on. This is how mathematics in Urdu would sound to a Hindi speaking mathematician (and the other way around), even though Hindi and Urdu share a base lexicon and the grammar.

The mathematics lexicons of Hindi, Telugu and Kannada suggest that a Sanskrit based vocabulary makes a powerful link across India. That vocabulary also makes Urdu the odd language out amongst Indian languages, despite its close relation to Hindi.

6 Discussion

Our results confirm that Hindi and Urdu share a grammar, but differ so much in vocabulary (even for travel and primary school) that they are now different languages in any but the most basic situation. With the various linguistic, cultural and political factors obtaining in India and Pakistan, a good guess is that the languages will diverge further.

A regular Sanskrit base for Hindi technical terms would cement this divergence from Urdu, but would give Hindi a more usual convergent relationship with other Indian languages, differing at the everyday level but coming together at higher registers. Indeed this situation might argue for Sanskritised Hindi as a national language, because for non-native Indian speakers this may be easier to understand than Hindi with more Perso-Arabic words.

(Paauw, 2009) says "Indonesia, virtually alone among post-colonial nations, has been successful at promoting an indigenous language as its national language." Pakistan may have similarly solved its national language problem, with a parallel situation of Urdu being the native language of a minority. A difference is that Urdu already has rich lexical and word-building resources, whereas Bahasa Indonesia did not. So the *Istilah* committee has over the decades standardised hundreds of thousands of terms. India does not need that many new terms, since it too has a rich shared lexical resource in Sanskrit, one that moreover has tremendous word-building capacity. But a standardising committee may help, since often the same Sanskrit word is used in different ways in different Indian languages. A standard pan-Indian lexicon for technical terms would allow for ease of translation, and might spur the usabilty of all Indian languages for science and technology.

Future Work

We hope to develop our Phrasebook and MGL tools, aiming for practical use. We also need to fix the remaining errors in our grammars, to do with continuous tenses, word order for some questions and negations, and the translation of English articles. Fixing these might be non-trivial. We have stated two other goals, to rebuild our resource grammars on a phonetic basis, and to do a progressive mathematics lexicon. We have started work on this last, which we believe will show an increasing divergence between Hindi and Urdu as we go to higher classes. The NCERT books are available in both Hindi and Urdu, so we have a ready made source for the lexicons.

Currently, popular articles and TV programs that need advanced vocabulary (e.g., music competitions or political debates) in Hindi take the terms needed from English, Urdu and Sanskrit sources, though these elements sit uncomfortably together, at least as of now. More examples are worth studying.

Acknowledgements

We thank our informants Anurag Negi, Vinay Jethava, and Azam Sheikh Muhammad for their painstaking comments.

Our paper originally used French and English as an example of the usual relationship: shared technical vocabulary but differing everyday words. We thank one of our anonymous referees for pointing out that we should rather take a pair closer to home - they suggested Malay-Indonesian (Paauw, 2009), but we chose Telugu-Kannada both because the first author speaks these and because we can link them to Hindi via Sanskrit.

References

Agnihotri, R. K. (2007). *Hindi: An Essential Grammar.* London/New York: Routledge.

Caprotti, O. and Saludes, J. (2012). The gf mathematical grammar library. In *Conference on Intelligent Computer Mathematics /OpenMath Workshop.*

Census-India (2001). *Abstract of Speakers' Strength of Languages and Mother Tongues.* Government of India. `http://www.censusindia.gov.in/Census_Data_2001/Census_Data_Online/Language/Statement1.htm`.

Census-Pakistan (1998). *Population by Mother Tongue.* `http://www.census.gov.pk/MotherTongue.htm`.

Chand, T. (1944). *The problem of Hindustani. Allahabad: Indian Periodicals.* `www.columbia.edu/itc/mealac/pritchett/00fwp/sitemap.html`.

Flagship (2012). *Undergraduate program and resource center for Hindi-Urdu at the University of Texas at Austin.* `http://hindiurduflagship.org/about/two-languages-or-one/`.

Hindi-WordNet (2012). *Hindi Wordnet. 2012. Universal Word – Hindi Lexicon.* `http://www.cfilt.iitb.ac.in`.

Joshi, M. M. (2012). Save Urdu from narrow minded politics. *Bombay: The Times of India, 19 Jan 2012.*

Kachru, Y. (2006). *Hindi (London Oriental and African Language Library).* Philadelphia: John Benjamins Publ. Co.

Martin-Löf, P. (1982). Constructive mathematics and computer programming. In Cohen, Los, Pfeiffer, and Podewski, editors, *Logic, Methodology and Philosophy of Science VI*, pages 153–175. North-Holland, Amsterdam.

Naim, C. (1999). *Introductory Urdu, 2 volumes. Revised 3rd edition.* Chicago: University of Chicago.

NCERT (2012). *Mathematics textbooks (English and Hindi).* New Delhi: National Council for Educational Research and Training.

Paauw, S. (2009). One land, one nation, one language: An analysis of Indonesia's national language policy. *University of Rochester Working Papers in the Language Sciences*, 5(1):2–16.

Ranta, A. (2004). Grammatical Framework: A Type-Theoretical Grammar Formalism. *Journal of Functional Programming*, 14(2):145–189.

Ranta, A. (2009). The GF Resource Grammar Library. *Linguistics in Language Technology*, 2. `http://elanguage.net/journals/index.php/lilt/article/viewFile/214/158`.

Ranta, A. (2011). *Grammatical Framework: Programming with Multilingual Grammars.* CSLI Publications, Stanford. ISBN-10: 1-57586-626-9 (Paper), 1-57586-627-7 (Cloth).

Ranta, A., Détrez, G., and Enache, R. (2012). Controlled language for everyday use: the molto phrasebook. In *CNL 2012: Controlled Natural Language*, volume 7175 of *LNCS/LNAI*.

Saludes, J. and Xambó, S. (2010). MOLTO Mathematical Grammar Library. `http://www.molto-project.eu/node/1246`.

Sarwat, R. (2006). *Language Hybridization in Pakistan (PhD thesis).* Islamabad: National University of Modern Languages.

Schmidt, R. L. (2004). *Urdu: An Essential Grammar.* London/ New York: Routledge.

Snell, R. and Weightman, S. (2003). *Teach Yourself Hindi.* London: Hodder Education Group.

Virk, S. M., Humayoun, M., and Ranta, A. (2010). An open source Urdu resource grammar. In *Proceedings of the Eighth Workshop on Asian Language Resouces*, pages 153–160, Beijing, China. Coling 2010 Organizing Committee.

Semantic Relation Extraction from a Cultural Database

Canasai KRUENGKRAI Virach SORNLERTLAMVANICH
Watchira BURANASING Thatsanee CHAROENPORN
National Electronics and Computer Technology Center
Thailand Science Park, Klong Luang, Pathumthani 12120, Thailand
{canasai.kru,virach.sor,watchira.bur,thatsanee.cha}@nectec.or.th

ABSTRACT
Semantic relation extraction aims to extract relation instances from natural language texts. In this paper, we propose a semantic relation extraction approach based on simple relation templates that determine relation types and their arguments. We attempt to reduce semantic drift of the arguments by using named entity models as semantic constraints. Experimental results indicate that our approach is very promising. We successfully apply our approach to a cultural database and discover more than 18,000 relation instances with expected high accuracy.

KEYWORDS: semantic relation extraction, cultural database.

1 Introduction

In this paper, we are interested in extracting certain basic facts from a cultural database derived from the Thai Cultural Information Center website[1]. The size of this cultural database has gradually increased to around 80,000 records (from November 2010 to October 2012). Each record contains a number of fields describing a specific cultural object. Figure 1 shows an excerpt of the front-end web page of the record no. 35860, which is about the Mid-River Pagoda. The content includes four main components: (1) cover image and thumbnails, (2) title, (3) description and (4) domain. We need to extract facts (hereafter referred to as relation instances) from the description. One can view relation instances as formal meaning representations of corresponding texts. These relation instances are useful for question answering and other applications. Using this record as an example, we could extract a relation instance ISLOCATEDAT(เจดีย์กลางน้ำ, ตำบลปากน้ำ) from the first text segment:

เจดีย์กลางน้ำตั้งอยู่ที่ตำบลปากน้ำ
(The *Mid-River Pagoda* is located at *Tambon Paknam*)

Recent research in semantic relation extraction has shown the possibility to automatically find such relation instances. Some approaches rely on high-quality syntactic parsers. For example, DIRT (Lin and Pantel, 2001) and USP (Poon and Domingos, 2009) discover relation instances based on the outputs from dependency parsers. Such parsers and annotated training corpora are difficult to obtain in non-English languages. Pattern-based approaches (Agichtein and Gravano, 2000; Pantel and Pennacchiotti, 2006; Banko et al., 2007) seem to be more practical for languages with limited NLP resources. For example, TEXTRUNNER (Banko et al., 2007) can efficiently extract relation instances from a large-scale Web corpus with minimal supervision. It only requires a lightweight noun phrase chunker to identify relation arguments. More advanced approaches like SNE (Kok and Domingos, 2008), RESOLVER (Yates and Etzioni, 2009) and SHERLOCK (Schoenmackers et al., 2010) exploit the outputs of TEXTRUNNER for learning.

Our cultural database allows us to make two assumptions:

(A1) Each record belongs to only one main cultural domain.
(A2) Each record has only one subject of relations.

The assumption (A1) seems to hold for most of records. We adopt the assumption (A2) from (Hoffmann et al., 2010) that try to extract infobox-like relations from Wikipedia. Also, the assumption (A2) seems to hold for our data since the description provides the details about one cultural object whose name is expressed in the record title.

Based on the above two assumptions, we propose our strategy to semi-automatically extract relation instances from the cultural database. We focus on unary relation extraction similar to (Hoffmann et al., 2010; Chen et al., 2011). We assume that the subject of the relation is the record title.[2] Each relation remains only one argument to be extracted. We describe our relation templates (Section 2.1) and how to effectively find relation texts in a large database (Section 2.2). We use named entities to reduce semantic drift of the target arguments (Section 2.3). We examine the effect of the distances between the relation surfaces and the target arguments (Section 3.1) and provide preliminary results of our experiments (Section 3.2). The results indicate that our strategy of semantic relation extraction is very promising for real-world applications.

[1] http://m-culture.in.th/

[2] In Figure 1, although the surface words of the *Mid-River Pagoda* are slightly different ("พระเจดีย์กลางน้ำ" vs. "เจดีย์กลางน้ำ"), they convey the same meaning and this assumption still holds.

Figure 1: An excerpt of the front-end web page of the record about the Mid-River Pagoda.

Domain	**Relation**	**Surface**	**Argument**
Cultural attraction	ISLOCATEDAT	ตั้งอยู่ที่	LOC
	ISBUILTIN	สร้าง(ขึ้น)*ใน สร้าง(ขึ้น)*เมื่อ ตั้ง(ขึ้น)*เมื่อ	DATE
	ISBUILTBY	สร้าง(ขึ้น)*โดย ตั้ง(ขึ้น)*โดย	PER, ORG
	HASOLDNAME	เดิมชื่อ ชื่อเดิม	LOC, ORG
Cultural person	MARRIEDWITH	สมรสกับ	PER
	HASFATHERNAME	บิดาชื่อ	PER
	HASMOTHERNAME	มารดาชื่อ	PER
	HASOLDNAME	เดิมชื่อ ชื่อเดิม	PER
	HASBIRTHDATE	เกิด(เมื่อ)*	DATE
	BECOMEMONKIN	อุปสมบทเมื่อ	DATE
Cultural artifact	ISMADEBY	ผลิต(ขึ้น)*โดย ทำ(ขึ้น)*โดย ผลงานโดย	PER, ORG
	ISSOLDAT	จำหน่ายที่	LOC, ORG

Table 1: Our relation templates.

2 Approach

2.1 Designing relation templates

Table 1 shows our relation templates. There are five main cultural domains in the database, and each main cultural domain has several sub-domains. In our work, we focus on three cultural domains, including attraction, person and artifact, as shown in the first column. Based on these cultural domains, we expect that the subject of relations in each record (i.e., the record title) should be a place, a human or a man-made object, respectively. As a consequence, we can design a set of relations that correspond to the subject. For example, if the subject is a place, we may need to know *where* it is, *when* it was built and *who* built it. We can formally write these expressions by ISLOCATEDAT, ISBUILTIN and ISBUILTBY. The second column shows our relations that are associated with the subject domains. The third column shows relation surfaces used for searching relation texts in which arguments may co-occur. The word in parentheses with an asterisk indicates that it may or may not appear in the surface.

The answers to *where*, *when* and *who* questions are typically short and expressed in the form of noun phrases. Using noun phrases as relation arguments can lead to high recall but low precision. For example, the noun phrase occurring after the relation ISBUILTIN could be a place (*is built in the area of*...) or an expression of time (*is built in the year of*...). In our case, we expect the answer to be the expression of time, and hence returning the place is irrelevant. This issue can be thought of as semantic drift. Here, we attempt to reduce semantic drift of the target arguments by using named entities as semantic constraints. The forth column shows named entity types[3] associated with the subject domains and their relations.

2.2 Searching relation texts

Searching text segments containing a given relation surface (e.g., "สร้างโดย" (*is built by*)) in a large database is not a trivial task. Here, we use Apache Solr[4] for indexing and searching the database. Apache Solr works well with English and also has extensions for handling non-English languages. To process Thai text, one just enables ThaiWordFilterFactory module in schema.xml. This module invokes the Java BreakIterator and specifies the locale to Thai (TH). The Java BreakIterator uses a simple dictionary-based method, which does not tolerate word boundary ambiguities and unknown words. For example, the words "สร้าง" and "ก่อสร้าง" occur in the Java's system dictionary. Both convey the same meaning (*to build*). We can see that the first word is a part of the second word. However, these two words are indexed differently. This means if our query is "สร้าง", we cannot retrieve the records containing "ก่อสร้าง". In other words, the dictionary-based search returns results with high precision but low recall.

In our work, we process Thai text in lower units called character clusters. A character cluster functions as an inseparable unit which is larger than (or equal to) a character and smaller than (or equal to) a word. Once the character cluster is produced, it cannot be further divided into smaller units. For example, we can divide the word "ก่อสร้าง" into 5 character clusters like "ก่-อ-ส-ร้า-ง". As a result, if our query is "สร้าง", we can retrieve the records containing "ก่อสร้าง". We refer to (Theeramunkong et al., 2000) for more details about character cluster based indexing. In our work, we implement our own ThaiWordTokinizeFactory module and plug it into Apache Solr by replacing the default WhitespaceTokenizerFactory. Our character cluster generator class is based on the spelling rules described in (Kruengkrai et al., 2009).

In Thai, sentence boundary markers (e.g., a full stop) are not explicitly written. The white spaces placing among text segments can function as word, phrase, clause or sentence boundaries (see the "รายละเอียด" section in Figure 1 for example). To obtain a relation text, which is not too short (one text segment) or too long (a whole paragraph), we proceed as follows. After finding the position of the target relation surface, we look up at most $\pm$ 4 text segments to generate relation texts. This length should be enough for morphological analyzer and named entity recognizer.

2.3 Learning named entities

We control semantic drift of the target arguments using named entities. We build our named entity (NE) recognizer from an annotated corpus developed by (Theeramunkong et al., 2010). The origi-

[3] We use four main named entity types: PER = persons, ORG = organizations, LOC = locations, DATE = dates (expressions of time).

[4] http://lucene.apache.org/solr/

(I): word 1,2 grams + label bigrams $\langle w_j \rangle, j \in [-2, 2] \times y_0$ $\langle w_j, w_{j+1} \rangle, j \in [-2, 1] \times y_0$ $\langle y_{-1}, y_0 \rangle$	**(III): (II) + POS 3 grams** $\langle p_j, p_{j+1}, p_{j+2} \rangle, j \in [-2, 0] \times y_0$
(II): (I) + POS 1,2 grams $\langle p_j \rangle, j \in [-2, 2] \times y_0$ $\langle p_j, p_{j+1} \rangle, j \in [-2, 1] \times y_0$	**(IV): (III) + k-char prefixes/suffixes** $\langle P_k(w_0) \rangle, k \in [2, 3] \times y_0$ $\langle S_k(w_0) \rangle, k \in [2, 3] \times y_0$ $\langle P_k(w_0), S_k(w_0) \rangle, k \in [2, 3] \times y_0$

Table 2: Our NE features.

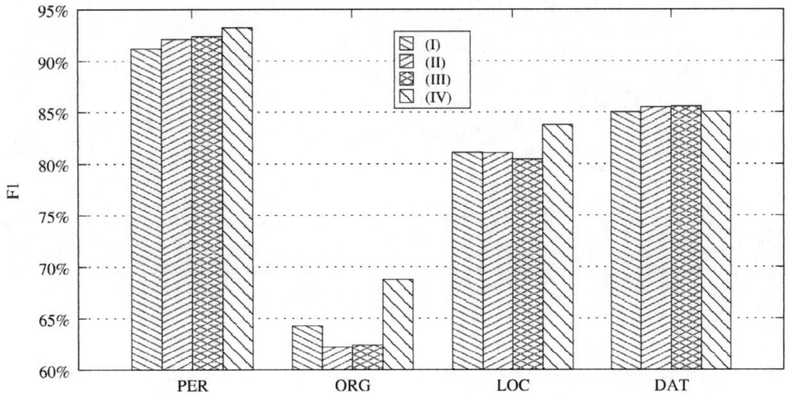

Figure 2: F1 results for our NE models.

nal contents are from several news websites. The corpus consists of 7 NE types. We focus on 4 NE types according to our relation templates in Table 1. Once we obtained the NE corpus, we checked it and found several issues as follows:

1. Each NE tag contains nested NE tags. For example, the person name tag contains the forename and surename tags.
2. The corpus does not provide gold word boundaries and POS tags.
3. Each NE type is annotated separately.

For the first issue, we ignored the nested NE tags and trained our model with top NE tags (PER, ORG, LOC, DATE). For the second issue, we used a state-of-the-art Thai morphological analyzer (Kruengkrai et al., 2009) to obtain word boundaries and POS tags. In this work, we trained the morphological analyzer using ORCHID corpus (Sornlertlamvanich et al., 1997) and TCL's lexicon[5] (Charoenporn et al., 2004). We then converted the corpus format into the IOB tagging style for NE tags. Thus, the final form of our corpus contains three columns (word, POS tag, NE tag), where the first two columns are automatically generated and of course contain a number of errors. For the third issue, we trained the model separately for each NE type. We obtained 33231, 20398, 8585, 2783 samples for PER, ORG, LOC, DATE, respectively.

To ensure that our NE models work properly, we split samples into 90%/10% training/test sets and conducted some experiments. We trained our NE models using k-best MIRA (Margin Infused Relaxed Algorithm) (Crammer et al., 2005). We set $k = 5$ and the number of training iterations to

[5]http://www.tcllab.org/tcllex/

Relation	Argument	Distance					
		0	1	2	3	4	5
Cultural attraction							
ISLOCATEDAT	LOC	356	574	591	624	678	757
ISBUILTIN	DATE	3825	11487	11538	11573	11633	11667
ISBUILTBY	PER, ORG	131	202	218	234	249	257
HASOLDNAME	LOC, ORG	0	9	21	26	27	29
Cultural person							
MARRIEDWITH	PER	132	177	177	177	177	177
HASFATHERNAME	PER	120	372	372	373	373	373
HASMOTHERNAME	PER	97	383	383	383	383	383
HASOLDNAME	PER	51	259	273	277	277	283
HASBIRTHDATE	DATE	4122	4745	4801	4947	4966	5075
BECOMEMONKIN	DATE	346	435	435	436	436	436
Cultural artifact							
ISMADEBY	PER, ORG	62	107	109	125	129	130
ISSOLDAT	LOC, ORG	31	31	56	59	62	64

Table 3: Numbers of relation instances when the distances are varied.

10. We denote the word by w, the k-character prefix and suffix of the word by $P_k(w)$ and $S_k(w)$, the POS tag by p and the NE tag by y. Table 2 summarizes all feature combinations used in our experiments. Our baseline features (I) include word unigrams/bigrams and NE tag bigrams. Since we obtained the word boundaries and POS tags automatically, we introduced them gradually to our features (II, III, IV) to observe their effects.

Figure 2 shows F1 results for our NE models. We used the `conlleval` script[6] for evaluation. We observe that PER is easy to identify, while ORG is difficult. Prefix/suffix features dramatically improve performance on ORG. Using all features (IV) gives best performance on PER (93.24%), ORG (68.75%) and LOC (83.78%), while slightly drops performance on DATE (85.06%). Thus, our final NE models used in relation extraction are based on all features (IV). Although these results are from the news domain, we could expect similar performance when applying the NE models to our cultural domains.

2.4 Summary

We summarize our strategy as follows. After selecting the subject domain, we send its relation surfaces (shown in the 3rd column of Table 1) to Apache Solr. We then trim the resulting record descriptions to obtain the relation texts (described in Section 2.2). Next, we perform word segmentation and POS tagging simultaneously using our morphological analyzer and feed the results into our NE models (described in Section 2.3). We invoke the appropriate NE model based on our relation templates (described in Section 2.1). Finally, our system produces outputs in the form of RELATION(a, b), where a is a record title, and b is an argument specified by its NE type in the templates.

[6] Available at http://www.cnts.ua.ac.be/conll2000/chunking/conlleval.txt.

Relation	Argument	# Samples	# Correct	# Incorrect	Accuracy
Cultural attraction					
ISLOCATEDAT	LOC	50	49	1	98%
ISBUILTIN	DATE	50	48	2	96%
ISBUILTBY	PER, ORG	50	48	2	96%
HASOLDNAME	LOC, ORG	27	23	4	85%
Cultural person					
MARRIEDWITH	PER	50	49	1	98%
HASFATHERNAME	PER	50	48	2	96%
HASMOTHERNAME	PER	50	49	1	98%
HASOLDNAME	PER	50	47	3	94%
HASBIRTHDATE	DATE	50	48	2	96%
BECOMEMONKIN	DATE	50	50	0	100%
Cultural artifact					
ISMADEBY	PER, ORG	50	44	6	88%
ISSOLDAT	LOC, ORG	50	49	1	98%

Table 4: Performance of our relation extraction.

3 Experiments

3.1 Effect of the distances between relation surfaces and arguments

In this section, we examine the number of extracted instances for each relation (without considering its accuracy). Our assumption is that the target argument tends to be relevant if it is adjacent (or close) to the relation surface. The relevance weakens with the distance. In our first example, the target argument "ตำบลปากน้ำ" (*Tambon Paknam*, a subdistrict name) is adjacent (distance = 0) to the relation surface "ตั้งอยู่ที่" (*is located at*). This target argument is relevant. Suppose there are intervening words[7] between them. The relevance tends to decrease. However, if we only select adjacent named entities to be the target arguments, the coverage may be limited. In our experiments, we varied the distances from 0 to 5 intervening words for observation.

Table 3 shows the numbers of relation instances when the distances are varied. For all relations, we observe that the numbers of relation instances do not significantly change after one word distance[8]. For example, we cannot extract more relation instances for MARRIEDWITH + PER, even we increased the distance. This indicates that using named entities helps to bound the number of possible arguments.

3.2 Preliminary results

To inspect the quality of relation instances extracted by our strategy, we randomly selected at most 50 instances of each relation for evaluation. Our evaluation procedure is as follows. Based on the assumptions (A1) and (A2), we expect that the subject (record title) of an instance should be relevant to its domain. We ignored instances whose subject is irrelevant. For example, the subject of the record no. 8026 is a person, but the volunteer assigned it to the cultural artifact domain. Note that this case rarely occurs, but exists. Next, a relation instance is considered to be correctly

[7]The intervening words include whitespace and punctuation tokens.

[8]This single word tends to be a whitespace token.

Record no.	Relation instance
	Cultural attraction
38481	ISLOCATEDAT(วัดโพธิ์ศรี, บ้านโพธิ์ศรี ต.อินทร์บุรี)
114585	ISBUILTIN(วัดเขาวงกฎ, ประมาณปี พ.ศ.2471-2573)
114333	ISBUILTBY(วัดปิตุลาธิราชรังสฤษฎิ์, กรมหลวงรักษ์รณเรศธ์)
61446	HASOLDNAME(วัดหนองกันเกรา, วัดหนองตะเกรา)
	Cultural person
14125	MARRIEDWITH(นายเนาวรัตน์ พงษ์ไพบูลย์, นางประคองกูล อิศรางกูร ณ อยุธยา)
32530	HASFATHERNAME(พระครูประยุตนวการ, นายเหยม เดชมาก)
45389	HASMOTHERNAME(หลวงพ่อลั้ง สุทสุสโน, นางพริ้ง แก้วแดง)
144574	HASOLDNAME(พระครูมงคลวรวัฒน์, สวัสดิ์ บุพศิริ)
145771	HASBIRTHDATE(อาจารย์ธนิสร์ ศรีกลิ่นดี, วันจันทร์ที่ 23 มกราคม 2494)
123678	BECOMEMONKIN(พระครูพิจิตรสิทธิคุณ, วันที่ ๑๖ เมษายน พ.ศ. ๒๕๒๘)
	Cultural artifact
160974	ISMADEBY(หนังสือประวัติคลองดำเนินสะดวก, พระครูสิริวรรณวิวัฒน์)
94286	ISSOLDAT(ข้าวเกรียบปากหม้อ, ตลาดเทศบาลพรานกระต่าย)

Table 5: Relation instances produced by our system.

extracted if its argument exactly matches the fact. For example, if our system only extracts the first name while the fact is the whole name, then we consider this instance to be incorrect. Finally, we set the maximum distance between the relation surface and its argument to 5. Table 4 shows the performance of our relation extraction. The overall results are surprisingly good, except those of HASOLDNAME and ISMADEBY. Table 5 shows some samples of relation instances produced by our system.

4 Related work

Named entity recognition has been applied to relation extraction. Hasegawa et al. (2004) propose an approach that discovers relations between two named entity types. Their approach clusters pairs of named entities using the similarity of context words intervening between them and assigns labels using frequent context words. In the Thai writing style, sentence boundary markers are absent, and subjects are often omitted. These two issues make it difficult to obtain two named entities in the same sentence. Our approach only considers one named entity and its preceding context words and uses simple templates to determine relation types.

Relation extraction can be simplified by focusing on unary relations. Hoffmann et al. (2010) present LUCHS, a self-supervised system that learns a large number of relation-specific extractors. Each extractor is trained according to an attribute of Wikipedia's infoboxes. Training data are created by matching attribute values with corresponding sentences. Their approach requires an article classifier to reduce the number of extractors to be invoked for prediction. The overall strategy fits well with Wikipedia data. Unfortunately, resources like infoboxes are not available in our data. Chen et al. (2011) propose an approach that learns relation types by using declarative constraints. The constraints capture regularities of relation expressions at various levels of linguistic structure, including lexical, syntactic, and discourse levels. To learn a model, their approach requires a constituent-parsed corpus, which is generated automatically using the Stanford parser (de Marneffe and Manning, 2008). Such a high-quality parser is difficult to obtain in languages with limited NLP corpora and tools like Thai.

5 Conclusion

We successfully applied our approach to a cultural database and could discover more than 18,000 relation instances with expected high accuracy. The outputs of our relation extraction can be useful for other applications such as question answering or suggesting related topics based on semantic relations.

In future work, we plan to extract more relations, especially in the cultural artifact domain. We are interested in some relations like ISMADEOF which requires the NE type like materials. However, this NE type is not available in the current NE corpus. We will explore other techniques to constrain the noun phrases to prevent the semantic drift problem.

References

Agichtein, E. and Gravano, L. (2000). Snowball: Extracting relations from large plain-text collections. In *In Proceedings of ICDL*, pages 85–94.

Banko, M., Cafarella, M. J., Soderl, S., Broadhead, M., and Etzioni, O. (2007). Open information extraction from the web. In *Proceedings of IJCAI*, pages 2670–2676.

Charoenporn, T., Kruengkrai, C., Sornlertlamvanich, V., and Isahara, H. (2004). Acquiring semantic information in the tcl's computational lexicon. In *Proceedings of the Fourth Workshop on Asia Language Resources*.

Chen, H., Benson, E., Naseem, T., and Barzilay, R. (2011). In-domain relation discovery with meta-constraints via posterior regularization. In *Proceedings of ACL-HLT*, pages 530–540.

Crammer, K., McDonald, R., and Pereira, F. (2005). Scalable large-margin online learning for structured classification. In *Proceedings of NIPS Workshop on Learning With Structured Outputs*.

de Marneffe, M.-C. and Manning, C. D. (2008). The stanford typed dependencies representation. In *Proceedings of the workshop on Cross-Framework and Cross-Domain Parser Evaluation*, pages 1–8.

Hasegawa, T., Sekine, S., and Grishman, R. (2004). Discovering relations among named entities from large corpora. In *Proceedings of ACL*.

Hoffmann, R., Zhang, C., and Weld, D. S. (2010). Learning 5000 relational extractors. In *In ACL*.

Kok, S. and Domingos, P. (2008). Extracting semantic networks from text via relational clustering. In *Proceedings of ECML-PKDD*, pages 624–639.

Kruengkrai, C., Uchimoto, K., Kazama, J., Torisawa, K., Isahara, H., and Jaruskulchai, C. (2009). A word and character-cluster hybrid model for thai word segmentation. In *Proceedings of InterBEST: Thai Word Segmentation Workshop*.

Lin, D. and Pantel, P. (2001). Dirt-discovery of inference rules from text. In *Proceedings of KDD*, pages 323–328.

Pantel, P. and Pennacchiotti, M. (2006). Espresso: leveraging generic patterns for automatically harvesting semantic relations. In *Proceedings of ACL*, pages 113–120.

Poon, H. and Domingos, P. (2009). Unsupervised semantic parsing. In *Proceedings of EMNLP*, pages 1–10.

Schoenmackers, S., Etzioni, O., Weld, D. S., and Davis, J. (2010). Learning first-order horn clauses from web text. In *Proceedings of EMNLP*, pages 1088–1098.

Sornlertlamvanich, V., Charoenporn, T., and Isahara, H. (1997). *ORCHID: Thai Part-Of-Speech Tagged Corpus*. Technical Report TR-NECTEC-1997-001, NECTEC.

Theeramunkong, T., Boriboon, M., Haruechaiyasak, C., Kittiphattanabawon, N., Kosawat, K., Onsuwan, C., Siriwat, I., Suwanapong, T., and Tongtep, N. (2010). Thai-nest: A framework for thai named entity tagging specification and tools. In *Proceedings of CILC*.

Theeramunkong, T., Sornlertlamvanich, V., Tanhermhong, T., and Chinnan, W. (2000). Character cluster based thai information retrieval. In *Proceedings of IRAL*, pages 75–80.

Yates, A. and Etzioni, O. (2009). Unsupervised methods for determining object and relation synonyms on the web. *Journal of Artificial Intelligence Research*.

Bengali Question Classification: Towards Developing QA System

Somnath Banerjee   Sivaji Bandyopadhyay
Department of Computer Science and Engineering
Jadavpur University, India
s.banerjee1980@gmail.com, sivaji_cse_ju@yahoo.com

ABSTRACT

This paper demonstrates the question classification step towards building a question answering system in Bengali. Bengali is an eastern Indo-Aryan language with about 230 million total speakers and one of the most spoken languages in the world. An important first step in developing a question answering system is to classify natural language question properly. In this work, we have studied suitable lexical, syntactic and semantic features to classify the Bengali question. As Bengali question classification is at early stage of development, so for simplicity we have proposed single-layer taxonomy which consists of only nine course-grained classes. We have also studied and categorized the interrogatives in Bengali language. The proposed automated classification work is based on various machine learning techniques. The baseline system based on Naïve Bayes classifier has achieved 80.65% accuracy. We have achieved up to 87.63% accuracy using decision tree classifier.

KEYWORDS : Bengali Question Classification, Question Classification, Machine Learning.

---

1 Introduction

Because of the high level of information overload on the Internet, research into question answering is becoming increasingly important. Question answering systems focus on how to respond to users' queries with exact answers. In recent years, many international question answering contests have been held at conferences and workshops, such as Text REtrieval Conference (TREC), Cross Language Evaluation Forum (CLEF) and NII Test Collection for IR Systems (NTCIR). Although Bengali is the sixth most spoken languages in the world, no QA contest in Bengali has been conducted so far.

Bengali (Bengali: বাংলা (Bangla)) is an eastern Indo-Aryan language. It is native to the region of eastern South Asia known as Bengal, which comprises present day Bangladesh, the Indian state of West Bengal, and parts of the Indian states of Tripura and Assam. Besides this region, there are also significant Bengali-speaking communities in: the Middle East (namely, UAE, Saudi Arabia, Bahrain, and Kuwait), Europe, North America, South-East Asia and Pakistan. It is written using the Bengali script. With about 193 million native and about 230 million total speakers, Bengali is one of the most spoken languages (ranked sixth[1]) in the world. The National song and the National anthem of India, and the National anthem of Bangladesh were composed in Bengali.

Along with other Eastern Indo-Aryan languages, Bengali evolved from the Magadhi Prakrit and Sanskrit languages. It is now the primary language spoken in Bangladesh and is the second most commonly spoken language in India. All the Indo-Aryan languages including Bengali, Hindi, Marathi, Gujrati are called the daughters of Sanskrit.

Question Classification (QC) is an important component of Question Answering System (QAS). The task of a question classifier is to assign one or more class labels, depending on classification strategy, to a given question written in natural language. For example for the question "What London street is the home of British journalism?", the task of question classification is to assign label "Location" to this question, since the answer to this question is a named entity of type "Location". Since we predict the type of the answer, question classification is also referred as answer type prediction. The set of predefined categories which are considered as question classes usually called question taxonomy or answer type taxonomy. Question classification has a key role in automated QA systems. Although different types of QA systems have different architectures, most of them follow a framework in which question classification plays an important role (Voorhees, 2001). Furthermore, it has been shown that the performance of question classification has significant influence on the overall performance of a QA system (Ittycheriah et. al., 2001; Hovy et. al., 2001; Moldovan et. al., 2003).

Basically there are two main motivations for question classification: locating the answer and choosing the search strategy. Knowing the question class not only reduces the search space need to find the answer, it can also find the true answer in a given set of candidate answers. For example, knowing that the class of the question "who was the president of U.S. in 1934?" is of type "human", the answering system should only consider the name entities in candidate passages which is of type "human" and does not need to test all phrases within a passage to see whether it can be an answer or not.

---

[1] http://en.wikipedia.org/wiki/Bengali_language

On the other hand, question class can also be used to choose the search strategy when the question is reformed to a query over information retrieval (IR) engine. For example, consider the question "What is a pyrotechnic display?". Identifying that the question class is "definition", the searching template for locating the answer can be for example "pyrotechnic display is a ..." or "pyrotechnic displays are ...", which are much better than simply searching by question words.

The remaining part of the paper is organized as follows- section 2 describes different approaches being used in question classification. Section 3 describes available language resources for Bengali language. Section 4 describes the various interrogatives present in Bengali questions. Section 5 describes taxonomies for question types. Section 6 explains the various features used in our work. Section 7 describes the classifiers used in the present work. Section 8 details the experiments conducted on our work and outlines the results. The last section concludes this work and its future work.

2 Related Work

A lot of researches on factoid question classification, question taxonomies, question features and question classifiers have been published continuously until now. Question classification in TREC QA has been intensively studied during the past decade. There are basically two different approaches used to classify questions- one is rule based and another is machine learning based. However, a number of researchers have also used some hybrid approaches which combine rule-based and machine learning based approaches (Huang et. al., 2008; Roy et. al., 2010; Silva et. al., 2011).

Rule based approaches used some manually handcrafted grammar rules to analyze the question to determine the answer type (Hull, 1999; Prager et. al., 1999). Though handcrafted rules have been used successfully for question classification, these approaches however, suffer from the need to define too many rules to determine specific types (Li et. al., 2004). Furthermore, while rule-based approaches may perform well on a particular dataset, they may have quite a poor performance on a new dataset and consequently it is difficult to scale them (Li et. al., 2004). So it is difficult to make a manual classifier with a limited amount of rules.

On the other hand, machine learning-based approaches perform the question classification by extracting some features from questions, train a classifier and predicting the question class using the trained classifier. Many successful learning-based classification approaches have been proposed. Many researchers have employed machine learning methods (e.g., maximum entropy and support vector machine) by using different features, such as syntactic features (Zhang et. al., 2003; Nguyen et. al., 2008) and semantic features (Moschitti et. al., 2007). However, these methods mainly focused on English factoid questions and confined themselves to classify a question into two or a few predefined categories (e.g., "what","how", "why", "when", "where" and so on).

There are also some notable studies that have used both rule-based and machine learning based approaches together. The most successful study (Silva et. al., 2011) that works on question classification, first match the questions with some pre-defined rules and then use the matched rules as features in the machine learning-based classifier. The same approach is used in the work by (Huang et. al., 2008). Machine learning-based and hybrid methods are the most successful approaches on question classification and most of the recent works are based on these approaches.

But in Bengali there is no such Question-Answering system available and this motivates us to classify questions for developing Bengali question-answering system in which user will pose a question in Bengali and also get answer in Bengali.

3 Overview of Language Resource

Compared to the question answering systems in English, because of the specificity on writing and grammar; and the lack of basic language processing resources Bengali question answering system is in development stage. Also, the availability of the experimentation corpus is very rare in the web.

Our classification work in Bengali uses Bengali Shallow Parser which is developed as part of the IL-ILMT Consortium[2]. The shallow parser gives the analysis of a sentence in terms of morphological analysis, POS tagging, Chunking, etc. Apart from the final output, intermediate output of individual modules is also available. All outputs are in Shakti Standard Format (SSF)[3].

4 Interrogatives in Bengali

People could determine the question type by the interrogative present in the question, such as the word 'why' in 'Why are you late?' describes that someone asks the reason. But not all questions type can be determined only by the interrogative. Bengali interrogatives not only describe important information about expected answer but also indicate the Number representations, i.e.- singular or plural.

Unlike English language there are many interrogatives present in the Bengali language. We have been classified it in three categories-

a) Simple Interrogative(SI) or Unit Interrogative(UI)

b) Dual Interrogative(DI)

c) Compound/Composite Interrogative(CI)

4.1 Simple Interrogatives or Unit Interrogatives

It is made up of a single interrogative word which can be considered an Interrogative unit. Further, a SI can be classified into two cases according to answer indication Number Representation. A SI can be indicating a Singular Answer (SA), Plural Answer (PA). If it indicates a SA then it is considered Singular Simple Interrogative (SSI) or Singular Unit Interrogative (SUI), otherwise it indicates a PA and it is considered Plural Single Interrogative (PSI). Sometimes SI indicates both (SA and PA) and sometimes it plays a neutral role. So, SI also can be considered as BSI (both) and NSI (neutral). Therefore, we have found four sub-categories of SI, i.e., SSI, PSI, BSI and NSI.

For example, SI/UI: কে('ke'), কারা ('kara'), কাদের ('kader'), কাহাকে ('kahake').

SSI/SUI: কে ('ke'), কাহাকে ('kahake') ;

PSI/PUI: কারা('kara'), কাদের('kader').

---

[2] http:// ltrc.iiit.ac.in/analyzer/bengali/

[3] http:// ltrc.iiit.ac.in/mtpil2012/Data/ssf-guide.pdf

BSI: কোন (*'kon'*), কত('koto'), কয়টি('koiti');

NSI:কিভাবে('kivabe'),কেন (keno).

4.2 Dual Interrogatives

Each dual interrogative (DI) is made up of using an SI/UI twice. But, all the SI/UI cannot be used to make DI. All the SSI/SUI can be used twice in a question to make DI.

For example,

DI: 'কে কে' ('ke ke'); using SSI কে ('ke')

DI: 'কার কার' ('kar kar'); using SSI কার ('kar')

DI: 'কি কি' ('ki ki'); using SSI কি ('ki')

Although a DI is consisting of one SSI twice, but each DI indicates Plural Answer (PA) only. So, কে('ke')indicates SA , but 'কে কে' ('ke ke') indicates PA. This implies that all DIs are implicitly PA.

4.3 Compound / Composite Interrogatives

Each compound interrogative (CI) is made up of using multiple Simple Interrogatives. As the CI is formed for getting multiple answers, so it is difficult to categorize it into SA or PA. Also, for this sort of questions simplification is needed. We have found only six CIs from corpus.

CI = { কে কবে, কারা কবে, কে কার, কবে কার, কে কখন, কে কোন }

Bengali Interrogatives are shown in Table-1.

Sl. No	Interrogative (Bengali)	Category	Number Representation
1	কে (ke)	SSI	Singular
2	কাকে (kake)	SSI	Singular
3	কাহাকে (kahake)	SSI	Singular
4	কে কে (ke ke)	PDI	Plural
5	কারা (kara)	PSI	Plural
6	কার (kar)	SSI	Singular
7	কার কার (kar kar)	DI	Plural

8	কাদের (kader)	PSI	Plural
9	কোন (kon)	BSI	Singular/Plural
10	কোন কোন (kon kon)	DI	Plural
11	কি (ki)	NSI	Neutral
12	কি কি (ki ki)	DI	Plural
13	কত (koto)	BSI	Singular/Plural
14	কয়টি (koiti)	BSI	Singular/Plural
15	কখন (kokhon)	NSI	Neutral
16	কোথায় (kothai)	NSI	Singular
17	কবে (kobe)	NSI	Neutral
18	কেন (keno)	NSI	Neutral
19	কিভাবে (kivabe)	NSI	Neutral
20	কেমন (kemon)	NSI	Neutral
21	কে কবে (ke kobe)	CI	Singular
22	কারা কবে (kara kobe)	CI	Plural
23	কে কখন (ke kokhon)	CI	Singular
24	কে কার (ke kar)	CI	Singular
25	কবে কার (kobe kar)	CI	Singular
26	কে কোন (ke kon)	CI	Singular

Table 1-Bengali Interrogatives

5 Question Type Taxonomies

The set of question categories (classes) are referred as question taxonomies or question ontology. Though different question taxonomies have been proposed in different works, but most of the recent learning-based and hybrid approaches are based on two layer taxonomy proposed by Li and Roth (Li et. al., 2002). This taxonomy consists of six course-grained classes and fifty fine-grained classes. The taxonomy proposed by Hermjakob (Hermjakob et al., 2002) consists of 180 classes which is the broadest question taxonomy proposed until now.

As Bengali question classification is at early stage of development, so for simplicity we used single-layer taxonomy for Bengali question type which consists of only eight course-grained classes and no fine-grained classes. Also, we do not consider two more classes namely list and yes-no-explain which have been introduced by Metzler and Croft (Metzler et. al., 2005). Table-2 lists this taxonomy.

Type	Description
PER	Person name i.e., name of human beings
ORG	Organization e.g., office, company etc.
LOC	Location related questions e.g., country , district, place etc.
TEM	Temporal e.g., date, time, year i.e., time related
NUM	Numerical e.g., statistical related questions
METH	Method e.g., procedure related questions
REA	Reason e.g., why related questions
DEF	Definition related questions
MISC	Miscellaneous ; river, mountain, hormone, bird, metal etc.

Table 2- Bengali Question Taxonomies

6 Features

In the task of question classification, there is always an important problem to decide the optimal set of features to train the classifiers. Different studies extracted various features with different approaches and the features in question classification task can be categorized into 3 different types: lexical, syntactical and semantic features (Loni, 2011). We also used three types of features used for question classification.

Loni and others (Loni et. al., 2011) also represented a question in question classification task similar to document representation in vector space model, i.e., a question is a vector which is described by the words inside it.

Therefore a question Q can be represented as:

$$Q = (W_1, W_2, \ldots, W_N)$$

Where,

W_I = frequency of term I in question Q;

N = total number of Term

Due to sparseness of feature vector only non-zero valued features are kept in feature vector. Therefore the size of samples is quite small despite the huge size of feature space. All lexical, syntactical and semantic features can be added to feature space and expand the above feature vector. The next subsections describe the features used for Bengali question classification.

6.1 Lexical Features

Lexical features of a question are generally extracted based on the context words of the question, i.e., the words which appear in a question. We have used five lexical features as below-

wh-word, *wh-word position* and *wh-type*: Question's *wh-word* or interrogative is one of the important lexical features and Huang (Huang et. al., 2008; Huang et. al., 2009) has shown that considering question *wh-words* as a feature can improve the performance of classification for English. As the free-word-order" nature of the Bengali language, the position of the wh-word has also been considered as another lexical feature. We considered the value of this feature according to the position {first, middle, last} in given question. We have also considered the interrogative type (*WH-type*) as another lexical feature.

Question length: (Blunsom et. al., 2006) introduced question's length as an important lexical feature which is simply the number of words in a question. We also considered this feature for Bengali classification.

End marker: End marker plays an important role in Bengali question classification that is either "?" or "।" in Bengali. If the end marker is "।", then it has been observed from the experimental corpus that the given question is definition question.

Word shape: Word shapes refer to apparent properties of single words. (Huang et. al., 2008) introduced five categories for word shapes: all digits, lower case, upper case, mixed and other. Word shapes alone is not a good feature set for question classification, but when they combined with other kind of features they usually improve the accuracy of classification(Huang et. al., 2008; Loni et. al., 2011). Capitalization feature is not present in Bengali; so we have considered the other three categories i.e., all digit, mixed and other.

Example: কে(*ke*) গৌড়(*goura*) প্রতিষ্ঠা(*protistha*) করেন(*Karen*) ?

Lexical features: *wh-word*: কে ; *wh-word position*: first ; *wh-type*: SSI; *question length*: 5; *end-marker*: ?

6.2 Syntactical Features

Different works extracted several syntactical features with different approaches. The most common syntactical features are Part of Speech (POS) tags and head words (Loni et. al., 2011).

POS tags: This indicate the part-of-speech tag of each word in a question such as NN (Noun), NP (Noun Phrase), VP (Verb Phrase), JJ (adjective), and etc.

We have added all POS tags of question in feature vector. Similar approach has been successfully used for English (Li and Roth, 2004; Blunsom et. al., 2006). This feature space sometimes referred as bag-of-pos tags. (Loni et. al., 2011) introduced a feature namely tagged unigram which is simply the unigrams augmented with pos tags. Considering the tagged unigrams instead of normal unigrams can help the classifier to distinguish a word with different tags as two different features (Loni et. al., 2011).

Head words: A head word is usually defined as the most informative word in a question or a word that specifies the object that question seeks (Huang et. al., 2008). Correctly identified headword can significantly improve the classification accuracy since it is the most informative word in the question. For example for the question "What is the oldest city in Canada?" the headword is "city". The word "city" in this question can highly contribute the classifier to classify this question as "LOC:city".

Extracting question's headword is quite a challenging problem and there is no research has been conducted so far for Bengali. But, we have considered three cases based on the position of question-word or interrogative in the question-

Case I: if *question-word* appears at beginning, then the first NP chunk after the question-word will be considered as head-word. For example-

কে(*ke*) গৌড়(*goura*) প্রতিষ্ঠা(*protistha*) করেন(*Karen*) ?

WQ NNP NN VM SYM

So, in the above example গৌড়(*goura*) is the head-word.

Case II: if the position of the *question-word* is in between of the question, then the immediate NP-chunk before the question-word will be considered as head-word. For example-

গৌড়(*goura*) কোথায়(*kothai*) অবস্হিত(*obosthita*) ?

NNP WQ JJ SYM

So, in the above example গৌড়(*goura*) is the head-word.

Case III: if *question-word* appears at last i.e., just before end marker, then the immediate NP-chunk before the question-word will be considered as head-word. For example-

বাংলাদেশে(*bangladeshe*) অর্থনীতি(*arthoniti*) কলেজ(*kolege*) কয়টি(*koiti*) ?

NNP (NN NN NN) WQ SYM

So, in the above example বাংলাদেশে(*bangladeshe*) অর্থনীতি(*arthoniti*) কলেজ(*kolege*) is the head-word

Now, if we consider the following example-

কে(*ke*) গৌড়(*goura*) প্রতিষ্ঠা(*protistha*) করেন(*Karen*) ?

Then, the syntactic features will be: [{WQ, 1}, {NNP, 1}, {NN, 1}, {VM, 1}]

6.3 Semantic Features

Semantic features can be extracted based on the semantic meaning of the words in a question. We have used *related word* and *named entities* as semantic features.

Related word: In the absence of Bengali WordNet a Bengali to Bengali dictionary[4] has been used to retrieve the related words. We have manually prepared three *related word* categories by analyzing the training data. The lists are as below-

date :{ জন্মদিন, জন্মতারিখ, দিন, দশক, ঘন্টা, সপ্তাহ, মাস, বছর... etc}

food :{ খাবার, মাছ, খাদ্য, মাখন, ফল, আলু, মিষ্টি, স্বাদ...etc}

human_authority :{নরপতি, রাজা, প্রধানমন্ত্রী, বিচারপতি, মহাপরিচালক, চেয়ারম্যান, জেনারেল, সুলতান, সম্রাট, মহাধ্যক্ষ...etc}

If a question word belongs to any category, then its category name will be added in the future vector.

কে(*ke*) গৌড়ের(*gourer*) স্বাধীন(swadhin) নরপতি(narapoti)[*human-authority*] ছিলেন(*chilen*) ?

For the above example the semantic feature can be added to the feature vector as: [{human-authority, 1}]

Named entities: Some studies (Li and Roth, 2004; Blunsom et. al., 2006) successfully used *named entities* as semantic feature. To identify the Bengali named entities in question text a Hidden Markov Model Based Named Entity Recognizer (NER) System (Ekbal et. al., 2007) has been used as Bengali NER system.

কে(*ke*) গৌড়(*goura*)[*Location*] প্রতিষ্ঠা(*protistha*) করেন(k*aren*) ?

For the above example the semantic feature can be added to the feature vector as: [{Location, 1}]

7 Classification Module

Though many supervised learning approaches have been proposed for question classification (Li et. al., 2002; Blunsom et. al., 2006; Huang et. al., 2008), but these approaches mainly differ in the classifier they use and the features they extract (Loni, 2011). We assume that a Bengali question is unambiguous, i.e., a question has only one class. So, we assign one label to a given question and can be described as follows-

C = {c1, c2, c3, c4, c5, c6, c7, c8};

Where, C is the set of possible classes

Q = {Q1, Q2, Q3… QN-1, QN};

Where, Q is the set of N given questions

The task of our question classifier is to assign the most likely class C_k to a question Q_m . Recent studies (Zhang et. al., 2003; Huang et. al., 2008; Silva et. al., 2011) also consider one label for one question.

---

4 http://dsal.uchicago.edu/dictionaries/biswas-bangala/

We have used Naive Bayes (NB), Kernel Naïve Bayes (KNB), Decision Tree (DT) and Rule Induction (RI) and DT has been performed the best among them.

7.1 Naïve Bayes (NB)

Naïve Bayes (NB) classifier is a simple probabilistic classifier based on applying Bayes' theorem with strong (naive) independence assumptions, i.e. assumes that the presence (or absence) of a particular feature of a class is unrelated to the presence (or absence) of any other feature, given the class variable.

Using the simplest assumption of a constant prior distribution, Bayes theorem leads to a straightforward relationship between conditional probabilities. Given a class label C with m classes, c_1, c_2, ..., cm, and an attribute vector x of all other attributes, the conditional probability of class label c_i can be expressed as follows:

$$P(C = c_i \mid x) = \frac{P(x \mid C = c_i)P(C = c_i)}{P(x)}$$

Where $P(C=c_i)$ is the probability of class label c_i and can be estimated from the data directly. The probability of a particular unknown sample, $P(x)$, does not have to be calculated because it does not depend on the class label and the class with highest probability can be determined without its knowledge.

7.2 Kernel Naïve Bayes (KNB)

Kernel Naïve Bayes classifier is modified version of NB classifier that uses estimated kernel density. Conditional probability $P(x \mid C = c_i)$ can be written as a kernel density estimate for class c_i

$$P(x \mid C = c_i) = f_i(x) \quad \text{And} \quad f_i(x) = \sum_{t=1}^{n} K_i(x, x_t);$$

Where, x_t are training points and $K_i(x,x_t)$ is a kernel function.

7.3 Rule Induction

Rule Induction (RI) learns a pruned set of rules with respect to the information gain. It works similar to the propositional rule learner named Repeated Incremental Pruning to Produce Error Reduction (RIPPER, Cohen 1995). Starting with the less prevalent classes, the algorithm iteratively grows and prunes rules until there are no positive examples left or the error rate is greater than 50%.

In the growing phase, for each rule greedily conditions are added to the rule until the rule is perfect (i.e. 100% accurate). The procedure tries every possible value of each attribute and selects the condition with highest information gain.

In the prune phase, for each rule any final sequences of the antecedents is pruned with the pruning metric p/(p+n).

7.4 Decision Tree

Decision trees are powerful classification methods which often can also easily be understood. In order to classify an example, the tree is traversed bottom-down. Every node in a decision tree is labelled with an attribute. The example's value for this attribute determines which of the out coming edges is taken. For nominal attributes, we have one outgoing edge per possible attribute value, and for numerical attributes the outgoing edges are labelled with disjoint ranges. This decision tree learner works similar to Quinlan's C4.5 or CART.

8 Experimentations and Results

8.1 Corpus

Though Bengali is one of the most spoken languages in the world, but there is no standard questions data available. So, we had to collected questions data from the web and we had selected the questions of different domains e.g., education, geography, history, science etc. available in BCSTAT.COM[5]. 1100 questions have been selected and processed to extract the features. Bengali shallow parser has been used to obtain the part of speech (POS). Two high qualified human annotators have been labelled the questions with an agreement score of 95.93%. We have used 770 questions (70%) for training and rest 330 questions (30%) to test the classification models.

8.2 Experiments

We have used four models i.e., Naive Bayes (NB), Kernel Naïve Bayes (KNB), Decision Tree (DT) and Rule Induction (RI) and used well known widely used Rapid Miner[6] Tool for experimentation. Performance of any classifier needs to be tested with some metric to assess the results. In our study, *classification accuracy* has been used to evaluate the results of the experiments.

Accuracy and *error* are widely used metrics to determine class discrimination ability of classifiers, and calculated using the following equation-

$$accuracy(\%) = \frac{TP + TN}{P + N}$$

$$error(\%) = 100 - accuracy$$

Where, TP = true positive samples; TN = true negative samples

P = positive samples; N = negative samples

It is a primary metric in evaluating classifier performances and it is defined as the percentage of test samples that are correctly classified by the algorithm.

Initially we have been only considering the lexical features of the questions. Naïve Bayes (NB) has been used as Baseline system for our experiment with classification accuracy of 80.65%. It has been found from the experiments that performance of baseline system drastically fall on ORG class (Precision-14.41%, Recall-41.18%) and MTHD class (Precision-34.62%, Recall-75.27%).

5 http://www.bcstest.com
6 http://www/rapid-i.com

Though, KNB classifier increased the accuracy but failed to produce better performance on ORG and MTHD classes. Rule Induction classifier not only increased the accuracy (83.31%) but also performed well on ORG and MTHD classes. Decision Tree has been performed the best among all classifiers (*accuracy* 84.19%) and has been exceptionally performed well on ORG, MTHD and others classes. The detail results have been shown on Table-3.

Features	Classifier	Accuracy	Error
Lexical	NB (*Baseline*)	80.65%	19.35%
	KNB	81.09%	18.91%
	RI	83.31%	16.69%
	DT	84.19%	15.81%

Table 3- Classifiers Performance

Next we have used lexical and semantic features together and applied NB, KNB, RI and DT classifiers respectively. It has been noted from experimental results that inclusion of semantic features improves the performance of all the said classifiers. The experiment results have been illustrated in table-4.

Features	Classifier	Accuracy	Error
Lexical + *Syntactical*	NB	81.34%	18.66%
	KNB	82.37%	17.63%
	RI	84.23%	15.77%
	DT	85.69%	14.31%

Table 4- Classifiers Performance

Finally, we have used lexical, syntactical and semantic features altogether and applied the four classifiers. Use of semantic features improves the performance of K-NB, NB classifiers on handling ORG and MTHD classes.

After inclusion of three features, NB classifier has been outperformed DT classifier handling NUM classes and RI classifier has been outperformed DT classifier handling TEMP classes. But overall DT classifier (*accuracy* 87.63%) has been performed well on classifying Bengali Questions. The detail results have been shown on Table-5.

Features	Classifier	Accuracy	Error
Lexical + *Syntactical* + *Semantic*	NB	81.89%	18.11%
	KNB	83.21%	16.79%
	RI	85.57%	14.43%
	DT	87.63%	12.37%

Table 5- Classifiers Performance

Conclusion and perspectives

This paper presents our research work on automatic question classification through machine learning approaches. The main contributions of this paper are as follows-

- We have studied the interrogatives and categorized them into three categories. We have also extracted the probable number representation i.e., singular or plural for each Bengali interrogative. 26 interrogatives have been identified from the experimented corpus.
- The baseline system based on Naïve Bayes classifier (using only lexical features) has achieved 80.65% accuracy. We have investigated the lexical, syntactic and semantic features for Bengali questions and the identified features performed well (achieved accuracy up to 87.63%) on Bengali Questions.
- We have experimented on four machine learning classifiers and shown that overall Decision Tree outperforms NB, KNB, RI methods for Bengali question classification.

The main future direction of our research is to exploit other lexical, semantic and syntactic features for Bengali question classification. In future an investigation can be performed on including new interrogatives using a large corpus. It may increase the count of Bengali interrogatives, particularly DI and CI. It is also worth investigating other types of machine learning algorithms. In the current work, we have prepared only three related word categories. So, the model performance can be improved in future by identifying new suitable categories.

References

Voorhees, E. M.(2001). Overview of the trec 2001 question answering track. *In Proceedings of the Tenth Text REtrieval Conference (TREC)*, pages 42–51.

Ittycheriah A., Franz, M., Zhu, W. J., Ratnaparkhi, A. and Mammone, R. J. (2001).*IBM's statistical question answering system. In Proceedings of the 9th TREC*, NIST.

Hovy, E., Gerber, L., Hermjakob, U., Lin, C. and Ravichandran, D. (2001). Toward semantics-based answer pinpointing .

Moldovan, D., Pa¸sca, M., Harabagiu, S. and Surdeanu, M. (2003). Performance issues and error analysis in an open-domain question answering system.*ACM Trans. Inf. Syst.*, 21:133–154.

Huang, Z., Thint, M. and Qin. Z. (2008). Question classification using head words and their hypernyms. *In Proceedings of EMNLP*, pages 927–936.

Ray, S. K., Singh, S. and B. P. Joshi. (2010). A semantic approach for question classification using wordnet and wikipedia. Pattern Recogn. *Lett.*,31:1935–1943.

Silva, J., Coheur, L., Mendes, A. and Wichert, A. (2011). From symbolic to sub-symbolic information in question classification. *Artifcial Intelligence Review*, 35(2):137–154.

Hull, D. A. (1999). Xerox TREC-8 question answering track report. *In Voorhees and Harman.*

Prager, J., Radev, D., Brown, E. and Coden, A. (1999). The use of predictive annotation for question answering in trec8. *In NIST Special Publication 500-246:TREC8*, pages 399–411.NIST.

Li, X. and Roth, D. (2004). Learning question classifiers: The role of semantic information. *In Proc. International Conference on Computational Linguistics (COLING)*, pages 556–562.

Zhang,D. and Lee,W.S. (2003). Question classification using support vector machines *In SIGIR.*

Nguyen, T., Nguyen, L., Shimazu, A. (2008). Using semi-supervised learning for question classification. *Journal of Natural Language Processing*, 15(1):3–21.

Moschitti, A., Quarteroni, S., Basili, R. and Manandhar, S. (2007). Exploiting syntactic and shallow semantic kernels for question/answer classification. *In ACL*, pages 776–783.

Li, X., and Roth, D. (2002). Learning question classifiers. *In Proceedings of the 19th international conference on Computational linguistics, COLING '02*, pages 1–7. Association for Computational Linguistics.

Hermjakob,U., Hovy, E. and Lin, C. (2002). Automated question answering in webclopedia - a demonstration. *In Proceedings of ACL-02.*

Metzler, D. and Croft, W. B. (2005). Analysis of statistical question classification for fact-based questions. *Inf. Retr.*, 8:481–504.

Loni, B., Tulder,G., Wiggers, P., Loog, M. And Tax, D. (2011).Question classification with weighted combination of lexical, syntactical and semantic features. *In Proceedings of the 15th international conference of Text,Dialog and Speech.*

Huang, Z., Thint, M. and Celikyilmaz, A. (2009). Investigation of question classifier in question answering. In *Proceedings of the 2009 Conference on Empirical Methods in Natural Language Processing, (EMNLP '09)*, pages 543–550.

Blunsom, P., Kocik, K. and Curran, J. R. (2006). Question classification with log-linear models. *In Proceedings of the 29th annual international ACM SIGIR conference on Research and development in information retrieval, SIGIR '06*, pages 615–616, NY, USA, ACM.

Loni, B. (2011). A Survey of State-of-the-Art Methods on Question Classification, *Literature Survey, Published on TU Delft Repository*.

Ekbal, A. and Bandyopadhyay, S. (2007). A Hidden Markov Model Based Named Entity Recognition System: Bengali and Hindi as Case Studies. *PReMI 2007*: 545-552.

Morphological Analyzer for Kokborok

Khumbar Debbarma[1] Braja Gopal Patra[2] Dipankar Das[3] Sivaji Bandyopadhyay[2]
(1) TRIPURA INSTITUTE OF TECHNOLOGY, Agartala, India
(2) JADAVPUR UNIVERSITY, Kolkata, India
(3) NATIONAL INSTITUTE_OF TECHNOLOGY, Meghalaya, India
khum_10jan@yahoo.co.in, brajagopal.cse@gmail.com,
dipankar.dipnil2005@gmail.com, sivaji_cse_ju@yahoo.com

ABSTRACT

Morphological analysis is concerned with retrieving the syntactic and morphological properties or the meaning of a morphologically complex word. Morphological analysis retrieves the grammatical features and properties of an inflected word. However, this paper introduces the design and implementation of a Morphological Analyzer for Kokborok, a resource constrained and less computerized Indian language. A database driven affix stripping algorithm has been used to design the Morphological Analyzer. It analyzes the Kokborok word forms and produces several grammatical information associated with the words. The Morphological Analyzer for Kokborok has been tested on 56732 Kokborok words; thereby an accuracy of 80% has been obtained on a manual check.

KEYWORDS : Morphology Analyzer, Kokborok, Dictionary, Stemmer, Prefix, Suffix.

1 Introduction

Kokborok is the native language of Tripura and is also spoken in the neighboring states like Assam, Manipur, Mizoram as well as the countries like Bangladesh, Myanmar etc., comprising of more than 2.5 millions[1] of people. Kokborok belongs to the Tibeto-Burman (TB) language falling under the Sino language family of East Asia and South East Asia[2]. Kokborok shares the genetic features of TB languages that include phonemic tone, widespread stem homophony, subject-object-verb (SOV) word order, agglutinative verb morphology, verb derivational suffixes originating from the semantic bleaching of verbs, duplication or elaboration. Kokborok is written in the script similar to Roman script.

In general, morphological analysis is the first step to analyze the source language whereas morphology is the field of linguistics that studies the structure of words. The Morphological Analyzer takes one word at a time and produces its structure, syntactic and morphological properties or sometimes the meaning of a morphologically complex word (Dhanalakshmi et al., 2009). The morphological structure of an agglutinative language is unique and capturing its complexity using machines and generate in presentable format is a challenging job. Various approaches are used for building morphological analyzers such as Brute force method, root driven approach, affix stripping etc. (Rajeev et al., 2007; Parakh and Rajesha, 2011).

However, a morphological analyzer is an essential and basic tool for building any language processing application for a natural language e.g., Machine Translation system. Morphological Analyzers are essential technologies for most text analysis applications like Information Retrieval (IR) and Summarization etc. The most obvious applications are found in the areas of lexicography and computational linguistics.

For example, with respect to the word "dogs", we can say that the "dog" is the root form, and‘s’ is the affix. Here the affix gives the number information of the root word. Thus, morphological analysis is found to be centered on the analysis and generation of the word forms. It deals with the internal structure of the words and how those words can be formed. Morphology also plays an important role in applications such as spell checking, electronic dictionary interfacing and information retrieving systems, where it is important that words that are only morphological variants of each other are identified and treated similarly. In natural language processing (NLP) and especially in machine translation (MT) systems, we need to identify words in texts in order to determine their syntactic and semantic properties (Parakh and Rajesha, 2011). Morphological study helps us by providing rules for analyzing the structure and formation of the words.

Several Morphological Analyzers have been developed in different languages using both rule based and statistical methods. Moreover, different approaches to Morphanalyzer for English have already been developed such as in (Minnen et al., 2001). On the other hand, many Morphological Analyzers for Indian Languages have also been developed such as in Hindi (Goyal and Lehal, 2008), Bengali (Das and Bandyopadhyay, 2010), Malayalam (Rajeev et al., 2007), Manipuri (Choudhury et al., 2004; Singh and Bandyopadhyay, 2005) and for four of the languages, viz., Assamese, Bengali, Bodo and Oriya (Parakh and Rajesha, 2011). Manipuri is quite similar to Kokborok as it falls under Sino language family and an accuracy of 75% was achieved in (Choudhury et al., 2004). To the best of our knowledge, no previous work has been done on

[1] http://tripura.nic.in/

[2] http://en.wikipedia.org/wiki/Kokborok

developing Morphological Analyzer for Kokborok language, though a stemmer has been developed for Kokborok language (Patra et al., 2011) and its reported average accuracy is 82.9%.

This paper focuses on designing of a database driven affix stripping based Morphological Analyzer in Kokborok. In general, the Kokborok words have complex agglutinative structures. In the present work, a Kokborok morphological analyzer has been developed to analyze the input Kokborok sentence and for each surface level word to produce the root word(s) and associated information like lexical category of the roots, the prefix and/or the suffix using three dictionaries namely root, prefix and suffix. The morphological analyzer uses the Kokborok root words and their associated information, e.g., part of speech information, category of the verbal bound root (action/ dynamic, static) from the Kokborok to English bilingual root dictionary.

The rest of the paper is organized in the following manner. Section 2 provides details of Kokborok word morphology whereas Section 3 provides an elaborative description of the Morphological Analyzer. Next, Section 4 describes the implementation of Morphological Analyzer while Section 5 presents the results and analysis. Finally, conclusions and future directions have been presented.

2 Kokborok Word Morphology

Kokborok language is highly agglutinative and rich in morphology. The verb morphology is more complex compared to noun morphology. Kokborok words can be easily formed by affixations.

2.1 Verb Morphology

Most verbs have a monosyllabic root, and the main method for processing verb phrases is to add suffixes to the root. Kokborok verbs always occur in bound form to which multiple affixes are added to give the tense, manner of action. The suffixes can be classified in three layers at least (Jacquesson, 2008):

- The immediate layer, just after the root, concerns for instance locative markers: the action may reach far away, or go from up to down etc.
- The medium layer after the locative information concerns actancy: this is the kingdom of factitive, passives, reciprocals etc.
- The outer layer is the so called Tense Aspect Modality (TAM) area, where indications of Tense, Aspect and Mode are given.

2.1.1 Inflectional Morphology

Inflectional morphology derives words from another word from acquiring certain grammatical features but maintaining the same part of speech or category. There are a number of inflectional suffixes indicating tense of the verb of a sentence. Inflectional morphology is more productive than derivational morphology. First, inflectional morphology is paradigmatic, i.e., every Kokborok verb exhibits a paradigm with each inflectional marker as illustrated in the Table 1.

Inflectional affix	Inflection type	Verb	English meaning
O	Aorist	Chaho	eats
Anə	Future	Chahanə	Will eat
Na	Verbal noun	Chahna	eat

TABLE 1 – Inflectional Paradigm of Verb Chah.

2.1.2 Derivational Morphology

The derivational morphology can be divided into three different levels viz., first level derivation, second level derivation and third level derivation as given in Tables 2, 3 and 4. There are non-category changing derivational suffixes and category changing derivational suffixes.

Suffix	Meaning	Use and Meaning
-sa-	Upwards <Up>	Look up
-khlai-	Downwards<Dw>	Look down
-laŋ-	Away from speaker<Lat>	take away
-gra-	First in order<Pri>	Go first

TABLE 2 – First Level Derivation.

Suffix	Meaning	Use and Meaning
-sa-	Upwards <Up>	Look up
-khlai-	Downwards<Dw>	Look down
-laŋ-	Away from speaker<Lat>	take away

TABLE 3 – Second Level Derivation.

Suffix	Meaning/ feature	Use and meaning
-o-	Aorist<Aor>	Go
-anə-	Near future<Ftp>	Will go(may be next year)
-nai-	Future<Fut>	Will go (on the verge of going)
-kha-	Past<Pf>	Went
-li-ja	Negative <Pf>Neg	Did not go
-kho-	Still<Pf>	Still
-ja-	Negative	Not go
-glak-	Negative	Will not be going

TABLE 4 – Third Level Derivation.

2.2 Noun Morphology

Monosyllabic nouns are relatively rare in Kokborok where bisyllabic formations are dominant. This is due to the widespread process of compounding, either true compounding when two lexical roots form a new word.

2.2.1 Inflectional Morphology

The sole nominal inflectional category is case marking. The category is highly productive, both formally and semantically. The following Table 5 shows the paradigmatic nature of case marking.

Inflectional Affix	Type	Surface Words
-ni	Genitive & ablative	*Nokni,musukni* 'from house,cows'
-no	Accusative & dative	*Chwngno ,bono* 'us,to him'
-o	Locative e& illative	*Or-o ,bisiŋ-o* 'here, inside'

TABLE 5 – Nature of Case Marking.

2.2.2 Derivational Morphology

Derivational morphology is not productive in that there are apparently arbitrary restrictions on which suffixes may occur with the different categories of nouns. There are no categories of gender and number in Kokborok. No accord of any kind on this respect. Gender is marked as number only when needed not when items have to be feminine or masculine, singular and plural.

- **Gender:** the male role is marked by suffix *–la* in *tokla* (cock). It is unlikely that *joŋgla* (frog) can be explained by this suffix. The suffix *–jək* denotes the feminine gender as in *sajək* (daughter).
- **Size:** However the suffixes *–ma* and *–sa* forms an antonymic couple specialized in big and small.since *–sa* also means offspring or young as in *toksa*(chicken), *təima*(river), *təisa*(stream).
- **Number:** plural is in *–rok* and mostly for animates and also used in pronouns. For example *cherai* (child), *cherairok* (children).

3 The Morphological Analyzer

The proposed architecture of Morphological Analyzer is shown in Figure 1. The Morphological Analyzer is composed mainly of three modules: Tokenizer, Stemmer and Morphological Analyzer.

- **Tokenizer**: This module breaks the Kokborok sentence in to its constituent words or tokens for analysis.
- **Stemmer:** it strips the word in to root and affixes.
- **Morphological analyzer**: it analyzes various types of word structures and combines the features associated with the affixes and tags the word.

3.1 Dictionary Development

3.1.1 Affix Dictionary

Altogether 91 affixes are there out of which 76 are suffixes and 19 are prefixes. The various affixes are associated with words belonging to different part of speech to give resultant words with a particular meaning. The statistics of affixes are given in Tables 6 and Table 7.

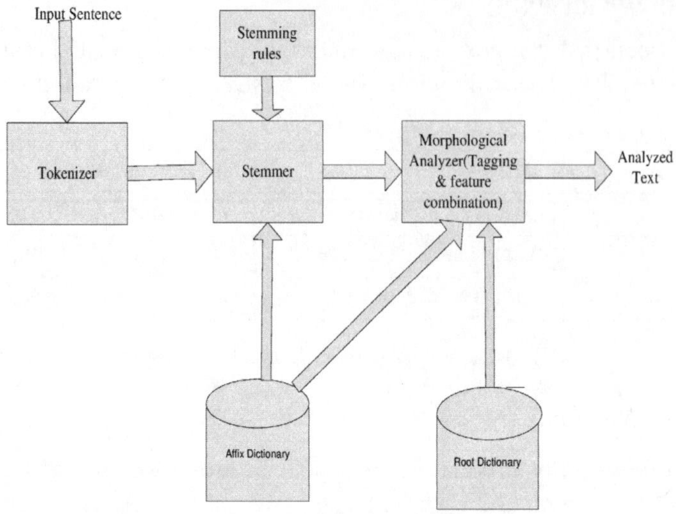

FIGURE 1 –Architecture of Morphological Analyzer for Kokborok

Type	No. of prefix	No. of suffix
Derivational	9	15
Inflectional	10	61

TABLE 6 – Statistics of Prefix types.

Lcat	No. of prefix	No. of Suffix
Noun	13	10
Verb	6	44
Adjective	0	22

TABLE 7 – Statistics of Suffix types.

Table 8 shows the affix dictionary entries where lcat, pers and emph are the features associated with each affix.

Kokborok_prefix	Icat	pers	Emph
Masema	Verb	2	Emph

TABLE 8 – Affix Dictionary Entries.

3.1.2 Root Dictionary

Altogether 2000 Kokborok root words have been collected, digitized and stored along with the associated information in root dictionary and the dictionary stores attribute of each Kokborok root words such as the part of speech (POS) and its English meaning. Root Dictionary has been developed by stemming the corpus collected from the Bible and the story books and the stemmed data are checked manually. Then we have assigned the POS and the English meaning manually.

The stemming algorithm used for the development of root dictionary is given below and Table 9 shows the root dictionary entries.

Kokborok	POS	English
Achuk	Verb	Sit

TABLE 9 – Root Dictionary Entries.

3.2 Stemming algorithm for generating Root Words

The algorithm is designed to remove both multiple suffixes as well as prefixes from the inflected words. It has been observed that the boundary of root words in Kokborok change after addition of suffixes (Patra et al., 2012). Thus we have added some rules in the algorithm as boundary changes after addition of suffixes. The algorithm is given below.

3.2.1 Prefix Stripping Algorithm

1. repeat the step 2 until all the prefixes are removed
2. read the prefix,
   if matched then store it in array and decrease the length of string
   else read another prefix.
3. If length of string >2 then go for suffix stripping, else exit

3.2.2 Suffix Stripping Algorithm

1. repeat the step 2 until all the suffixes are removed
2. read the largest suffix,
   if matched then check for rules.
   then store it in array and decrease the length of string
   else read another suffix.
3. exit.

We have achieved an accuracy of 85.5% by maximum suffix striping algorithm, where we striped maximum suffix first. There is no case of under stemming seen as we striped largest suffix first. The overall statistics of accuracies on major categories like verb, noun, adjective and adverbs are given in Table 10. In this case out of the total error, there are 69.3% mis-stemming and 30.7% over-stemming. For example,

Over- stemming: *sumano*(input) →*suma+no*(output)

Desired output: *suman+o*

Mis-stemming: *tongo*(input)= *tonk +o* (output)

Desired output: *tong+o*

Categories	Accuracy
Noun	72%
Verb	79%
Adjective	87%
Adverbs	96%

Table 11 – Results of Morphological Analyzer.

We have observed more number of errors in case of proper nouns or nouns, because the occurrence of proper nouns or nouns is more in the sentences. Some words have alphabet pairs similar to the affixes leading to over stemming for example:
Mis-stemming: *Kothmano*→ *Kothman+o* (after stemming which is incorrect)
Desired output: *Kothma+no*
In case of verbs, error occurs due to the order of stemming of word for example
Mis-stemming: *Malwi* → *ma+lwi*(error if prefix stemmed first)
Desired output: *Mal+wi*(correct)
There are less number of errors in Adjectives and those are due to presence of alphabets similar to affix in the word. For example *bw+rwichwk* (error since bw is in prefix list), but "bwrwichwk" is a single words. Numbers of errors in case of adverbs are negligible.

4 Implementation Details

The Morphological Analyzer has been used in the present work for identification of word class features and sentence type. Broadly, there are five types of words that can be handled by this Morphological Analyzer.

Free words are formed without any affixation or compounding. E.g. Borok (people). Words with multiple prefixes and suffixes, such word occurs in the pattern given below. Where P, RW, S stands for prefix, root word and suffix respectively.

P + RW	For e.g., ***bu**pha* (my father)
RW+S	For e.g., *Khumbar**no*** (to Khumbar)
P+RW+S.	For e.g. ***Bu**kumui**ni*** (His/Her Brother In Law"s)
P+RW+S+S...	For e.g., *Ma(P)+thang (to go)+lai(S)+nai(S)* →***Ma**thang**lainai***(need to go)
RW+RW...	For e.g., *Khwn (Flower)+Lwng(Garden)*→*Khwmlwng*(Flowergarden)
RW+S+RW+S.	For e.g., *Hui(RW)(to hide)+jak(S)+hui(RW)+jak(S)+wi(S)* → *Hujakhujakwi* (Without Being Seen)

Compound words are formed by compounding among various words belonging to different part of speech. The various pattern of compounding is given below.
Noun + Noun
Noun + Adjective
Pronoun + Noun + Noun

4.1 Algorithm for implementing the Morphological Analyzer

1. Give input Kokborok sentences to the tokenizer module.
2. Tokenize each sentence to words
3. Repeat from step 4 to 7 until each word is analysed
4. Check if the word is in dictionary
5. If match not found stem the word in to root and affixes
6. Check for the pattern given above with the help of root and affix dictionary. If match is found apply rules, combine grammatical features and tag the word. If not found then send the word to complex word handler.

7. Complex word handler will stem the word with the help of root dictionary. If match found then will tag accordingly, otherwise tag it a unknown words.
8. Exit.

The flow chart of the Morphological Analyzer is shown in Figure. 2.

5 Evaluation

In the segmentation of words, we tested two methods: (i) First affix isolation, then detection of root and (ii) First detection of root, then isolation of affixes. In the former case there is overhead due to repeated access to the root dictionary. On the other hand, the later approach needs a single pass in the root dictionary. The first approach handles the orthographic complexity well and the second strategy is much faster in comparison with the former. The Morphological Analyzer has been tested using the corpus. The unanalysed words have been tagged by the analyzer as unknown (unk) and after manual check it has been found out that maximum number of unknown words belong to proper noun, thus later on it was tagged as NNP. The Morph Analyzer was tested again and it has seen that it is giving a better result. Errors have been calculated on the basis of words wrongly tagged, unanalyzed words and words tagged as unk out of total input words. Correctness of Kokborok Morphological Analyzer is shown in Table 11. There are some unknown words which could not be analyzed based on rules available and due to unavailability of root word dictionary, are effectively reducing the performance of Morphology Analyzer. The words in Kokborok can be easily formed by affixations and compounding, so the number of unknown words are relatively large. The accuracy of the Morphanalyzer can be further improved by introducing more numbers of linguistic rules and adding more root words to the dictionary.

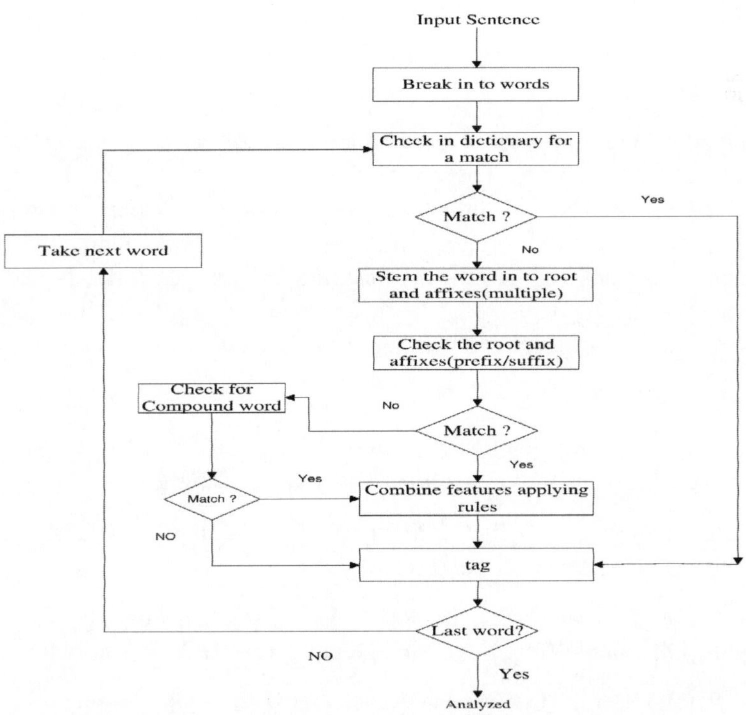

FIGURE 2 – Flowchart of Kokborok Morphological Analyzer.

	Based on unanalyzed words tagged as UNK	After UNK words tagged as NNP
Total input words	56732	56732
Analyzed words	42549	45386
Unanalyzed words	14183	11346
%age of analysed words	75%	80%
%age of errors	25%	20%

TABLE 11 – Results of Morphological Analyzer.

Conclusion and Future Work

In the present work, the development of a Kokborok Morphological Analyzer has been described. The analyzer uses three dictionaries of morphemes viz., root, prefix and suffix. The root dictionary stores the related information of the corresponding roots. The stemmer performs with an accuracy of 85.5% considering the inflectional and derivational suffixes. The Analyzer can classify the word classes and sentence types based on the affix information. In Kokborok, word category is not so distinct except Noun. The verbs are under bound category. The verb morphology is more complex than that of noun. The distinction between the noun class and verb classes is relatively clear; the distinction between nouns and adjectives is often vague. Thus, the assumption made for word categories depend upon the root category and affix information. Currently, we use a sequential search of a stem from the root dictionary because of its smaller size. Further a part of root may also be a prefix which leads to wrong tagging. In the stripping of the morphemes the various morphemes pattern combinations are tested. The morphology driven Kokborok POS tagging is very much dependent on the morphological analysis and lexical rules of each category.

The Natural Language Processing tools need more text corpus with better transfer rules and techniques to achieve quality output. The performance of the various Kokborok NLP tools that have been developed in the present work need to be improved by experimenting with various machine learning approaches with more training data. Future works include the developments of automatic Morphological Analyzer using some machine learning algorithms. The exploration and identification of additional linguistics factors that can be incorporated into the Morphological Analyzer to improve the performance is an important future task.

References

Choudhury, S., Singh, L., Borgohain, S. and Das, P. (2004). Morphological analyzer for Manipuri: Design and Implementation. *Applied Computing*, 123-129.

Das, A. and Bandyopadhyay, S. (2010). Morphological Stemming Cluster Identification for Bangla. *Knowledge Sharing Event-1: Task, 3.*

Debbarma, Binoy and Debbarma, Bijesh (2001). Kokborok Terminology P-I, II, III, English-Kokborok-Bengali. Language Wing, Education Dept., TTAADC, Khumulwng, Tripura.

Debbarma, K., Patra, B. G., Debbarma, S., Kumari, L. and Purkayastha, B. S. (2012). Morphological analysis of Kokborok for universal networking language dictionary. In

Proceedings of 1st International Conference on Recent Advances in Information Technology (RAIT), pages 474-477. IEEE.

Dhanalakshmi, V., Kumar, M. A., Rekha, R. U., Kumar, C. A., Soman, K. P. and Rajendran, S. (2009). Morphological Analyzer for Agglutinative Languages Using Machine Learning Approaches. In *Proceedings of International Conference on Advances in Recent Technologies in Communication and Computing (ARTCom'09)*, pages 433-435. IEEE.

Goyal, V. and Lehal, G. S. (2008). Hindi Morphological Analyzer and Generator. In *Proceedings of First International Conference on Emerging Trends in Engineering and Technology (ICETET'08).* pages 1156-1159. IEEE.

Jacquesson, F. (2008). A Kokborok Grammar. Published by Kokborok tei Hukumu Mission.

Minnen, G., Carroll, J. and Pearce, D. (2001). Applied morphological processing of English. *Natural Language Engineering*, *7*(3), 207-223.

Parakh, M. and Rajesha, N. (2011). Developing Morphological Analyzers for Four Indian Languages Using A Rule Based Affix Stripping Approach. In *Proceedings of Linguistic Data Consortium for Indian Languages, CIIL, Mysore.*

Patra, B. G., Debbarma, K., Debabarma, S., Das, D., Das, A. and Bandyopadhyay, S. (2012). A light Weight Stemmer for Kokborok. In *Proceedings of the 24th Conference on Computational Linguistics and Speech Processing (ROCLING 2012)*, pages 318-325, Yuan Ze University, Chung-Li, Taiwan.

Rajeev, R. R., Rajendran, N. and Sherly, E. (2007). A Suffix Stripping Based Morph Analyzer for Malayalam Language. *Morph Analyzer Science Congress.*

Singh, T. D. and Bandyopadhyay, S. (2005). Manipuri morphological analyzer. In *Proceedings of the Platinum Jubilee International Conference of LSI*. University of Hyderabad, India.

Comparing Different Criteria for Vietnamese Word Segmentation

Quy T. Nguyen[1] *Ngan L.T. Nguyen*[2] *Yusuke Miyao*[2]
(1) University of Informatics, Hochiminh city, Vietnam
(2) National Institute of Informatics, Chiyoda-ku, Tokyo, Japan
quynt@uit.edu.vn, ngan@nii.ac.jp, yusuke@nii.ac.jp

Abstract

Syntactically annotated corpora have become important resources for natural language processing due in part to the success of corpus-based methods. Since words are often considered as primitive units of language structures, the annotation of word segmentation forms the basis of these corpora. This is also an issue for the Vietnamese Treebank (VTB), which is the first and only publicly available syntactically annotated corpus for the Vietnamese language. Although word segmentation is straight-forward for space-delimited languages like English, this is not the case for languages like Vietnamese for which a standard criterion for word segmentation does not exist. This work explores the challenges of Vietnamese word segmentation through the detection and correction of inconsistency for VTB. Then, by combining and splitting the inconsistent annotations that were detected, we are able to observe the influence of different word segmentation criteria on automatic word segmentation, and the applications of word segmentation, including text classification and English-Vietnamese statistical machine translation. The analysis and experimental results showed that our methods improved the quality of VTB, which positively affected the performance of its applications.

Title and Abstract in another language, L_2 (optional, and on same page)

So sánh các tiêu chí tách từ khác nhau thông qua ứng dụng

Trong bài báo này, chúng tôi khảo sát những nhãn ranh giới từ được đánh dấu trong ngữ liệu cây cú pháp tiếng Việt gọi tắt là VTB. Từ việc khảo sát những trường hợp bị gán nhãn không nhất quán, chúng tôi xác định một số trường hợp khó khăn của bài toán tách từ. Dựa trên những trường hợp này, chúng tôi xây dựng và khảo sát một số tiêu chí tách từ khác nhau. Cụ thể, chúng tôi đã đánh giá các các tiêu chí này thông qua bộ tách từ tự động, và hai ứng dụng: dịch tự động Anh-Việt theo phương pháp thống kê và phân loại văn bản tiếng Việt. Kết quả thí nghiệm cho thấy: (1) các tiêu chí tách từ khác nhau có ảnh hưởng đến độ chính xác của ứng dụng, (2) việc nâng cao chất lượng cho VTB là cần thiết để xây dựng ứng dụng có chất lượng cao.

Keywords: treebank, inconsistency detection, word segmentation, Vietnamese.

Keywords in L_2: ngữ liệu gán nhãn cú pháp, phát hiện nhãn không nhất quán, tách từ, tiếng Việt.

---

1 Introduction

Treebanks, which are corpora annotated with syntactic structures, have become more and more important for language processing. In order to strengthen the automatic processing of the Vietnamese language, the Vietnamese Treebank has been built as a part of the national project, "Vietnamese language and speech processing (VLSP)" (Nguyen et al., 2009c). However, in our preliminary experiment with VTB, when we trained the Berkeley parser (Petrov et al., 2006) and evaluated it by using the corpus, the parser achieved only 65.8% in F-score. This score is far lower than the state-of-the-art performance reported for the Berkeley parser on the English Penn Treebank, which reported 90.3% in F-score (Petrov et al., 2006). There are two possible reasons to explain this outcome. One reason for this outcome is the difficulty of parsing Vietnamese, which requires new parsing techniques. The second reason is the quality of VTB, including the quality of the annotation scheme, the annotation guidelines, and the annotation process.

The Vietnamese Treebank (VTB) contains 10.433 sentences (274.266 tokens) annotated with three layers: word segmentation, POS tagging, and bracketing. This paper focuses on the word segmentation, since *words* are the most basic unit of a treebank[1] (Di Sciullo and Edwin, 1987), and defining words is the first step (Xia, 2000b,a; Sornlertlamvanich et al., 1997, 1999). For languages like English, defining words is almost trivial, because the blank spaces denote word delimiters. However, for an isolating language like Vietnamese, for which blank spaces play a role of syllable delimiters, defining words is not a trivial problem. For example, the sentence "*Học sinh học sinh học (students learn biology)*[2]" is composed of three words "*học sinh (student)*", "*học (learn),*" and "*sinh học (biology)*". Word segmentation is expected to break down the sentence at the boundaries of these words, instead of splitting "*học sinh (student)*" and "*sinh học (biology).*" Note that the terminology *word segmentation* also refers to the task of extracting "words" statistically without concerning a gold-standard for segmentation, as in (Seng et al., 2009; Ha, 2003; Le et al., 2010). In such a context, the extracted "words" are more appropriate for building a dictionary, rather than for corpus-based language processing, which are outside of the scope of this paper. Because of the discussed characteristics of the language, there are challenges in establishing a gold standard for Vietnamese word segmentation.

The difficulties in Vietnamese word segmentation have been recognized by many researchers (Ha, 2003; Nguyen et al., 2004, 2006; Le et al., 2010). Although most people agree that the Vietnamese language has two types of words: single and compound, there is little consensus as to the methodology for segmenting a sentence into words. The disagreement occurs not only because of the different functions of blank spaces (as mentioned above), but also because Vietnamese is not an inflectional language, as is the case for English or Japanese, for which morphological forms can provide useful clues for word segmentation . While similar problems also occur with Chinese word segmentation (Xia, 2000b), Vietnamese word segmentation may be more difficult, because the modern Vietnamese writing system is based on Latin characters, which represent the pronunciation, but not the meaning of words. All these characteristics make it difficult to perform word segmentation for Vietnamese, both manually and automatically, and have thus resulted in different criteria for word segmenation. However, so far there have been few studies on the challenges in word segmentation, and the comparison of different word segmentation criteria.

[1] In this paper, the terminology *word* is used with the meaning *the most basic unit of a treebank.*

[2] The English translation for a Vietnamese example text is given in parentheses following the text.

In this paper, a brief introduction of the Vietnamese Treebank (VTB) and its annotation scheme are provided in Section 2. Then, we described our methods for the detection and correction of the problematic annotations in the VTB corpus (Section 4.2). We classified the problematic annotations into several patterns of inconsistency, part of which were manually fixed to improve the quality of the corpus. The rest, which can be considered as the most difficult and controversial instances of word segmentation, were used to create different versions of the VTB corpus representing different word segmentation criteria. Finally, we evaluated these criteria in automatic word segmentation, and its application in text classification and English-Vietnamese statistical machine translation in Section 4.

This study is not only beneficial for the development of computational processing technologies for Vietnamese, a language spoken by over 90 million people, but also for similar languages such as Thai, Laos, and so on. This study also promotes the computational linguistic studies on how to transfer methods developed for a popular language, like English, to a language that has not yet intensively studied.

2 Word segmentation in VTB

Word segmentation in VTB aims at establishing a standard for word segmentation in a context of multi-level language processing. VTB specifies 12 types of units that should be identified as words (Table 1) (Nguyen et al., 2009b), which can be divided up into three groups: single, compound, and special "words." Single words contain only one token. The terminology *tokens* refers to text spans that are separated from each other by blank spaces. Compound words have two or more tokens, and are divided into four types: compound words composed by semantic coordination (semantic-coordinated compound), compound words composed by semantic subordination (semantic-subordinated compound), compound words with an affix, and reduplicated words. Special "words" include idioms, locutions, proper names, date times, numbers, symbols, sentence marks, foreign words, or abbreviations. The segmentation of these types of words forms a basis for the POS tagging, with 18 different POS tags, as shown in Table 2 (Nguyen et al., 2009d).

Each unit in Table 1 goes with several example words; English translations are given in parentheses. Furthermore, we added a translation for each token, where possible, so that readers who are unfamiliar with Vietnamese can have an intuitive idea as to how the compound words are formed. The subscript of a token translation is the index of that token in the compound word. However, for some tokens, we could not find any appropriate English translation, so we gave it an empty translation marked with an asterisk. Note that a Vietnamese word or a token in context can have other meanings in addition to the given translations.

A classifier noun, denoted by the part-of-speech Nc in Table 2, is a special type of word in Vietnamese. One of the functions of classifier nouns is to express the definiteness. For example, the common noun "*bàn*" generally means tables in general, while "*cái bàn*" means a specific table, similar to "the table" in English.

3 Inconsistency detection for word segmentation annotation of VTB

In this section, we analyzed the VTB corpus to determine whether the difficulties in Vietnamese word segmentation affected the quality of VTB annotations. The analysis revealed several types of inconsistent annotations, which are also problematic cases for

Type	Example
Simple word	*ba (father), cá (fish)*
Semantic-coordinated compound	*quần áo / trousers$_1$ shirt$_2$ (clothes)*
Semantic-subordinated compound	*xe đạp / vehicle$_1$ pedal$_2$ (bicycle)*
Compound word with affix	*bất lương / not$_1$ honest$_2$ (dishonest)*
Reduplicated word	*long lanh / *$_1$ *$_2$ (glistening)*
Idiom	*có thực mới vực được đạo* *(a hungry belly has no ears)*
Locution	*nói tóm lại (in short)*
Proper name	*Việt Nam (Vietnam)*
Date time, number, symbol	*30-4-1975 (April 30, 1975),* *15% (fifteen percent)*
Sentence marks	. , !
Foreign word	*internet, chat*
Abbreviation	*WTO*

Table 1: Word types in VTB word segmentation guidelines

	Label	Name	Example
1	N	Noun	*tiếng (syllable), nhân dân (people), chim muông (birds)*
2	Np	Proper noun	*Việt Nam, Nguyễn Du*
3	Nc	Classifier noun	*con, cái, bức*
4	Nu	Unit noun	*mét (meter), nhúm (pinch), đồng (VND)*
5	V	Verb	*ngủ (sleep), ngồi (sit), suy nghĩ (think)*
6	A	Adjective	*tốt (good), đẹp (beautiful), cao (high)*
7	P	Pronoun	*tôi (I), hắn (he), nó (it)*
8	L	Determiner	*mỗi (every), những, mấy*
9	M	Number	*một (one), vài (a few), rưỡi (half)*
10	R	Adverb	*đã, sẽ, đang*
11	E	Preposition	*trên (on), dưới (under), trong (in)*
12	C	Conjunction	*và (and), tuy nhiên (however)*
13	I	Exclamation	*ôi, chao, a ha*
14	T	Particle	*ạ, ấy, chăng*
15	B	Foreign word	*internet, email, video, chat*
16	Y	Abbreviation	*APEC, WTO, HIV*
17	S	Affix	*bất, vô, đa*

Table 2: VTB part-of-speech tag set

Vietnamese word segmentation. Our analysis is based on two types of inconsistencies: variation and structural inconsistency, which are defined below.

Variation inconsistency: is a sequence of tokens, which has more than one way of segmentation in the corpus. For example, "*con gái/girl*" can remain as one word, or be segmented into two words, "*con*" and "*gái*". A variation can be an annotation inconsistency, or an ambiguity in Vietnamese. While ambiguity cases reflect the difficulty of the language, annotation inconsistencies are usually caused by the confusion in the decision of annotators, which should be eliminated in annotation. We use the term *variation instance* to refer to a single occurrence of a variation.

Structural inconsistency: happens when different sequences have similar structures, thus should be split in the same way, but are segmented in different ways in the corpus. For example, "*con gái/girl*" and "*con trai/boy*" have similar structures: a combination of a classifier noun and a common noun Nc + N, so when "*con gái/girl*" is split, and "*con trai/boy*" is not, it is considered as a structural inconsistency of Nc. It is likely that structural inconsistency at the word segmentation level complicates the higher levels of processing, including POS tagging and bracketing.

3.1 Variation inconsistency detection

3.1.1 Detection method

N-gram	Number of variations	Number of variation instances
2-gram	157	2686 (92.9%)
3-gram	31	177 (6.1%)
4-gram	7	28 (1.0%)
Total	195	2891 (100.0%)

Table 3: Statistics of N-gram variations

POS sequences	Count	Examples
N-N	83	*vụ việc/ $*_1$ job$_2$ (event),* *quê nhà/ native place$_1$ house$_2$ (hometown)*
V-N	33	*nói chuyện/ say$_1$ story$_2$ (say),* *cho phép/ give$_1$ permission$_2$ (permit)*
V-V	25	*ra vào/ go out$_1$ go in$_2$ (go in and out)*
N-A	22	*đường mòn/ path$_1$ worn$_2$ (trail),* *năm xưa/ year$_1$ old$_2$ (long ago)*
N-V	20	*nhà ở/ house$_1$ live$_2$ (house),* *câu hỏi/ sentence$_1$ question$_2$ (question)*
Nc-N	16	*niềm tin/ $*_1$ believe$_2$ (belief),* *bà mẹ/ Mrs.$_1$ mother$_2$ (the mother)*
A-A	13	*đen trắng/ black$_1$ white$_2$ (black and white),* *đúng mức/ suitable$_1$ level$_2$ (moderate)*
V-R	11	*trở lại/ go$_1$ back$_2$ (return)*
N-P	9	*trước đây/ before$_1$ now$_2$ (previous)*
A-N	8	*cao tầng/ high$_1$ storey$_2$ (multi-storey)*

Table 4: Top 10 POS sequences of 2-gram variation inconsistencies

The detection method for variation inconsistency is based on N-gram sequences and the phrase structures in the VTB, following the definition for variation inconsistency, above. In detail, we counted N-gram sequences of different lengths in VTB that have two or more ways of word segmentation, satisfying one of the following two conditions:

- N tokens are all in the same phrase, and all have the same depth in phrase. For

POS pattern	Count
N-	148
V-	79
A-	27
Nc-	21
R-	17
E-	12
S-	11
C-	10
M-	10
P-	7
Np-	3
Nu-	2
L-	1
T-	1
Total	349

Table 5: Counts of POS sequences of 2-gram variation inconsistencies grouped by the first POS

POS pattern	Count
-N	166
-V	53
-A	45
-P	40
-R	16
-M	9
-Np	8
-C	4
-X	2
-T	2
-Nc	1
-S	1
-Nu	1
-Nb	1
Total	349

Table 6: Counts of POS sequences of 2-gram variation inconsistencies grouped by the second POS

example, the 3-gram "*nhà tình nghĩa (house of gratitude)*" in this structure "*(NP (Nc-H căn) (N nhà) (A tình nghĩa)),*" OR

- N tokens are all in the same phrase, and some token can appear in an embedded phrase which contains only one word. For example, "*nhà tình nghĩa*" in this structure "*(NP (Nc-H căn) (N nhà) (ADJP (A tình nghĩa))),*" where the ADJP contains only one word.

3.1.2 Evaluation and results

Table 3 shows the overall statistics of the variation inconsistency detected by method described above. Most of the difficult cases of word segmentation occur in two-token variations, occupying the majority of variations (92.9%). This ratio of 2-gram variations is much higher than the average ratio of two-token words in Vietnamese, as reported in (Nguyen et al., 2009a), which is 80%. Variations that have lengths of three and four tokens occupy 6.1% and 1.0%, respectively.

We estimated the precision of our method by randomly selecting 130 2-gram variation instances, extracted from the method described above, and manually checked whether the inconsistencies are true. We found that 129 cases occupying 99.2% of all extracted 2-grams are true inconsistencies. Only one instance of inconsistency was an ambiguous sequence *giá cả*, which is one word when it means *price*, and two words *giá/price cả/all* in *đều có giá cả/all have (their own) price.* The precision of our method is high, so we can use the extracted variations to provide insights on the word segmentation problem.

3.1.3 Analysis of 2-gram variations

We further analyzed the 2-gram variations to understand what types of 2-grams were most confusing for annotators. The analysis results showed that compound nouns, compound verbs, and compound adjectives are the top difficult cases of word segmentation.

We classified the 2-gram variations according to their POS sequences in case the tokens in the 2-gram are split. There are a total of 54 patterns of POS sequences. The top 10 confusing patterns, their counts of 2-gram variations, and examples are depicted in Table 4. Table 5 and Table 6 show the POS patterns that are a specific POS tag appearing at the beginning or ending of the sequence.

Investigating the inconsistent 2-grams extracted, we found that most of them are compound words according to the VTB guidelines (Section 2). One of the reasons why the compound words are sometimes split, is because the tokens in those compound words have their own meanings, which seem to contribute to the overall meaning of the compounds. This can be seen through the examples provided in Table 4, where the meanings of tokens are given with a subscript. This scenario has proven to be problematic for the annotators of VTB.

Furthermore, by observing the POS patterns in Table 5 and Table 6, we can see the potential for structural inconsistency, particularly for closed-set POS tags. Among them, classifier nouns (Nc) and affixes (S) are two typical cases of structural inconsistency, which will be used in several settings for our experiments. The same affix or classifier noun can modify different nouns, so when they are sometimes split, and combined in the variations, we can conclude that classifier nouns and affixes involve in structural inconsistencies. In the following section, we present our detection method for structural inconsistency for classifier nouns and affixes.

3.2 Structural inconsistency detection for classifier nouns and affixes

3.2.1 Detection method

We collected all affixes and classifier nouns in the VTB corpus, and then extracted 2-grams containing these affixes or classifier nouns, which they are also structural inconsistencies. For example, since "*con*" is tagged as a classifier noun in VTB, we extracted all 2-grams of "*con*" including both "*con gái/girl*" and "*con trai/boy*".

Even though the sequence, "*con trai*" is always split into two words throughout the corpus, it can still be an inconsistency, if we consider similar structures such as "*con gái*". In other words, by this method, we extract sequences that may be consistent at the surface level, but are not consistent, if we consider the higher analysis levels, such as POS tagging.

According to the VTB POS-tagging annotation guidelines (Nguyen et al., 2009d), classifier nouns should be separated from the words they modify. However, in practice, when a classifier noun can be standalone as a meaningful single word, it may be difficult for annotators to decide whether to split, or to combine it with the noun it modifies to form a semantic-subordinated compound. For example a classifier noun, e.g., "*con*" in "*con trai (boy)*", or "*con gái (girl)*", can also be a simple word, which means "*I (first person pronoun used by a child when talking to his/her parents)*", or part of a complex noun "*con cái (children)*". Therefore, in our experiments, we want to evaluate the "splitting" and "combining" of these cases, in order to see whether the solution is successful for applications of the corpus.

Type	Number of combinations	Number of instances
Affix	345	1289
Nc	2715	10445

Table 7: Statistics of targeted structural inconsistency

3.3 Correction of inconsistency in annotations of special characters

By examining the variations extracted by the variation inconsistency detection, we found that there are cases when a special character like a percentage (%) in "30%", is split or combined with "30". Such inconsistent annotations are manually fixed based on their textual context.

By checking structural inconsistencies of these special characters, including percentages (%), hyphens (-), and other symbols, we found quite a significant number of inconsistent annotations. For example, the character, %, in "30%" is split, but is combined with a number in "50 %", which is considered to be a structural inconsistency. Note that it can be argued that splitting "N%" into two words or combined in one word is dependent on the blank space in-between N and "%". Higher-levels of annotation such as POS tagging is significant, because we may need one or two different POS tags for the different methods of annotation. Therefore, we think that it is better to carefully preprocess text and segment these special characters in a consistent way.

To improve the quality of the VTB corpus, we extracted the problematic sequences using patterns of the special characters, and manually fixed this type of inconsistency. Automatic modification is difficult, since we must check the semantics of the special characters in their contexts. For example, hyphens in date expressions like "5-4-1975", which refers to the date, "the fifth of April, 1975," are combined with the numbers. However, when the hyphen indicates "(from) to" or "around ... or", as in "*2-3 giờ sáng*" meaning "around 2 or 3 o'clock in the morning", we decided to separate it from the surrounding numbers. As a result, we have fixed 685 inconsistent annotations of 21 special characters in VTB.

4 Comparing different word segmentation criteria

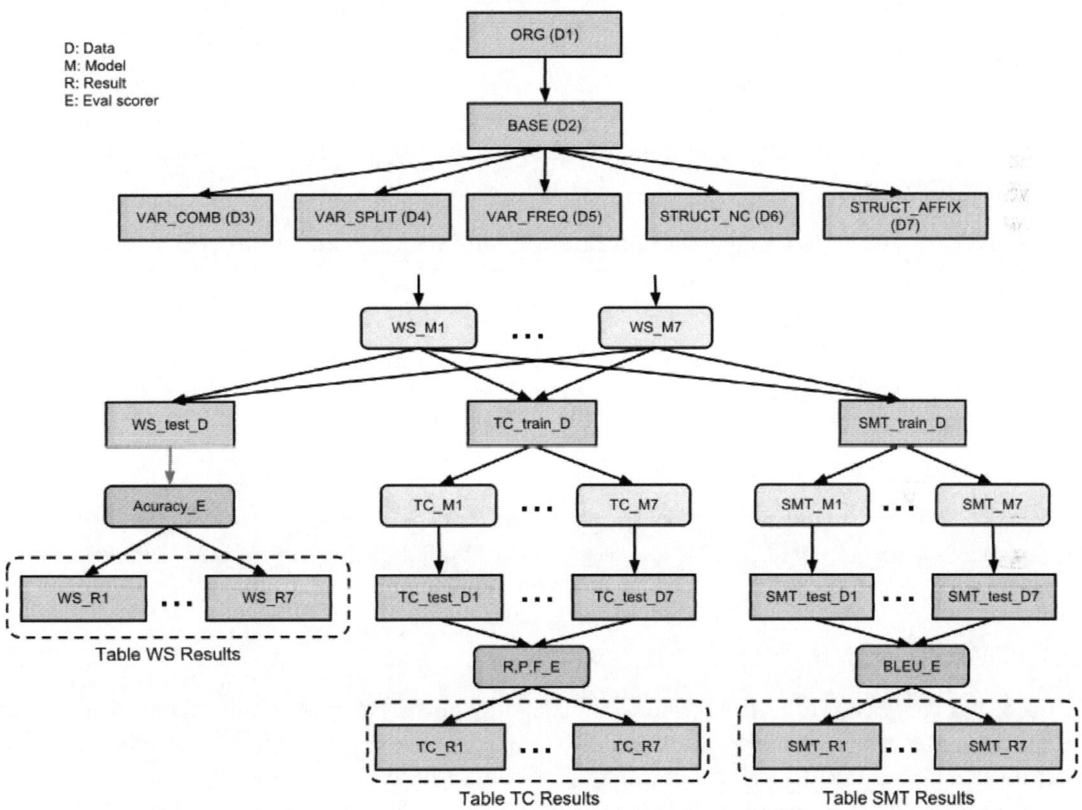

Figure 1: Experimental diagram showing how different word segmentation criteria are encoded in our experiments.

The variation inconsistency and structural inconsistency found in Section 3 can also be seen as representatives of different word segmentation criteria for Vietnamese. We organized the inconsistency detected in seven configurations of the original VTB corpus. Then, by using these data sets, we could observe the influence of the different word segmentation criteria on three tasks: automatic word segmentation, text classification, and English-Vietnamese statistical machine translation.

4.1 Data preparation for experiments on word segmentation criteria

Seven data sets corresponding to different segmentation criteria are organized as follows.

- ORG : The original VTB corpus.
- BASE : The original VTB corpus + Manual modification of special characters done in Section 3.3.
- VAR_SPLIT : BASE + split all variations detected in Section 3.1.
- VAR_COMB : BASE + combine all variations detected in Section 3.1.
- VAR_FREQ : BASE + select the segmentation with higher frequency among all variations detected in Section 3.1.
- STRUCT_NC : BASE + combine all classifier nouns detected in Section 3.2 with the words they modify.
- STRUCT_AFFIX : BASE + combine all suffixes detected in Section 3.2 with the words they modify.

These data sets are used in our experiments as illustrated in Figure 1. The names of the data sets are also used to label our experimental configurations.

4.2 Experimental settings

In this section, we briefly describe the task settings and the methods used for word segmentation (WS), text classification (TC), and English-Vietnamese statistical machine translation (SMT).

4.2.1 Word segmentation (WS)

We used YamCha (Kudo and Matsumoto, 2003), a multi-purpose chunking tool, to train our word segmentation models. The core of YamCha is the Support Vector Machine (SVM) machine learning method, which has been proven to be effective for NLP tasks. For the Vietnamese word segmentation problem, each token is labeled with standard B, I, or O labels, corresponding to the beginning, inside, and outside positions, respectively. The label of each token is determined based on the lexical features of two preceding words, and the two following words of that token. Since the Vietnamese language is not inflectional, we cannot utilize inflection features for word segmentation.

Each of the seven data sets is split into two subsets for training and testing our WS models. The training set contains 8443 sentences, and the test set contains 2000 sentences.

4.2.2 Text classification (TC)

Text classification is defined as a task of determining the most suitable topic from the predefined topics, for an input document. We implemented a text classification system similar to the system presented in (Nguyen et al., 2012). The difference is that we performed the task at the document level, instead of at the sentence level.

The processing of the system is summarized as follows. An input document is preprocessed with word segmentation and stop-word removals. Then, the document is represented in the form of a vector of weighted words appearing in the document. The weight is calculated using standard tf-idf product. An SVM-based classifier predicts the most probable topic for the vector, which also is the topic for the input document. In our experiment, for comparison of different word segmentation criteria in topic classification, we only vary the word segmentation model used for this task, while fixing other configurations.

News articles of five topics: music, stock, entertainment, education, and fashion are used. The sizes of the training and test data sets are summarized in Table 8.

Topic	Training (documents)	Test (documents)
Music	900	813
Stock	382	320
Entertainment	825	707
Education	821	707
Fashion	412	302
Total	3340	2849

Table 8: Data used in the text classification experiment

4.2.3 Statistical machine translation (SMT)

A phrase-based SMT system for English-Vietnamese translation was implemented. In this system, we used SRILM (Stolcke, 2002) to build the language model, GIZA++ (Och and Ney, 2003) to train the word-aligned model, and Moses (Holmqvist et al., 2007) to train the phrase-based statistical translation model. Translation results are evaluated using the word-based BLEU score (Papineni et al., 2002). Both training and test data are word-segmented using the word segmentation models achieved. For the experiment, we used the VCL_EVC bilingual corpus (Dinh and Hoang, 2005), 18000 pairs of sentences for training, and 1000 pairs for testing.

4.3 Experimental results and analysis

	Recall	Precision	F-score
ORG	95.89	95.44	95.66
BASE	96.00	95.60	95.80
VAR_COMB	96.05	95.69	95.87
VAR_SPLIT	96.53	96.27	**96.40**
VAR_FREQ	96.20	95.85	96.02
STRUCT_NC	95.08	94.79	94.93
STRUCT_AFFIX	96.03	95.59	95.81

Table 9: Evaluation results of automatic word segmentation with different WS criteria

Evaluation of word segmentation models trained on different versions of the VTB are given in Table 9. The experimental results with text classification and English-Vietnamese

	Recall	Precision	F-score
ORG	98.20	97.90	98.05
BASE	98.63	98.79	**98.71**
VAR_COMB	98.45	98.63	98.54
VAR_SPLIT	98.60	98.72	98.66
VAR_FREQ	98.68	98.65	98.67
STRUCT_NC	98.34	98.35	98.34
STRUCT_AFFIX	98.61	98.67	98.64

Table 10: Evaluation results of text classification with different word segmentation methods

	BLEU
ORG	36.36
BASE	36.44
VAR_COMB	36.03
VAR_SPLIT	**36.91**
VAR_FREQ	36.75
STRUCT_NC	35.41
STRUCT_AFFIX	36.36

Table 11: Evaluation results of SMT with different word segmentation methods

statistical machine translation are shown in Table 10 and Table 11, respectively. There are two important conclusions that can be drawn from these tables: (1) The quality of the treebank strongly affects the applications, since our BASE model and most of the other enhanced models improved the performance of TC and SMT systems; (2) "Splitting" seems to be a good solution for word segmentation of controversial cases, including the split of variations, affixes, and classifier nouns.

According to the result in Table 9, the VAR_SPLIT criterion gives the highest WS performance. With the exception of STRUCT_NC, all of the modifications to the original VTB corpus increase the performance of WS. However, the word segmentation criterion with higher performance is not necessarily a better criterion, but a criterion should also be judged through applications of word segmentation. In both SMT and TC experiments, the BASE model, which is based on the manually-modified inconsistency of special characters, achieved better results than the ORG model. In particular, in the TC experiment, the BASE model achieved 0.66 point higher than ORG, which is a significant improvement. The results support the conclusion that the quality of the word-segmentation corpus is very important for building NLP applications.

The SMT results show that three out of six augmented models, VAR_SPLIT, VAR_FREQ and BASE, performed better than the ORG configuration. Among them, the best-performing model, VAR_SPLIT achieved 36.91 BLEU score, which is 0.55 higher than ORG. In TC results, all six augmented models achieved higher results than ORG. In general, the augmented models performed better than the ORG. Additionally, because our automatic methods for inconsistency detection could not cover all of the types of inconsistencies in word segmentation annotation, further improvement of corpus quality is demanded.

Comparing the results of STRUCT_AFFIX and STRUCT_NC with BASE in WS, TC, and SMT, we can observe that combining affixes with their head nouns resulted in slightly better results for WS and TC, and did not change the performance of SMT. However, the combination of classifier nouns with their head nouns had negative effects on WS and SMT.

Another part of the scope of our experiment is to compare two solutions for controversial cases of word segmentation, splitting and combining. Splitting and combining variations are reflected by VAR_COMB and VAR_SPLIT, while STRUCT_AFFIX and STRUCT_NC represent the combination of affixes or classifier nouns with the words that they modify. STRUCT_AFFIX and STRUCT_NC are contrasted with BASE where affixes and classifier nouns remain untouched. Comparing VAR_COMB and VAR_SPLIT in both the TC experiment and SMT experiment, we see that the VAR_SPLIT results are better in both cases. Since the ratio of combined variations in the ORG corpus is 60.9%, it can be observed that splitting seems to be better than combining for WS, TC and SMT.

5 Conclusion

In this paper, we have provided a quantitative analysis of the difficulties in word segmentation, through the detection of problematic cases in the Vietnamese Treebank. Based on the analysis, we automatically created data that represent the different word segmentation criteria, and evaluated the criteria indirectly through their applications.

Our experimental results showed that manual modification, done for annotation of special characters, and most other word segmentation criteria, significantly improved the performances of automatic word segmentation, text classification and statistical machine translation, in comparison with the use of the original VTB corpus. Since the VTB corpus is the first effort in building a treebank for Vietnamese, and is the only corpus that is publicly available for NLP research, this study contributes to further improvement of the corpus quality, which is essential for building efficient NLP systems in future.

References

Di Sciullo, A. M. and Edwin, W. (1987). On the definition of word. *The MIT Press.*

Dinh, D. and Hoang, K. (2005). Building an annotated english-vietnamese parallel corpus for training vietnamese-related nlps. *Mon-Khmer Studies: A Journal of Southeast, Asian Languages and Cultures*, 35:21–36.

Dinh, Q. T., Le, H. P., Nguyen, T. M. H., Nguyen, C. T., Rossignol, M., and Vu, X. L. (2008). Word segmentation of vietnamese texts: a comparison of approaches. In Nicoletta Calzolari (Conference Chair), Khalid Choukri, B. M. J. M. J. O. S. P. D. T., editor, *Proceedings of the Sixth International Conference on Language Resources and Evaluation (LREC'08)*, Marrakech, Morocco. European Language Resources Association (ELRA). http://www.lrec-conf.org/proceedings/lrec2008/.

Ha, L. A. (2003). A method for word segmentation in vietnamese. In *Proceedings of Proceedings of Corpus Linguistics*, pages –, Lancaster, UK.

Hoang, C. D. V., Dinh, D., Nguyen, L. N., and Ngo, Q. H. (2007). A comparative study on vietnamese text classification methods. In *IEEE International Conference: Research, Innovation and Vision for the Future*, pages 267 – 273.

Holmqvist, M., Stymne, S., and Ahrenberg, L. (2007). Getting to know moses: initial experiments on german–english factored translation. In *Proceedings of the Second Work-*

shop on Statistical Machine Translation, StatMT '07, pages 181–184. Association for Computational Linguistics.

Kudo, T. and Matsumoto, Y. (2003). Fast methods for kernel-based text analysis. In *Proceedings of the 41st Annual Meeting on Association for Computational Linguistics - Volume 1*, ACL '03, pages 24–31, Stroudsburg, PA, USA. Association for Computational Linguistics.

Le, H. P., Nguyen, T. M. H., Roussanaly, A., and Vinh, H. T. (2008). Language and automata theory and applications. chapter A Hybrid Approach to Word Segmentation of Vietnamese Texts, pages 240–249. Springer-Verlag, Berlin, Heidelberg.

Le, T. H., Le, A. V., and Le, T. K. (2010). An unsupervised learning and statistical approach for vietnamese word recognition and segmentation. In *Proceedings of the Second international conference on Intelligent information and database systems: Part II*, ACIIDS'10, pages 195–204, Berlin, Heidelberg. Springer-Verlag.

Nguyen, C. T., Nguyen, T. K., Phan, X. H., Nguyen, L. M., and Ha, Q. T. (2006). Vietnamese word segmentation with crfs and svms: An investigation. In *Proceedings of the 20th Pacific Asia Conference on Language, Information, and Computation (PACLIC)*.

Nguyen, D. (2009). Using search engine to construct a scalable corpus for vietnamese lexical development for word segmentation. In *Proceedings of the 7th Workshop on Asian Language Resources*, ALR7, pages 171–178, Stroudsburg, PA, USA. Association for Computational Linguistics.

Nguyen, G. S., Gao, X., and Andreae, P. (2009a). Vietnamese document representation and classification. In *Proceedings of the 22nd Australasian Joint Conference on Advances in Artificial Intelligence*, AI '09, pages 577–586, Berlin, Heidelberg. Springer-Verlag.

Nguyen, P. T., Vu, X. L., and Nguyen, T. M. H. (2009b). Vtb word segmentation guidelines (vlsp project, report sp 8.2).

Nguyen, P. T., Vu, X. L., Nguyen, T. M. H., Dao, M. T., Dao, T. M. N., and Le, K. N. (2009c). Vtb bracketing guidelines (vlsp project, report sp 7.3).

Nguyen, P. T., Vu, X. L., Nguyen, T. M. H., Nguyen, V. H., and Le, H. P. (2009d). Building a large syntactically-annotated corpus of vietnamese. In *Proceedings of the Third Linguistic Annotation Workshop*, ACL-IJCNLP '09, pages 182–185, Stroudsburg, PA, USA. Association for Computational Linguistics.

Nguyen, Q., Nguyen, A., and Dinh, D. (2012). An approach to word sense disambiguation in english-vietnamese-english statistical machine translation. In *The 9th IEEE - RIVF International Conference and Communication Technologies*, pages 125–129.

Nguyen, T. B., Nguyen, T. M. H., Romary, L., and Vu, X. L. (2004). Lexical descriptions for Vietnamese language processing. In *The 1st International Joint Conference on Natural Language Processing - IJCNLP'04 / Workshop on Asian Language Resources*, page 8 p, Sanya, Hainan Island, China. none. Colloque avec actes et comité de lecture. internationale. A04-R-031 || nguyen04b A04-R-031 || nguyen04b.

Nguyen, T. M. H., Hoang, T. H. L., and Vu, X. L. (2009e). Vtb part-of-speech tagging guidelines (vlsp project, report sp 7.3).

Och, F. J. and Ney, H. (2003). A systematic comparison of various statistical alignment models. *Comput. Linguist.*, 29(1):19–51.

Papineni, K., Roukos, S., Ward, T., and Zhu, W.-J. (2002). Bleu: a method for automatic evaluation of machine translation. In *Proceedings of the 40th Annual Meeting on Association for Computational Linguistics*, ACL '02, pages 311–318, Stroudsburg, PA, USA. Association for Computational Linguistics.

Petrov, S., Barrett, L., Thibaux, R., and Klein, D. (2006). Learning accurate, compact, and interpretable tree annotation. In *Proceedings of the 21st International Conference on Computational Linguistics and the 44th annual meeting of the Association for Computational Linguistics*, ACL-44, pages 433–440, Stroudsburg, PA, USA. Association for Computational Linguistics.

Seng, S., Besacier, L., Bigi, B., and Castelli, E. (2009). Multiple text segmentation for statistical language modeling. In *10th International Conference on Speech Science and Speech Technology (InterSpeech 2009)*, pages 2663–2666.

Sornlertlamvanich, V., Charoenporn, T., and Isahara, H. (1997). Orchid: Thai part-of-speech tagged corpus. technical report orchid tr-nectec-1997-001. Technical report, National Electronics and Computer Technology Center.

Sornlertlamvanich, V., Takahashi, N., and Isahara, H. (1999). Building a thai part-of-speech tagged corpus (orchid). *The Journal of the Acoustical Society of Japan (E)*, 20(3):189–140.

Stolcke, A. (2002). Srilm - an extensible language modeling toolkit. pages 901–904.

Tran, T. O., Le, A. C., and Ha, Q. T. (2010). Improving vietnamese word segmentation and pos tagging using mem with various kinds of resources. *Information and Media Technologies*, 5(2):890–909.

Xia, F. (2000a). The part-of-speech tagging guidelines for the penn chinese treebank (3.0).

Xia, F. (2000b). The segmentation guidelines for the penn chinese treebank (3.0).

Xue, N., Xia, F., Huang, S., and Kroch, A. (2000). The bracketing guidelines for the penn chinese treebank (3.0).

A Light Weight Stemmer for Urdu Language: A Scarce Resourced Language

Sajjad Ahmad Khan[1], *Waqas Anwar*[1], *Usama Ijaz Bajwa*[1], *Xuan Wang*[2]
(1) COMSATS Institute of Information Technology, Abbottabad, Pakistan
(2) Harbin Institute of Technology, Shenzhen Graduate School, P.R.China
Sajjad_ak78@yahoo.com, waqas@ciit.net.pk, usama@ciit.net.pk, wangxuan@insun.hit.edu.cn

ABSTRACT

Stemming is a procedure that conflates morphologically related terms into a single term without doing complete morphological analysis. Urdu language raises several challenges to Natural Language Processing (NLP) largely due to its rich morphology. The core tool of information retrieval (IR) is a Stemmer which reduces a word to its stem form. Due to the diverse nature of Urdu, developing its stemmer for an IR system is a challenging task. This paper presents a light weight stemmer for Urdu text, which uses rule based approach. Exceptional lists are developed to enhance the accuracy of the stemmer. The result of the stemmer is quite enough and can be effective in IR system.

KEYWORDS : Information Retrieval, Light weight stemmer, Exceptional Lists, Suffix and prefix list

1 Introduction

Urdu is an Indo-Aryan language. It is the national language of Pakistan and is one of the twenty-three official languages of India. It is written in Perso-Arabic script. The Urdu vocabulary consists of several languages including Arabic, English, Turkish, Sanskrit and Farsi (Persian) etc. Urdu's script is right-to-left and form of a word's character is context sensitive, means the form of a character varies in a word because of the position of that character in the word (start, end, medial, independent).

According to (Al-Khuli, M. 1991), Morphology deals with the internal structure of words. Hundreds thousands of words are contained in every human language and constantly fresh words are incorporated. These words are formed from a group of smaller components. In morphology, its main building blocks are morphemes. Morpheme is the smallest component in a language having some meaning[1]. There are two types of morphemes i.e. free and bound morphemes.

Morphemes which exists freely (alone) are called free morphemes whereas bound morphemes are made as a result of combination with another morpheme. The affixes are bound morphemes. Those morphemes that produce the grammatical formation of a word are called Inflectional morphemes[2]. Deriving new words from the existing ones is called derivational morphemes. In derivation, a different part-of-speech class is created by adding a bound morph to a stem.

In Urdu language, morphological processing becomes particularly important for IR. IR system is used to ensure easy access to stored information. Inside IR, the information data which is stored and receives search calls usually corresponds to the lists of identifiers recognized as key terms, keywords. One of the attempts to make the search engines more efficient in IR is the use of

[1] http://www.ielanguages.com/linguist.html
[2] http://introling.ynada.com/session-6-types-of-morphemes

stemmer. Stem is the base or root form of a word. Stemmer is an algorithm that reduces the word to their stem/root form e.g. jumping, jumped and jumps to the stem "jump". Similarly the Urdu stemmer should stem the words بدنصیبی (unlucky), نصیب دار (lucky), بدنصیب (luckless) to Urdu stem word نصیب (luck).

The stemmer is also applicable to other natural language processing applications needing morphological analysis for example spell checkers, word frequency count studies, word parsing etc. The rest of the paper organization is as follows: In section 2, different stemming approaches and rule based stemming algorithms are discussed, in section 3, Orthographic features of Urdu is discussed, in section 4, the Urdu morphology is discussed, section 5 discusses light weight stemmer, section 6 discusses the Proposed Urdu Stemmer and finally the evaluation of the stemmer is discussed in section 7.

2 Stemming approaches and algorithms

There are four kinds of stemming approaches (Frakes, et al.1992): table lookup, affix removal, successor variety and n-grams. Table lookup method is also known as brute force method, where every word and its respective stem are stored in table. The stemmer finds the stem of the input word in the respective stem table. This process is very fast, but it has a disadvantage i.e. large memory space required for words and their stems and the difficulties in creating such tables. The affix removal stemmer eliminates affixes from words leaving a stem. The successor variety stemmer is based on the determination of morpheme borders, i.e., it needs information from linguistics, and is more complex than affix removal stemmer. The N-grams stemmer is based on the detection of bigrams and trigrams.

The study (J.B. Lovins, 1968) discussed the first English stemmer and used about 260 rules for stemming the English language. The study, suggested a stemmer consisting of two-phases. The first stage removes the maximum possible match from the suffix list sorted on the base of word lengths. The spelling exceptions are covered in the second stage.

The Porter stemmer (M.F. Porter, 1980) developed the stemmer on the truncation of suffixes, by means of list of suffixes and some restrictions/conditions are placed to recognize the suffix to be detached and generating a valid stem. Porter Stemmer performs stemming process in five steps. The Inflectional suffixes are handled in the first step, derivational suffixes are handled through the next three steps and the final step is the recoding step. Porter simplified the Lovin's rules upto 60 rules.

Different stemmers have also been developed for Arabic language. The study (S. Khoja, et al. 1999) explains an Arabic stemmer called a superior root-based stemmer. This stemming algorithm truncates prefixes, suffixes and infixes and then uses patterns for matching to pull out the roots. The study (Thabet, N. 2004) described a stemmer, which performs on classical Arabic in Quran to produce stem. For each Surah, this stemmer generates list of words. These words are checked in stop word list, if they don't exist in this list then corresponding prefixes and suffixes are removed from these words.

The study (E.T. Al-Shammari, et al. 2008) proposed the Educated Text Stemmer (ETS). It is a simple, dictionary free and efficient stemmer that decreases stemming errors and needs lesser storage and time.

Bon was the first stemmer developed for Persian language (M. Tashakori, et al. 2002). Bon is an iterative longest matching stemmer. The iterative longest matching stemmer truncates the longest possible morpheme from a word according to a set of rules. This procedure is repeated until no more characters can be eliminated. The study (Mokhtaripour, et al. 2006) proposed a Persian stemmer that works without dictionary. This stemmer first removes the verb and noun suffixes from a word. After that it starts truncation of prefixes from that word.

Till date only one stemmer i.e. *Assas-band*, has been developed for Urdu language (Q. Akram, et al. 2009). This stemmer extracts the stem/root word of only Urdu words and not of borrowed words i.e. words from Arabic, Persian and English used in Urdu. This algorithm removes the prefix and suffix from a word and returns the stem word.

3 Orthographic features of Urdu

According to (Malik, M. G. Abbas, et al. 2008), Urdu alphabet consists of 35 simple consonants, 15 aspired consonants, 10 vowels, 15 diacritical marks, 10 digits and other symbols

3.1 Consonants

Consonants are divided into two groups i.e. Aspirated consonants and non aspirated consonants.

There are 15 aspirated consonants in Urdu language. These consonants are shown by a grouping of a simple consonant to be aspirated. A special letter called Heh Doachashmee (ھ) is used to mark the aspiration. Aspired Consonants are بھ, پھ, تھ, ٹھ, جھ, چھ, دھ, ڈھ, کھ, گھ, رھ, ڑھ, مھ, نھ, لھ .Urdu language consists of 35 non aspirated consonant signs that represent 27 consonant sounds. Various scripts are employed to show the similar sound in Urdu, For example: Sad (ص), Seen (س) and Seh (ث) represent the sound [s].

3.2 Vowels

Urdu has ten vowels. Seven of them contain nasalized forms. Out of these seven, four long vowels are represented by Alef Madda (آ), Alef (ا), Choti Yeh (ی) and Vav (و) and three short vowels are represented by Arabic Kasra (Zer), Arabic Fatha (Zabar) and Arabic Damma (Pesh). In Urdu language, the Vowel demonstration is context sensitive. For example, the Urdu Choti Yeh (ی) and Vav (و) can also be used as a consonant (Malik, M. G. Abbas, et al. 2008).

3.3 Diacritical marks

The diacritical marks are those marks that are added to a letter to change the pronunciation of a word or to differentiate among similar words. It is also called as accent mark or diacritic.[3]

There are 15 diacritical accent marks in Urdu (Malik, M. G. Abbas, et al. 2008). Diacritical marks (Zabar, Zer, Pesh, Ulta Pesh, Do-Zabar, Do-Zer, Do-Pesh etc) represent vowel sounds. These are placed above or below of an Urdu word. The diacritical marks are very rarely used by people in writing Urdu. When the diacritic of a character in a word is changed then it could entirely change its meaning. For example the word (بیل) has two meanings i.e. a "creeping plant" as well as it means "bull". To remove the doubt between these two words, there should be Zabar after Beh (ب) for deducing the meaning as "bull".

[3] http://www.the-comma.com/diacritics.php

4 Urdu morphological structure

Urdu verbs, nouns and adjectives are discussed in the following sections as in (Sabzwari, S, 2002):

4.1 Urdu verb

Verb (فعل) corresponds to occurrence or performing of something. That verb which does not take object is called intransitive verb (فعل لازم). When a verb needs a direct object then it is called transitive verb and we can called it (فعل متعدی) in Urdu. A root form is that morpheme of Urdu verb which is not changed among different morphological forms and it is also called base form. When a suffix (نا) is removed from the verb's lexicon form (infinitive form) then the left over part of an infinitive form will be a root, which is also called (مادہ) in Urdu. Causative Stem Form of verb can be achieved through adding of suffixes to root form. The Causative verb forms /transitivitized verb forms can be obtained through the roots of lower valency verb by adding Urdu suffixes: –aa (ا), –waa (وا) to the root form of verb. The causative verb types are known as stem forms. The infinitive (مصدر) is that kind of verb which has the suffix "نا". This form of the verbs also can be used in place of noun. Usually this form of the verb has a masculine suffix "نا". For feminine infinitive form the suffix "نے" and the suffix "نی" for oblique infinitive form are used. The repetitive form (استمراری) also known as imperfect or habitual form that is produced by appending suffixes to the root as: تا, تے, تی, تیں.

4.2 Urdu noun

A word which is the name of anything is called Noun, i.e. person's name, a place, an animal, thing, a concept, time, a situation etc.

Initially nouns are classified into proper and common nouns. Proper noun (اسم معرفہ) is the name of particular person, thing or place, e.g. Hafsa, Del Laptop , Karachi etc. The Common noun (اسم نکرہ) is the common name for any person, thing or place e.g. woman, pen, village, etc. The Common nouns are further divided into state, spatial, group, instrumental and temporal nouns. There are four fundamental properties related with Urdu nouns i.e. Gender, Number, Form and Case. The masculine and feminine gender is accepted by the Urdu's Nouns. For inanimate nouns, to get its gender categorization in Urdu, there is no common rule. Generally powerful, huge, dominant, heavy and larger items are masculine, whereas lighter, weak and smaller are feminine. Generally, masculine are shown through bigger nouns (اسم مکبر), whereas feminine are shown through smaller nouns (اسم مصغر). The Urdu nouns have two possibilities for number. One is called singular and second is called plural. In Normal form, when Urdu noun is listed in dictionary is called nominative form. When Nouns are followed by a postposition then it can be viewed in oblique form. Those Urdu nouns which belong to human being and sometimes other animate nouns contain a different form used to call/ address person, this type is called vocative.

4.3 Urdu adjective

An adjective express the status or action, quality that a noun refers to e.g. نیک آدمی(Pious man) , (Fresh banana) تازہ کیلا .Descriptive Adjective is the most common and significant type of adjective. It express attributes of the noun they qualify in terms of its color, size, dimensions, shape, sound, shade, personal trait, time, and quality. When the descriptive adjectives directly lead a nominal head as modifiers, in that case they are called attributive adjectives e.g. (Cruel king) ظالم بادشاہ ,سفید گیند (White ball).

The Possessive adjectives are used to show the ownership and the ownership relation is understand in two ways; whether, in noun phrases, adjectives lead the head noun as modifiers or they may be lead by a proper form of the genitive postposition (کا،کے،کی) e.g. حفصہ کا نیلا دوپٹہ (Hafsa's blue veil).

5 Light weight stemmer

Light weight stemming is to find the representative indexing form of a word by the application of truncation of affixes (Imed Al-Sughaiyer, et al. 2004). The core objective of light weight stemmer is to preserve the word meaning intact and so increases the retrieval performance of an IR system.

In this paper, a light stemmer for Urdu text is proposed. Various lists are developed that help in finding a stem of an Urdu word. This stemmer is rule based and works by truncating all possible affixes from a word. The problem in this light weight stemming is that in some cases there is ambiguity e.g. a particular string of letters may or may not play a function of affix. A method is introduced for detecting such type of ambiguity that finds if a specific sequence in an affix is part of the original word. For this purpose Global Prefix Exceptional and Global Suffix Exceptional Lists are developed which are discussed in the coming sections.

6 Proposed Urdu Stemmer

During morphological analysis of Urdu text, it is noticed that there could be upto sixty different forms of a single verb (Rizvi, S, et al. 2005). Therefore reducing these forms to their stem forms is very important during IR tasks. Affixes perform an important role in making inflection and derivation of words. When these affixes are removed from a word, it gives a stem word. We have developed different lists for our stemmer. The details of these lists are given below.

6.1 Stop word list

Stop words are those words that occur frequently. For English stemmers, a stop word list is already maintained, similarly, it is necessary for Urdu stemmer, that there must be a stop word list. Therefore, to accomplish this task, various Urdu books and literature were studied and finally 150 stop words are generated for Urdu. Some of the stop words in Urdu are نے،کا،کے،سے،میں.

6.2 Prefix list

Prefix is that morpheme which is attached to the start of a word. The prefix may consist of only a single character, two or more than two characters and sometimes a complete word. After consulting many grammar books 180 prefixes were collected. A sample of these prefixes are بد،زبر،با،خار.

6.3 Suffix list

The suffix is that morpheme that is added to the end of a word. The suffix may consist of a character, more than a single character or a complete word. A list of suffixes, consisting of 750 suffixes for Urdu text is collected after consulting relevant literature. Samples of such suffixes are ات،باش،بندی،پسند،خانہ.

6.4 Global prefix exceptional list

There are some words that contain a prefix, in fact it is not a prefix but it is the part of that word e.g. in the word "نایاب", this word contain a prefix "نا" , if it is removed then it produces a word "یاب", which is incorrect from stemming point of view. Therefore, such type of words must need to be identified in advance and to be treated as an exceptional case. For our stemmer an exceptional list for prefixes (about 13000) is created called Global Prefix Exceptional List (GPEL). Samples of such type of words are اعتماد،اتفاق،ازل،درج .

6.5 Global suffix exceptional list

In some cases, when a suffixe is removed from a word and actually that suffix was the part of a stem word that should not be detached. An erroneous result will be produced due to irrelevant truncation of suffix e.g. in the word "نانا", when the suffix "نا" is removed then it produces stem "نا", which is incorrect. Therefore such type of words should be treated as an exceptional case. Samples of such type of words are فوت،دستیاب،لیاقت،مرد. For our stemmer an exceptional list for suffix (of length about 16000) is created.

6.6 Characters add-list (normalization of stem)

When affix stripping algorithm is applied on Urdu words, then some time we get an incomplete word, e.g. after stripping affixes from a word "خوبصورتی" (Beautifulness), we get stem "صور", which is incorrect stem. Therefore, this word should be added with the character "ت" to form correct stem form i.e. "صورت" (appearance). For this reason five types of list are maintained for five characters; (ا،ہ،ت،ی،ن).

6.7 Stem dictionary

To check the accuracy of any stemmer, there should be a stem word dictionary. After studying relevant literature, it is noted that there is no stem dictionary available for Urdu text. Therefore, we developed a stem dictionary for Urdu words having 3500 words.

6.8 Proposed algorithm of Urdu stemmer

The *longest-match* theory regarding affix removal states that when more than one affixes result as a match, the one which is longest should be removed. This method is applied by first sorting the affixes in any class in order of decreasing length. In case of suffix removal, if *-ional* is removed when there is another match *-ational,* then more work has to be done to eliminate *-at,* that is, for another order-class. To avoid this extra order-class, *-ational* should precede *-ional* in the prefix/suffix exception list.

An algorithm based on the principle of longest-match uses only one order-class. The entire feasible combinations of affixes are compiled and then ordered based on their length, so the longest word comes first. When a match is not found on longer suffixes / prefixes, shorter ones are scanned.

```
A-   INPUT Word for stemming
     Initially Word = (Prefix)-stem-(Suffix)
B-   Search in Stop word list
     IF Word exists in Stop word list
          Return to step A (for next word)
     ELSE go to step C
C-   Search in Global Prefix Exceptional List   (GPEL)
     IF Word exists in GPEL
          THEN go to step E
     ELSE go to step D
D-   OPEN Urdu prefixes file
     READ prefix one by one from the file until EOF is
     reached
     IF there is a match
          THEN remove prefix from word
          So Word = stem-(Suffix)

E-   Search in  Global Suffix Exceptional List
     (GSEL)
     IF Word exist in GSEL
          THEN output Word = stem
          go to step H
     ELSE go to step F

F-   OPEN Urdu suffixes file
     READ suffix one by one from the file Until EOF
     reached
     IF there is a match
          THEN remove suffix from word
          So Word = stem
          go to step G
     ELSE go to step H
G-   Search in Characters-Add List (CAL) file
     IF Word exists in CAL file
           THEN Add the respective
                character to the word
           So Word = stem (normalized)
     ELSE
           Word=stem
H-   End
```

The proposed stemmer extracts the stem by removing the prefixes and suffixes having maximum length from a word. Thus for this purpose, the prefix and suffix lists are sorted in descending order before any prior operation.

To understand the proposed algorithm, please refer to Figure 1. Our proposed algorithm first checks the entered word that whether it is a stop word? If so then no processing will be done on that word and next word will be entered. When a word is not a stop word then the word is checked in global prefix exceptional list, if it exists then it means that the word has prefix(s) but should not be removed from the word because they are the part of stem. On the other hand if it does not exist in global prefix exceptional list then it means it has some prefix (s), thus prefix rules are applied to remove the maximum prefix from the word.

The word is now checked in global suffix exceptional list, if it exists then it is marked as the stem. But if it does not exist in the list then it means this word has some suffix (s). Therefore suffix rules are applied to remove the maximum suffix from the word.

To normalize the word form, the word is checked in five different lists maintained for (ا،ہ،ت،ی،ن) characters i.e. Characters-Add list. When a word is found in any of the five lists then respective character is added to produce a normal word form. Thus marks this resultant word as the stem.

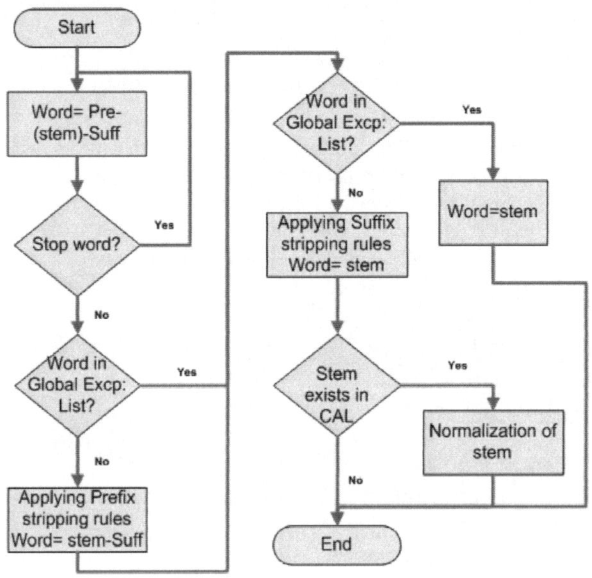

Figure 1: Flow chart of Proposed Urdu Stemmer

7 Evaluation

We evaluated the proposed Urdu stemmer on three corpora[4] i.e. corpus-1 (9200 words), corpus-2 (27000 words) and corpus-3 (30000 words). These corpora include data in the form of verbs, nouns, adjectives, punctuations, numbers, special symbols etc. When the corpus-1 is fed to the stemmer, then in pre-processing step, the stemmer removed all stop words, numbers and punctuation marks. Thus after pre-processing steps, there were 4268 words left. Stemming is performed on 4268 words that produce 39.4% precision, 71.1% recall and 50.70% F1-Measure.

The low accuracy obtained is due to the occurrence of various issues in stemming Urdu words e.g. Compounding, Tokenization, Transliteration and Infixation. It is very difficult to classify the compound words as a single or multiple words e.g. مرہم پٹی (bandaging), خط وکتابت (correspondence). Some times the reduplication also produces ambiguity; whether it is treated as single or double word e.g. جگہ جگہ،آہستہ آہستہ،ساتھ ساتھ(together, slowly, at every place)

English language generally uses white spaces or punctuation marks for the identification of word boundaries. Although in Urdu, space character is not present but with increasing usage of computer, it is now being used, for generating right shaping and to break up words. Tokenization process should be error free, hence producing correct tokens before applying an Urdu stemmer. It

[4] http://www.crulp.org/software/ling_resources/UrduNepaliEnglishParallelCorpus.htm

is also observed that these corpora include Urdu transliteration of English words e.g. فیملیز (families), پروگرامنگ (programming). There is no prefix and suffix morpheme available in our developed lists for such type of words. We cannot get stem word of an Urdu word by only stripping off prefixes and (or) suffixes e.g. اقوام (nations) , مساجد (mosques) , علوم (knowledge). These words contain infixes and large amount of such type of words are present in Urdu. Thus light weight stemmer cannot handle words having infixes. Due to insufficient words in Character Add lists, it leads to error in stemming. Proper nouns and abbreviations also contribute in the error of stemming e.g. یو-ایس-اے (USA), لندن (London).

The same stemmer is applied on corpus-2 that produced 18378 words after pre-processing. It gives 49% precision, 78.6% recall and 60.36% F1-Measure. When corpuse-3 is fed to the stemmer it produces 19351 words after pre-processing. Our light weight stemmer produced precision 73.55%, recall 90.53% and 81.16% F1-Measure. The summary of the three corpora and evaluation of the stemmer after applying stemmer is given in table 1.

Characteristics	Corpus (1)	Corpus (2)	Corpus (3)
Words after Pre-processing	4268	18378	19351
Already stemmed Words	2233	10674	12428
Words to be Stemmed	2035	7704	6923
Correct Stemmed Words	802	3775	5092
Results			
Precision	39.4%	49%	73.55%
Recall	71.1%	78.6%	90.53%
F1-Measure	50.70%	60.36%	81.16%

Table-1: Description of corpora after pre-processing and evaluation of stemmer

Conclusion

Morphologically Urdu is a complex language. There exist a number of variants in this language for a single word. Urdu language is rich in both inflectional and derivational morphologies.

In this paper, a light weight stemmer for Urdu text is proposed. The proposed stemmer handles inflectional morphology. This stemmer removes prefixes and suffixes from a word to get stem word but before removing the affixes, the stemmer checks the exceptional cases. The stemmer gives 73.55% precision, 90.53% recall and 81.16% F1-Measure and it was also compared with *Assas-band*, the only available Urdu stemmer.

Generally stemmer increases recall at the cost of decreased precision. Our study proves that maximum matching affix approach is more suitable for developing the stemmer for Urdu language. Other regional languages of Pakistan (Punjabi, Pashtu, Sindi, and Kashmiri etc) are similar to Urdu in morphology. It would be interesting to observe whether similar techniques can be used to develop stemmers for these languages.

References

Al-Khuli, M. (1991). A dictionary of theoretical linguistics: English-Arabic with an Arabic-English glossary. Published by Library of Lebanon.

E.T. Al-Shammari, Jessica Lin, (2008). Towards an error-free Arabic stemming. *17th Conference on Information and Knowledge Management, iNEWS'08*, pages 1–6,Napa Valley, California, USA.

Frakes, R.Baeza-Yates, (1992). *Information Retrieval: Data Structures and Algorithms*. New Jersey, Prentice Hall PTR.

Imed Al-Sughaiyer, Ibrahim Al-Kharashi. (2004). Arabic morphological analysis techniques: a comprehensive survey. *Journal of the American Society for Information Science and Technology*, 55(3):189 – 213.

J.B. Lovins, (1968). Development of a stemming algorithm. *Mechanical Translation and Computational Linguistics*, 11(1 and 2):22–31.

Malik, M. G. Abbas,B.C. Bhattcharyya, P. (2008). Hindi Urdu machine transliteration using finite-state transducers. *proceedings of COLING* 2008, pages 537–544, Manchester, UK.

M.F. Porter. (1980). An algorithm for suffix stripping. Program, 14(3): 130–137.

Mokhtaripour and S. Jahanpour, (2006). Introduction to a new Farsi stemmer. *CIKM Proceedings of the 15th ACM international conference on Information and knowledge management*, pages 826-827,Arlington, Virginia, USA.

M. Tashakori, M. Meybodi & F. Oroumchian, (2002). Bon: first Persian stemmer. *Lecture Notes on Information and Communication Technology*, pages 487-494.

Q. Akram, A. Naseer and S. Hussain, (2009). Assas-band, an affix- exception-list based Urdu stemmer", *Proceedings of the 7th Workshop on Asian Language Resources*, pages 40–47, Singapore.

Rizvi, S. & Hussain, M. (2005), "Analysis, Design and implementation of Urdu morphological analyzer. *Engineering Sciences and Technology, SCONEST*, pages 1-7.

Sabzwari, S. (2002). *Urdu Quwaid.* Sang-e-Meel Publication.

S. Khoja and R. Garside. (1999). Stemming Arabic Text, Lancaster, UK, Computing Department, Lancaster University.

Thabet, N. (2004). Stemming the Qur'an. In the *Proceedings of the Workshop on Computational Approaches to Arabic Script-based Languages*, pages 85-88.

Morpheme Segmentation for Kannada Standing on the Shoulder of Giants

Suma Bhat
Beckman Institute, University of Illinois, Urbana-Champaign, IL 61801, USA
spbhat2@illinois.edu

ABSTRACT
This paper studies the applicability of a set of state-of-the-art unsupervised morphological segmentation algorithms for the problem of morpheme boundary detection in Kannada, a resource-poor language with highly inflectional and agglutinative morphology. The choice of the algorithms for the experiment is based in part on their performance with highly inflected languages such as Finnish and Bengali (complex morphology similar to that of Kannada). When trained on a corpus of about 990K words, the best performing algorithm had an F-measure of 73% on a test set. The performance was better on a set of inflected nouns than on a set of inflected verbs. Key advantages of the algorithms conducive to efficient morphological analysis of Kannada were identified. An important by-product of this study is an empirical analysis of some aspects of vocabulary growth in Kannada based on the word frequency distribution of the words in the reference corpus.

KEYWORDS: Unsupervised morphological segmentation, Kannada language.

1 Introduction

With the ongoing quest for developing language processing techniques and tools for under-resourced languages there is an emerging need to study various aspects of these languages. Kannada, with nearly 70 million speakers is one of the 40 most spoken languages in the world. It is one of the scheduled languages of India and the official and administrative language of the state of Karnataka in South India. Its rich literary heritage has endowed the language with an immense written resource and efforts are currently underway to bring them to web scales. However, available computational tools for Kannada are only in their incipient stages. Simultaneously, there is an ever increasing number of internet users who are creating online materials in Kannada. As more information becomes available it becomes imperative to develop language processing tools that help us organize, search and understand information in Kannada. One such task is that of information retrieval and the time is ripe for developing efficient information retrieval algorithms for Kannada.

The role of stemming to improve retrieval effectiveness, particularly for highly inflected languages and monolingual retrieval has been well documented in (Larkey and Connell, 2003). Consequently, with the goal of developing a suitable stemmer for Kannada, the focus of this study is an exploration of the suitability of current state-of-the-art unsupervised morphological analyzers (studied for English and Finnish) for the task of morphological segmentation of words and eventual stemming in Kannada. In this sense, we see Kannada as a dwarf sitting on the shoulder of giants such as English and Finnish.

More specifically, we study the usefulness of a set of unsupervised learning of morphology (ULM) approaches towards addressing the problem of morpheme boundary analysis for Kannada. Our empirical study uses two corpora in Kannada and we compare the performance of the approaches with respect to addressing some of the challenges of Kannada morphology. A by-product of this study is an analysis of the word frequency distributions for the purpose of creating stop words in Kannada as also to quantify the productive processes of Kannada morphology. In this study, we restrict ourselves to studying morpheme segmentation noting the fact that eventual stemming is not a distant goal once we have reasonably segmented a word into its constituent morphemes.

The rest of this paper is organized as follows. In Section 2 we present a description in brief of the morphological analyzers for Kannada proposed thus far. Section 3 deals with an overview of the unsupervised methods we consider in this study and the challenges in Kannada morphological analysis. A description of our experiment is found in Section 4 with its subsections describing the corpora used, the evaluation methods and the results. Section 5 deals with the discussion of the results and error-analyses of the experiment. In Section 6 we analyze some aspects of Kannada with reference to its word frequency distribution. We conclude the paper with our conclusion and remarks in Section 7.

2 Related Prior Work

There is some amount of work done on morphological analysis in Kannada. Vikram and Urs (Vikram and Urs, 2007) present their prototypical morphological analyzer for Kannada based on finite state machines. There is a mention of its ability to handle 500 distinct noun and verb stems of Kannada.

Antony et al (Antony et al., 2010) outline the development of a paradigm-based morphological analyzer for Kannada verbs with the ability to handle compound verb morphology achieves a very competitive accuracy of 96.25% for Kannada verbs.

In (Ramasamy et al., 2011), Ramasamy et al. describe their implementation of a morphological analyzer and generator for Kannada. It is a rule-based finite state transducer with relevant morphological feature information of Kannada words and well defined morphophonemic (sandhi) rules governing word generation.

The morphological analyzer for Kannada described by Shambhavi et al. (Shastri, 2011) is a rule based approach which stores the possible paradigms for the roots available in a lexicon in a computationally efficient trie data structure. A given word is analyzed by matching it with the corresponding paradigm. It also performs a morphophonemic analysis of a word that does not reside in the lexicon by proceeding with suffix stripping and lexicon look-up iteratively. The developed system has the capability to can handle up to 3700 root words and around 88000 inflected forms.

Murthy (Murthy, 1999) describes a finite-state network based morphological analysis and generation system, MORPH, for Kannada. In essence, the system segregates the procedural and declarative processing between its two components, the network component - which has the capability of handing the analysis, and the process component - which has the capability of handing the morphophonemic decisions. The analysis proceeds in a series of affix stripping steps, from the input word to the root which is then checked against its stored lexicon. The performance of the system is reported to be 60 to 70% on general texts.

However, as of this study, the few attempts towards morphological analysis available in the literature have only marginal details about the studies, broad mentions about performance and no form of discussion or error-analysis via insights gained for word classes or methods that worked (or those that did not work) is available. What is clear from available literature is that all the above methods have pursued a rule-based and completely supervised approach. There have been no studies to understand the capabilities/limitations of an unsupervised approach to morphological segmentation in Kannada nor are other corpus-based analyses about Kannada available.

Consequently, this study is an attempt to fill the lacuna and has the following two goals - first, we explore the applicability of state-of-the-art models for unsupervised learning of morphology in Kannada. Here our focus is not only to analyze the performance in general but also to study their behavior handling the morphological complexities in Kannada as pointers in the direction of leveraging their results. Second, we perform an empirical analysis of one of the largest publicly available corpora in Kannada. To the extent of our knowledge, this is the first study exploring unsupervised techniques for Kannada and consequently, we expect it to drive future efforts towards developing further tools/algorithms that address the broader problem of stemming in Kannada.

3 Methods for Unsupervised Morphological Analysis

Being the most researched language in the natural language processing community, several unsupervised morphological analysis techniques have been implemented and studied for English. In the recent years, however, with the inclusion of other highly inflected European languages such as Finnish in the language processing to-do list, unsupervised methods are expanding to analyze morphologies more complex than that of English. For the purpose of our experiment, we focus our attention on three main approaches where the choice is based in part owing to their success with highly inflected languages such as Finnish and Bengali(complex morphology) and popularity in available literature. The methods that we will consider for our study are:

1. Goldsmith's method of unsupervised learning of morphology (Goldsmith, 2001),
2. Morfessor Categories-MAP (Creutz and Lagus, 2007), and,
3. High-Performance, Language-Independent Morphological Segmentation (Dasgupta and Ng, 2006, 2007).

3.1 Linguistica

Goldsmith's method of unsupervised learning of morphology (popularly known by the name of the tool, Linguistica[1] that implements this technique) is centered around the idea of minimum description length (MDL). Very broadly, MDL of the data is a combination of the length of morphology (in information theoretic terms) and length of compressed data (or compressed length of the corpus, given by probabilities derived from morphology). The learning heuristic then proceeds in steps of discovering basic candidate suffixes of the language using weighted mutual information, using these to find a set of suffixes, then using MDL to correct errors generated by heuristics. It starts with a corpus of unannotated text and produces a set of signatures, a signature being a pattern of affixes (prefixes or suffixes) that a stem takes (Goldsmith, 2001). An example suffix signature in English could be NULL.ed.ing.s, which combines with the stem *mark* to create the words *mark, marked, marking* and *marks*. In addition to this, the algorithm gives a list of stems, prefixes and suffixes with corresponding frequency information. This method will henceforth be referred to as Linguistica.

3.2 Morfessor Categories-MAP

Morfessor is an unsupervised method for the segmenting words into morpheme-like units. The idea behind the Morfessor model is, like Linguistica, to discover as compact a description of the data as possible. Substrings occurring frequently enough in several different word forms are proposed as morphs and the words are then represented as a concatenation of morphs. An optimal balance is sought between compactness of the morph lexicon versus the compactness of the representation of the corpus. For our study we use the most general of the currently available morfessor implementations of the generative probabilistic models designed for highly inflecting and compounding languages (Creutz and Lagus, 2007).

In Morfessor Categories, the segmentation of the corpus is modeled using a Hidden Markov Model (HMM) with transition probabilities between categories and emission probabilities of morphs from categories. Three categories are used: prefix, stem, and suffix and an additional non-morpheme (or noise) category. Some distributional properties of the morphs in a proposed segmentation of the corpus are used for determining category-to-morph emission probabilities. An important improvement in this model (compared to its predecessors) is that the morph lexicon contains hierarchical entries. That is, a morph can either consist of a string of letters (as in the previous models) or of two submorphs, which can recursively consist of submorphs. This in turn supports the agglutinative word structure of complex words. The Morfessor Categories algorithm has one parameter (the perplexity threshold b) that needs to be set to an appropriate value for optimal performance. Being a Maximum a Posteriori (MAP) model, an explicit probabilty is calculated for both the lexicon and the representation of the corpus

[1]Linguistica is publicly available at http://humanities.uchicago.edu/faculty/goldsmith/Linguistica2000/

conditioned on the lexicon. Current versions of Morfessor attain an F-measure value of about 70% for the languages Turkish, Finnish and English. We will refer to this model by its family name, Morfessor.

3.3 Language-Independent Morphological Segmentation

The third algorithm we consider here (henceforth referred to as UnDivide from the name of the program accompanying the publication(Dasgupta and Ng, 2007)[2]) is an extension of Keshava and Pitler's algorithm (Keshava and Pitler, 2006) on language-independent techniques for morpheme induction. It is possibly the first to apply unsupervised learning to morphological parsing of an Indo-Aryan language (Dasgupta and Ng, 2006). At its core is the step for inducing morphemes using the heuristics in Keshava and Pitler's algorithm[3]. The induced morpheme list is then modified via three extensions -

- Employing a length-dependent threshold to prune the list of candidate affixes - here the rationale is that shorter morphemes (of length one or two) are likely to be more erroneous than their longer counterparts;
- Detecting composite suffixes via suffix strength and word-level similarity; and,
- Improving root induction via a simple but novel idea of using relative corpus frequency of the candidates.

The important features of this algorithm are its ability to move beyond one-slot morphology to handle words with multiple suffixes and the identification of inappropriate morpheme attachments. It achieves an F-score of 83.29% on Bengali.

The first two of the algorithms studied here are similar in that they have information theoretic optimization criteria and the heuristics are guided by probabilistic methods. The last of these is based on heuristics pertinent to word formations in general. The above algorithms seem attractive candidates for studying unsupervised morphological segmentation for Kannada owing to the fact that they have very few or no language dependent parameters and because of their reasonable performance with Bengali and Finnish (with morphological complexities such as that of Kannada).

3.4 Challenges to Morphological Analysis in Kannada

Kannada is one of the four major literary languages of the Dravidian family. Kannada is mainly an agglutinating language of the suffixing type. Nouns are marked for number and case and verbs are marked, in most cases, for agreement with the subject in number, gender and person. This makes Kannada a relatively free word order language. Morphologically rich languages such as Kannada, are characterized by a large number of morphemes in a single word, where morpheme boundaries are difficult to detect because they are fused together. In addition, rampant morphophonemic processes (sandhi), productive compounding and agglutinating morphology of inflectional and derivational suffixes (the latter mostly with words

[2]Its implementation is available at http://www.hlt.utdallas.edu/ sajib/.

[3]The key idea in this paper is to use words that appear as substrings of other words and transitional probabilities together to detect morpheme boundaries

of Sanskrit origin naturalized into Kannada) drive the prolific word formation processes of the language(Sridhar, 1990).

Another challenge at the level of word formations is that Kannada is diglossic - the formal or the literary variety differs significantly from the spoken (informal) or the colloquial variety. For example, the first person singular form of the verb 'tinnu' (eat) in the non-past tense is 'tinnuttEne' in the literary variety and 'tinnuttIni' (which gets further simplified to 'tiMtIni') in the spoken variety. Here we restrict ourselves to the analysis of the literary variety but it must be pointed out that informal written materials (including plays, short stories or humorous articles) can include a lot of spoken forms.

It may be worth noting here that effective language processing techniques for a language like Kannada cannot a rely on a purely rule-based or a purely stochastic approach, since the former demands subtle linguistic expertise and elaborate hand coding whereas the latter a large and diverse corpus. What is needed is an efficient combination of both approaches.

4 Experiments

4.1 Data

For purposes of experimentation, we use two corpora whose sizes are tabulated in Table 1.

1. A collection of stories for children, *dinakkoMdu kathe* written in Kannada [4] by one of the leading writers Dr. Anupama Niranjana. This corpus being a collection of children's stories, is informal in nature as a result of which, includes a widespread use of informal constructions. Although our focus in this study is on the formally constructed word forms, efforts needed to clean the data prevent us from excluding the informal constructions from the corpus.

2. The set of written documents in Kannada from the EMILLE-CIIL corpus (EMI).The documents comprise a collection of essays on diverse topics including commerce, leisure, social sciences and literature.

Corpus name	No. of word tokens	No. of word types
Story collection (**DINA**)	96370	24851
EMILLE (**EMIL**)	997012	210368

Table 1: Data size of Kannada corpora.

Vocabulary creation: We then preprocess each of these data sets (romanized) by tokenizing (we follow the standard tokenization of counting word tokens as units delimited by spaces) and removing punctuations and other unwanted character sequences. The remaining words are then used to create our vocabulary, which consists of 24851 word types for the story collection and 210368 for the EMILLE set. Unlike morphological analysis for many European languages, however, we do not take the conventional step of removing proper nouns from our word list, because we do not have a named entity identifier for Kannada.

[4] We would like to acknowledge the help of the members of Sriranga Digital Software Technologies - Prof. C. S. Yogananda and D. Shivashankar, in Srirangapatna, Karnataka, India, who made this corpus available.

Test set preparation: To create our test set, we first get a list of common words in the vocabularies of the two corpora. We then manually removed the proper nouns, informal forms for verbs *hyAge,naMge*, words with spelling mistakes and high frequency stop words from the common word list before performing hand-segmentation of the words. In the absence of a complete knowledge-based morphological parsing tool and a publicly available hand-tagged morphological database for Kannada, we had to annotate on a subset of the common word list for generating our test cases. The test set consists of 53 inflected noun forms and 50 verb forms amounting to a total of 103 words. The verb forms included are those with one of the several aspectual auxiliaries, e.g. *hArihOyitu*(also termed as vectors, (Sridhar, 1990)), as well as those with various tense, aspect and PNG markers. The noun forms are those with the form noun+case ending, or noun+plural+case.

Gold standard: We obtain the gold standard by segmenting the words in the test set and for the purpose of this study we are looking for a surface-level segmentation. That is, the segmented word form must contain exactly the same letters as the original, unsplit word. Thus there may be multiple surface-level segmentations for a given word. For instance, the inflected verb form *ODidaru* has three surface segmentations - OD idaru, OD id aru and ODi daru all considered valid for this study.

4.2 Evaluation of the Chosen Methods

We run the algorithms separately for the two corpora with their default parameters. We then evaluate the results by comparing the segmentation of the words in the test set with that in the gold segmentation. The algorithms were run in their default parameter settings since a large enough gold standard to tune the parameters of the algorithms was unavailable.

The evaluation is based on the placement of morpheme boundaries and follows the guidelines set by the Morphochallenge competition[5]. We use F-score to evaluate the performance of the segmentation algorithms on the test set. F-score is the harmonic mean of recall and precision, which are computed based on the placement of morpheme boundaries as below.

- Precision is the number of hits (H) divided by the sum of the number of hits and insertions (I): Precision = H/(H+I).
- Recall is the number of hits divided by the sum of the number of hits and deletions (D): Recall = H/(H+D).
- F-Measure is the harmonic mean of precision and recall: F-Measure = 2H/(2H+I+D).

Here a hit occurs for every correctly placed boundaries between morphemes, an insertion for every incorrect boundary between morphemes, and a deletion for every missed boundaries between morphemes - all with respect tot the gold segmentation.

In many cases, it is difficult to come up with one single correct morpheme segmentation. However, we will use the provided gold standard as the only correct answer. For some words, there are multiple interpretations in the gold standard. All of them are considered correct, and the alternative that provides the best alignment against the proposed segmentation is chosen.

[5]For details see http://research.ics.aalto.fi/events/morphochallenge2005/evaluation.shtml.

4.3 Results

Linguistica and UnDivide in their default settings exclude the least frequent words (those seen only once in the corpus) in their analysis. Consequently, we first run all the algorithms with words that occur at least twice in the corpus. The corresponding results are summarized in Table 2

	DINA			EMIL		
Algorithm	P	R	F	P	R	F
Linguistica	62.64	47.11	53.77	45.63	38.21	41.59
Morfessor-CatMAP	73.63	59.82	**66.01**	67.86	68.47	68.16
UnDivide	63.75	45.13	52.85	72.348	71.58	**71.96**

Table 2: Evaluation results (reported in terms of precision (P), recall (R) and F-score (F))

Based on the results, it appears that the UnDivide algorithm by far outperforms the other algorithms for the large data set (EMILLE), whereas Morfessor is the best performing algorithm for the small data set.

In order to assess the performance of the segmentation algorithm on specific word categories (noun/verb), we do the following. We split the test set into two - a set of inflected nouns and another that of inflected verbs and evaluate the performance for the 6 data set and algorithm combinations. As tabulated in Table 3, we observe that for inflected nouns, UnDivide emerges as the best performer for EMIL whereas, Morfessor emerges as the best performer for DINA. In the case of inflected verbs, however, we notice that UnDivide is the best performing algorithm for both the data sets.

	DINA			EMIL		
Algorithm	P	R	F	P	R	F
Linguistica	67.92	59.02	63.16	40.98	47.17	43.86
Morfessor-CatMAP	93.33	73.68	**82.35**	80.36	80.36	80.36
UnDivide	64.86	42.11	51.06	79.25	85.71	**82.35**

Table 3: Evaluation results for inflected nouns (reported in terms of precision (P), recall (R) and F-score (F)).

	DINA			EMIL		
Algorithm	P	R	F	P	R	F
Linguistica	55.26	35.00	42.86	44.00	35.48	39.29
Morfessor-CatMAP	54.35	45.45	49.50	55.36	55.36	55.36
UnDivide	62.79	47.37	**54.00**	63.41	55.32	**59.09**

Table 4: Evaluation results for inflected verbs (reported in terms of precision (P), recall (R) and F-score (F)).

Noting that several morphological variants of more frequent stems belong to the set of words occurring only once, we extend the input data to include them and use all words in the analysis. The resulting change in performance is shown in Table 5 where we compare the results using the trimmed data set (no singletons) with those obtained using the full data set. Here we would like to mention the fact that Morfessor showed a bigger change in performance compared to UnDivide[6] the other results are not tabulated. In both instances we notice an increased recall and hence an increase in the F-measure.

	Trimmed			**Full**		
Algorithm	P	R	F	P	R	F
Morfessor (EMIL)	67.86	68.47	68.16	67.18	80.00	73.03
Morfessor (DINA)	73.63	59.82	66.01	66.91	82.73	73.98
UnDivide(EMIL)	72.348	71.58	71.96	68.97	73.39	71.11
UnDivide(DINA)	63.75	45.13	52.85	63.75	45.13	52.85

Table 5: Evaluation results including all words in the corpus(reported in terms of precision (P), recall (R) and F-score (F)) for Morfessor and UnDivide. We notice an improved F-measure owing to an increase in recall in all the cases except for DINA with UnDivide. Linguistica did not show any change.

5 Discussion and Error Analysis

5.1 Effect of Data size

With the exception of Linguistica, we notice improved morpheme boundary detection (in terms of increased F-measure) with increase in data sizes. A plausible explanation is that with increased data sizes, more morphological variants are available permitting better stochastically motivated decisions. In the case of Linguistica, however, we noticed that only about 65% of the input data was analyzed (recall that the training data excludes words occurring only once) and so data sparsity with inadequate access to morphological variants was an obvious reason for poor performance.

The improved performance resulting from an increased recall (as seen from Table 5) can be explained as follows. With access to more inflected forms of the same stem, the algorithm has an improved ability to segment the morphemes. As an example with the segmentation by Morfessor, consider the form *mADuttA* which in the trimmed case, was not segmented but in the full case was segmented as *mADutt A*. Again, consider the case of *janarige* which in the trimmed case was not segmented, but in the full was segmented as *jana ri ge*. This has the potential to decrease the number of deletions and in turn cause a corresponding increase in the number of hits (refer back to Section 4.2 for the meaning of hits and deletions in this context).

5.2 Morpheme Boundary Detection

We will now highlight some observations based on the segmentation output of the algorithms underscoring some special cases that were handled/not handled by the algorithms.

As shown in Table 6, we notice that Linguistica only separates the final suffix, which in this example is the plural ending; Morfessor shows a tendency to overly segment the words.

In another instance, the word *lekkaparishOdhakarAgalAraru* was not analyzed either by UnDivide or by Linguistica. Morfessor, however, produced the following segmentation:

[6] UnDivide and Linguistica in their default settings ignore singleton word types. It was possible to change two parameters of UnDivide to accept this change, but such a change was not possible with Linguistica 3.

Algorithm	jagaLavADatoDagidaru	aNNatammaMdiriddaru
Linguistica	jagaLavADatoDagida+ru	aNNatammaMdiridda+ru
Morfessor-CatMAP	jagaLa+vADa+toDagida+ru	aNNatammaMdir+idda+ru
UnDivide	jagaLa+vADatoDagidaru	aNNa+tammaMdiriddaru

Table 6: Sample of detected morpheme boundaries for the three algorithms for two words *jagaLavADatoDagidaru* and *aNNatammaMdiriddaru*.

$$lekka/STM + pari/STM + shOdha/STM + ka/SUF + rAga/STM + lAra/STM + ru/SUF$$

Based on the sample and other segmentations, we observe the ability of Morfessor to deal with the complex morphology of Kannada. In particular, the instance of not splitting the compound *aNNatammandiru* (meaning 'brothers') interesting. However, there are also cases of over-segmentation as seen in the last example here, where *lekkaparishOdhaka*, a compound, has been segmented. It appears that a more data-driven analysis leading to a careful choice of the perplexity parameter b is necessary to tune the model.

5.3 Algorithm-specific Features

We will now consider some features we observe when analyzing the segmentation output of each of the algorithms.

5.3.1 Linguistica

A closer examination of Linguistica output reveals that it is particularly weak at segmenting Kannada compound words and its complex verbal inflectional system. Kannada being a highly inflected language with a wide variety of inflectional and derivational morphology acting upon the stems to produce valid words, the single-slot capability of Linguistica is a serious shortcoming of the model. With word formation processes in Kannada governed by compounds, phonotactics (sandhi), prefixation and serial suffixation (from its agglutinative characteristics), the one-slot procedure seems rather simplistic to capture the wide spectrum of word formation processes. Nevertheless, looking at the signatures and the stems taking the signatures, a general framework of a paradigm can be induced and is likely to be more descriptive with a very large data set.

5.3.2 UnDivide Algorithm

- The algorithm was successfully able to generate the following (character-change) rules by a single character replacement, addition and deletion at morpheme boundaries as instantiated below. For the noun stems, *guDisalu, hAvu, hUvu, haDagu, kADu, kAlu, mAtu, nIru, pAlu*

  1. the stem final *u* becomes *i* before the dative case marker *ge*;
  2. the stem final *u* becomes *i* before the genitive case marker *na*; and
  3. the stem final *u* becomes *i* before the dative case marker *niMda*

  which are incipient rules of noun declension (paradigm generation) for Kannada.

- The list of the top suffixes learned by the algorithm includes: *gaLannu, yannu, nnu, vannu, da, lli, nige, gaLu, nannu, ru, ya, diMda, na, ge, yalli, dalli, koMDu*. One can identify these to be the noun endings.
- The algorithm correctly analyzed instances of derivational affixes. As an example, we see that suffixes *shAhi* in *adhikArashAhi* and *kAra* in *itihAsakAra* and *kUlikAra* were identified.
- Although the heuristics to detect composite suffixes seems plausible for Kannada with the successful detection (and segmentation) of composite suffixes *kkiruva* in *pUrvakkiruva* as *kke* and *ruva*, a more reasonable analysis should likely take into consideration the morphophonemic (internal sandhi) rules.

It is also worth pointing out here that despite the claim of the language-independence of the algorithm, the 16 parameters in the algorithm need tuning for a better capturing the morphological nuances of the language under consideration.

5.3.3 Morfessor Categories-MAP

- Upon closer inspection, we noticed that the algorithm has only generated 37 suffixes, which seems very small given the size of the data. However, owing to the small test set, the performance does not reflect this shortcoming. In the larger data, the algorithm generated 196 suffixes.
- The algorithm has the capability to identify prefixes (with its dedicated category for a prefix, apart from stem and suffix). While it correctly identified the prefixes *vi* in *viBinna*, *A* in *AdEsha*, *saM* in *saMpUrNa* and *a* in *amUrta*, it incorrectly segmented *ADuvudu* as *A* - Prefix and *Duvudu* - Stem.
- As in the case of the algorithm UnDivide, a few instances of derivational morphology were successfully analyzed by the algorithm. e.g: The suffix *shAhi* in *adhikArashAhi* and *kAra* in *itihAsakAra* and *kUlikAra* were identified.

Unfortunately owing to the fact that no sufficient segmented data was available to tune the parameters, we are unable to make further language specific generalizations on the items mentioned above. Testing the systems on a large collection of words from real world data is the only way to discover some of the potential problems or interesting segmentation patterns.

6 Analysis of Word Frequency Distributions

We now digress slightly from the unsupervised morphological analysis set up and consider some aspects of Kannada in the light of analyses derived from its word frequency distribution obtained from the EMIL corpus considered in the study. In this context we ask the following questions that we think are important from an IR point of view.

1. We know that in English, one can safely say that the most frequent word in a corpus is 'the' and will likely not be very far from truth to say that 'of' and 'and' follow 'the' in the most frequent list of words. Analogously, what words in Kannada are most frequent?
2. We know that Kannada has a richer morphology compared to English. Is it possible to obtain a quantitative comparison of the relative complexities? For instance, how do their vocabulary growths compare?

3. In the realm of IR a stopword list contains nonsignificant words that are removed from a document or a request before beginning the indexing process. What would a list of stopwords for Kannada look like?

The answers to these questions will be the material we explore in this section.

First we consider the word frequency distribution for the word types in the EMILLE corpus (with size about a million word tokens) and obtain the frequency of occurrence of the word types in the corpus. A snapshot of the frequencies of the top ten and the bottom ten are shown in the Table 7.

10 most frequent words		10 least frequent words	
10993	mattu	1	beMbalavAgirisikoLLabEkiruvudariMda
8007	oMdu	1	vyavasthApakarAgiruvadillavAddariMda
5374	A	1	AdEshisalpaTTavugaLu
4803	athavA	1	sURyacaMdranakSatragaLiruvavarege
4608	eMdu	1	AtaMkagaLannuMTumADuvavaruivarella
4525	mEle	1	prItivAtsalyavuLLavarAgiruttAre
3692	Adare	1	toMdaregIDAgiruvavareMdare
3388	tanna	1	nayanamanOharavAgirabEkallade
3370	hAgU	1	paThyapustakagaLaMthavirabEkeMbudannu

Table 7: The most frequent and least frequent words in the EMILLE corpus for Kannada.

We notice that the high frequency slots are occupied by conjunctions, articles, number words, postposition and pronouns - words that are right candidates for being included in the stopword list. The words in the other column, the singleton words, may belong to various categories, but what is salient among them is their length. While some are results of typographical errors, others are true words formed from internal sandhi processes or compounding or a combination of both. These singletons account for nearly 66% of the corpus. Successful morphological analysis of these words cannot be achieved by paradigm look-up alone since their stems are outcomes of the productive word-formation processes in Kannada and by their very nature, they cannot all be found in a lexicon. On the other hand, owing to their sparse occurrence in corpora, taken by themselves, they are not amenable to be considered in statistical analyses. Processing them requires a combination of rule-based and stochastic approaches deriving the benefits of linguistic expertise (for rule-based methods) and access to large, diverse and permuted corpora (for stochastic techniques).

Having obtained a frequency list of the word types we observe that the most frequent word, *mattu*, accounts for about 1.3% of all word occurrences, the second most frequent word, *oMdu*, accounts for slightly over 1% of all words, followed by the third which accounts for about 0.8% of all words. Going down the frequency list, we notice that it takes 3458 word types to account for half the corpus (in terms of word tokens).

Now consider these numbers in the light of the following fact that in the Brown Corpus, the word *the* is the most frequently occurring word, and by itself accounts for nearly 7% of all word occurrences (69,970 out of slightly over 1 million). True to Zipf's Law, the second-place word *of* accounts for slightly over 3.5% of words (36,410 occurrences), followed by "and" (28,854).

Only 135 vocabulary items are needed to account for half the Brown Corpus[7].

Using the two facts, we make the following important observations towards making a guesstimate of the size of a stopword list for Kannada.

- Comparing the number of word types required to cover 50% of the corpus (3458 types in Kannada vs. 135 in English) and noting that the corpora are roughly of the same size (and assuming that the genres are similar), we notice that the number of word types for Kannada is about 25 times that for English. Thus we need to look farther than the number of stopwords in English to generate a reasonable list of stop words.

- Shifting our attention to the other end of the frequency distribution, we now consider the growth of vocabulary comparing the proportion of *hapax legomena* or the number of words occurring once in the corpus. Baayen ((Baayen, 2001), pp. 49-50) shows how the growth rate of the vocabulary (the rate at which the vocabulary size increases as sample size increases), can be estimated as, the ratio of the number of *hapax legomena* to the number of tokens. Intuitively, this means that the proportion of hapax legomena encountered up to the N th token is a reasonable estimate of how likely it is that word $N+1$ will be a hapax legomenon, i.e., a word that we have not seen before and one that will consequently increase vocabulary size.

  For the Brown corpus, the number of *hapax legomena* is 24375 and given its corpus size to be 1015945, we have an estimate of vocabulary growth rate for the Brown corpus is $24375/1015945 = 0.024$. Now consider a similarly diverse corpus, EMIL with the number of *hapax legomena* $= 140353$ and a corpus size $= 997012$. An estimate of the vocabulary growth rate for EMILLE(Kannada) is then $140353/997012 = 0.14$. Discounting foreign words (words with consonant endings are good candidates) totaling to about 4585 words, the estimate of vocabulary growth rate comes to 0.136. Thus, even at a corpus size of nearly 1 million, we notice that the growth of vocabulary for Kannada is roughly about 6 times that of English. This could be construed as an approximate quantitative comparison of the relative complexities in vocabulary between English and Kannada and one could attribute this difference to the rich and complex morphology of Kannada compared to English.

7 Conclusion

In this study we have seen that a set of unsupervised methods of morpheme induction perform morpheme boundary segmentation reasonably well. When trained on a corpus of size of about 990K words, the best performing algorithm (Morfessor) had an F-score of 73%. A key feature of these methods is that they have no language specific rules - the heuristics are language independent and probabilistic relying only on the training corpus, but are nonetheless able to capture some important features of the morphology of Kannada. However, we also saw that for a reasonable coverage of the productive morphological processes, we would need an approach that captures the productive process. This is possible by a synergistic approach to morphological analysis that combines a linguistically grounded, rule-based approach with a stochastic method.

So, where do we go from here? In the comprehensive survey article on unsupervised learning of morphology (ULM)(Hammarström and Borin, 2011), the authors, summarizing the general

[7] Source: http://www.edict.biz/textanalyser/wordlists.htm

strengths and weaknesses of the methods, state "typically word segmentation algorithms perform on an insufficient level, apparently due to the lack of any notion of morphotactics. On the other hand, typical morphology learning algorithms have problems because the ingrained assumptions they make about word structure are generally wrong (i.e., too strict) for Finnish or for other highly inflecting or compounding languages. In short, they cannot handle the possibly high number of morphemes per word."

Continuing their analysis on whether ULM is of any use, "most ULM approaches reported in the literature are small proof-of-concept experiments, which generally founder on the lack of evaluation data. The MorphoChallenge series does provide adequate gold-standard evaluation data for Finnish, English, German, Arabic, and Turkish as well as task-based Information Retrieval (IR) evaluation data for English, German, and Finnish. It can be seen that ULM systems are mature enough to enhance IR, but so far, ULM systems are not close to full accuracy on the gold standard."

So if our immediate goal is stemming for IR in Kannada, there is some hope in the pursuit of a hybrid (unsupervised and rule-based) stemmer for Kannada utilizing the key ideas of the algorithms considered in this study. Standing on the shoulder of giants such as English and Finnish (and possibly Turkish) we should look for models attempted and benefit from the knowledge advances achieved for making progress in the task of morphological segmentation of words and eventual stemming in Kannada.

Acknowledgements

We would like to acknowledge the help of the members of Sriranga Digital Software Technologies - Prof. C. S. Yogananda and D. Shivashankar, who not only made the corpus of a collection of short stories in Kannada available for this study but also made it computation friendly with the use of their unicode to ASCII converter.

References

The emille/ciil corpus, catalogue reference: Elra-w0037.

Antony, P., Kumar, M., and Soman, K. (2010). Paradigm based morphological analyzer for kannada language using machine learning approach. *International Journal on Advances in Computational Sciences and Technology ISSN*, pages 0973–6107.

Baayen, R. (2001). *Word frequency distributions*, volume 18. Springer.

Creutz, M. and Lagus, K. (2007). Unsupervised models for morpheme segmentation and morphology learning. *ACM Transactions on Speech and Language Processing*, 4(1):3.

Dasgupta, S. and Ng, V. (2006). Unsupervised morphological parsing of bengali. *Language Resources and Evaluation*, 40(3):311–330.

Dasgupta, S. and Ng, V. (2007). High-performance, language-independent morphological segmentation. In *Proceedings of NAACL HLT*, pages 155–163.

Goldsmith, J. (2001). Unsupervised learning of the morphology of a natural language. *Computational linguistics*, 27(2):153–198.

Hammarström, H. and Borin, L. (2011). Unsupervised learning of morphology. *Comput. Linguist.*, 37(2):309–350.

Keshava, S. and Pitler, E. (2006). A simpler, intuitive approach to morpheme induction. In *Proceedings of 2nd Pascal Challenges Workshop*, pages 31–35.

Larkey, L. S. and Connell, M. E. (2003). Structured queries, language modeling, and relevance modeling in cross-language information retrieval. In *Information Processing and Management Special Issue on Cross Language Information Retrieval*.

Murthy, K. (1999). A network and process model for morphological analysis/generation. In *ICOSAL-2, the Second International Conference on South Asian Languages, Punjabi University, Patiala, India*.

Ramasamy, V., Antony, P., Saravanan, S., and Soman, K. (2011). A rule based kannada morphological analyzer and generator using finite state transducer. *International Journal of Computer Applications*, 27(10):45–52.

Shastri, G. (2011). Kannada morphological analyser and generator using trie. *IJCSNS*, 11(1):112.

Sridhar, S. (1990). *Kannada*. Routledge.

Vikram, T. and Urs, S. (2007). Development of prototype morphological analyzer for the south indian language of kannada. asian digital libraries. looking back 10 years and forging new frontiers. *Lecture Notes in Computer Science Springer*.

Manipuri Morpheme Identification

Kishorjit Nongmeikapam[1] *Vidya Raj RK*[2] *Yumnam Nirmal* [2] *Sivaji Bandyopadhyay*[3]
(1) Department of Comp. Sc. & Engg., MIT, Manipur University, Imphal, India
(2) Department of Comp. Sc., Manipur University, Imphal, India
(3) Department of Comp. Sc. & Engg., Jadavpur University, Kolkata, India
kishorjit.nongmeikapa@gmail.com, vidyarajrk@gmail.com,
yumnamnirmal@gmail.com, sivaji_cse_ju@yahoo.com

ABSTRACT

The Morphemes of the Manipuri word are the real bottleneck for any of the Manipuri Natural Language Processing (NLP) works. It is one of the Indian Scheduled Language with less advancement so far in terms of NLP applications. This is because the nature of the language is highly agglutinative. Segmentation of a word and identifying the morphemes becomes necessary before proceeding for any of the Manipuri NLP application. A highly inflected word may sometimes consist of ten or more affixes. These affixes are the morphemes which change the semantic and grammatical structure. So the inflexion in a word plays an important role. Words are segmented to the syllables and are examined to extract a morpheme among the syllables. This work is implemented in the Manipuri words written with the Meitei Mayek (script). This is because the syllable formations are distinct comparing to the Manipuri written with Bengali script. The combination of 2-gram or bi-gram and the Standard Deviation technique are used for the identification of the morphemes. This system gives an output with the recall of 59.80%, the precision of 83.02% and the f-score of 69.52%.

KEYWORDS : Manipuri, Morpheme, Segmentation, Syllable, Bi-gram, Standard Deviation

1 Introduction

Manipuri or Meiteilon which is synonymous with the Manipuri language is a highly agglutinative Indian scheduled language. A single root word can sometimes have 10 or more affixes which are attached one after another. For example, different suffixes can be agglutinated to the root word ꯄꯨ(pu) in order to produce the word ꯄꯨꯁꯤꯟꯍꯟꯖꯔꯝꯒꯗꯕꯅꯤꯗꯀꯣ(pusinhənjərəmgədəbənidəko), which means "I wish (I) myself would have caused to bring in the article". Here 10 suffixes are being attached to a bound verbal root (Nonigopal, 2006). Separation of the morphemes in the word are as follows: ꯄꯨꯁꯤꯟꯍꯟꯖꯔꯝꯒꯗꯕꯅꯤꯗꯀꯣ = ꯄꯨ/pu + ꯁꯤꯟ/sin + ꯍꯟ/hən + ꯖ/jə + ꯔꯝ/rəm + ꯒ/gə + ꯗ/də + ꯕ/bə + ꯅꯤ/ni + ꯗ/də + ꯀꯣ/ko

Morphology is the identification, analysis and description of the structure of morphemes and other units of meaning in a language such as words, affixes, part of speech etc (Denial J et.al. 2008). Morphemes are the smallest conceptual meaningful component of a word that has semantic meaning.

In this work, first the syllables are identified which is followed by the morpheme identification among the syllables. It is not guaranteed that all the syllables are morphemes. Manipuri usages two script a borrowed Bengali script and the original Manipuri script which is also known as the Meitei Mayek. This work is implemented in the Meitei Mayek Manipuri words. This is because the syllable formations are distinct comparing to the Bengali Script Manipuri.

The paper is organised with the related works in section 2, word segmentation into syllables in section 3, the system design in section 4 which is followed by experiment and evaluation in section 5 and at the last section 6 conclusions is drawn.

2 Related work

Morphological works in Germanic and other European languages can be found in (Braschler et.al, 2004). The various stemming algorithms comparative analysis for nine European Languages is presented in the survey report by (Tomlinson, 2003).

Some of the other works on Indian Language can be found in the work of (Utpal et. al., 2002a) where unsupervised learning technique is implemented for highly inflectional language. Another work of (Utpal et. al., 2008b) deals about acquisition of morphology of an Indic language from text corpus. Oriya morphological analyser design is reported in (Mohanty et. al., 2008).

Morpheme detection will of great help for Manipuri which is a highly agglutinative Indian Language. It is because these morphemes are meaningful units and the affixation of these morpheme changes semantic and POS of a word. This identification may lead us to an easy way for Machine translation. So far, identification of syllabic unit for Manipuri words are reported in the work of (Kishorjit et. al, 2012a). The work of Manipuri morphological analyser is reported in (Sirajul et.al, 2004). Stemming works of Manipuri is also reported in (Kishorjit et. al.,2011b). Morphological driven Manipuri POS tagging are also reported in (Singh et. al., 2008).

3 Word Segmentation into syllables

Word Segmentation in this context refers to the process of division of words into phonemic units or syllables that forms the whole word. It is an operation for dividing words into unit syllables by automatic means (Kalyani et. al., 2009). It is also known as *syllabification* (Bernd, 1998).

Segmentation may be used in a variety of applications which need the unit prosodic cues of the words, or need the proper understanding of the structural construction of the words (Jean-Luc, 2007). The word segmentation of Manipuri follows the algorithms and the systems mention in (Kishorjit et. al., 2012b) with certain modifications.

3.1 A brief about Meitei Mayek characters

It will be better if the characters used in the Meitei Mayek are discussed in brief. The work is based on the 27 scripts approved by the State Government of Manipur. which is also published in (Kangjia, 2003). The characters used in Meiteilon (Manipuri language) can be classified into five different categories.

- Iyek Ipee : This character set consists of 27 letters which are mainly major consonants, out of which three are used to produce vowel sounds (ꯑ, ꯏ, ꯎ). This category is considered as major consonants in the sense that letters are used in their full form at the initial position of a syllabic unit. Moreover, associations with Cheitap Iyek are permitted with these characters only.
- Cheitap Iyek (Matras): These are associative symbols which can be found only in association with Iyek Ipee character sets. Association with Iyek Ipee characters follow a one to one relationship i.e. no two (or more) symbols is found to be associated with one letter in Iyek Ipee. Consecutive occurrence is also not permitted.
- Cheising Iyek (Numerals): This set contains the numeral figures and follow the decimal system.
- Lonsum Iyek: There are 8 characters in this set and these characters can be considered to be derivative form of 8 distinct letters in Iyek Ipee. In one sense, these letters can be regarded as half consonants as they cannot be associated with any symbols in Cheitap Iyek and cannot initiate formation of a syllable. This character set can only be present in the syllabic final position. Recurrence or clusters of these characters i.e. consecutive occurrence of these characters are also not permitted in the language.
- Khudam Iyek (Symbols): Usage of special characters is limited in this language and as such few symbols suffice the need in expression.

    Examples:

    '॥' - Cheikhei (Full Stop)

    '.' - Lum Iyek (Sign of intonation) eg. ꯆ.ꯕ (*cha.ba* (to eat)) falling intonation and ꯆꯕ (*cha.ba* (swimming/floating)) rising intonation.

    '_' - Apun Iyek (Sign of Ligature) eg. ꯆꯝꯄ꯭ꯔꯥ (*cham.pra* (lemon))

Other symbols are as internationally accepted symbols.

Before going deep into the syllabic structure it is important to discuss the usage of Apun Iyek for better understanding. This symbol is used to indicate clustering of Iyek Ipee characters to produce a combined sound.

ꯆꯝꯄ꯭ꯔꯥ	→	cəm.pra (lemon)
ꯆꯠꯈ꯭ꯔꯦ	→	cət.khre (gone)

Important thing to be noted is that clustering of more than two characters in Iyek Ipee is rare and Cheitap Iyek, if present (along with Apun Iyek), are found in association with the second Iyek Ipee character.

3.2 Syllabic unit structure in Meitei Mayek Manipuri

A hand craft structure is identified. This rule is used to identified the formation of a mono syllable Manipuri origin words without occurrence of consonant clusters. Basically, the structure consists of three cells: the initial position, intermediate position and the final position.

FIGURE 1 – The character set and positions of syllabic unit structure in Meitei Mayek Manipuri

3.2.1 Pattern of Character Sets in Different Positions in Mono Syllable

In this section, occurrences of different character sets in different position contributing to the formation of syllables are discussed along with exceptional cases.

3.2.1.1 Initial Position

The initial position should always be a character from Iyek Ipee. The conditions apply to every syllable in a Meiteilon origin word, regardless of exceptions.

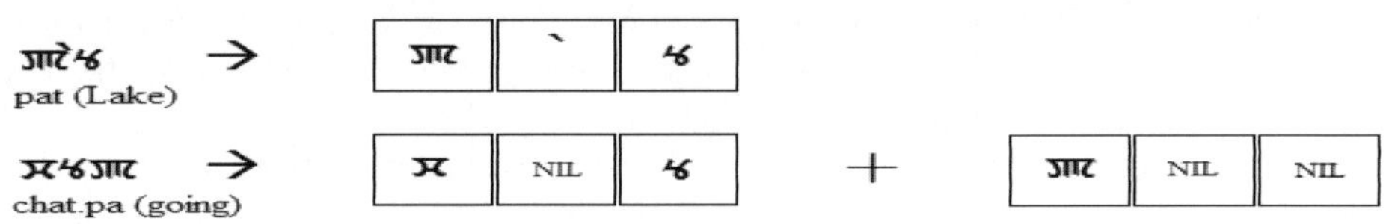

FIGURE 2 – Illustration of Initial Position with examples.

The first example is a mono syllabic word, in which the initial position is occupied by the character ‘ꯄ’ belongs to Iyek Ipee.

The second example is a word formed by two syllables where in both cases the character in initial position belongs to Iyek Ipee character set.

3.2.1.2 Intermediate Position

The intermediate position, generally, is occupied by the character set in Cheitap Iyek. This condition may not apply in case of consonant clustering and exceptional cases. Moreover, it is not necessary that this position be occupied.

In the first example shown in Fig 3.3, the occurrence of ‘ ` ’ , a character in Cheitap Iyek in the intermediate position is illustrated, while in the second example the nonexistent state in this position is shown in **Figure 3.3**.

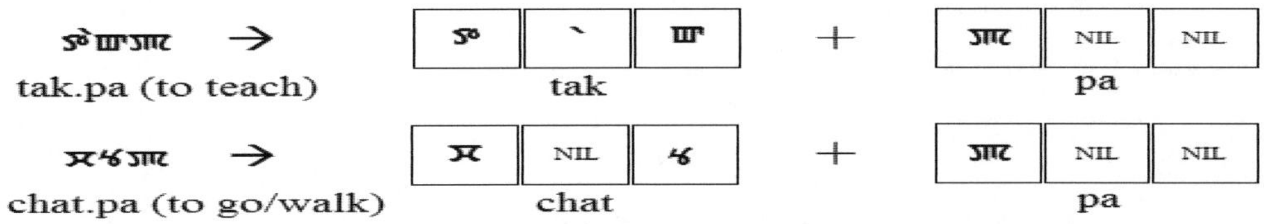

FIGURE 3 – Illustration of Intermediate Position with examples.

3.2.1.3 Final Position

Normally, the final position is filled in by characters from the Lonsum Iyek character set, but, as in the previous case, it is not a necessary condition. Syllables with nonexistent final position are common in the language.

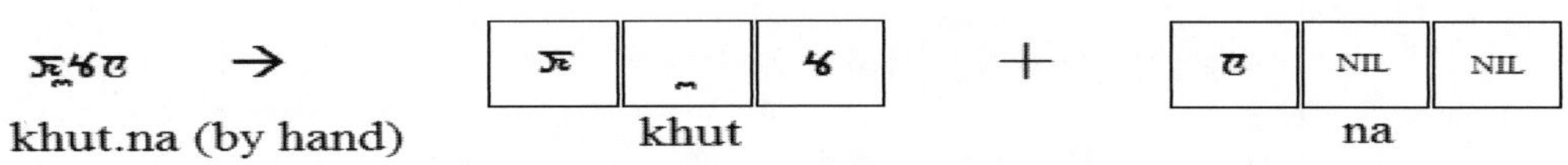

FIGURE 4 – Illustration of Final Position with examples.

In this example, the final position of the first syllable is occupied by Lonsum Iyek character ' ꯠ ' whereas in the second syllable the position is empty.

3.2.1.4 Occurrence of Exceptional Characters in Final Position

In Meiteilon some exceptional characters belonging to Iyek Ipee are found to occur in the final position of a syllable. Special attention is to be given to each and every letter in this group because understanding the correct utilization of these letters is important for correct and proper command over the language.

One such character is the letter ' ꯏ '(i). This letter is present in both Iyek Ipee character set as well as Lonsum Iyek. So, if it initializes a syllable, should it be considered as a major consonant, and if it finalizes the syllable, should it be considered as Lonsum Iyek? This issue is purely linguistic in nature. But from a computational view this is a character which has the capability to initiate as well as finalize syllable and its importance should be kept in mind while developing algorithm.

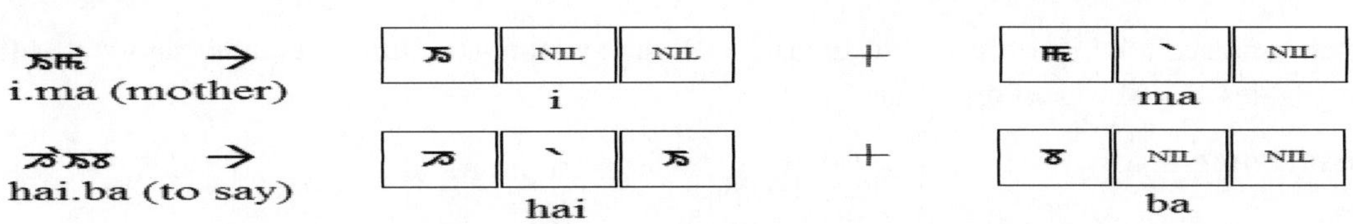

FIGURE 5 – Illustration of Exceptional cases with examples.

Similarly, the letters [illegible] are found to be used in both initial and final positions, but these letters do not have their derivative counterparts in Lonsum Iyek character set.

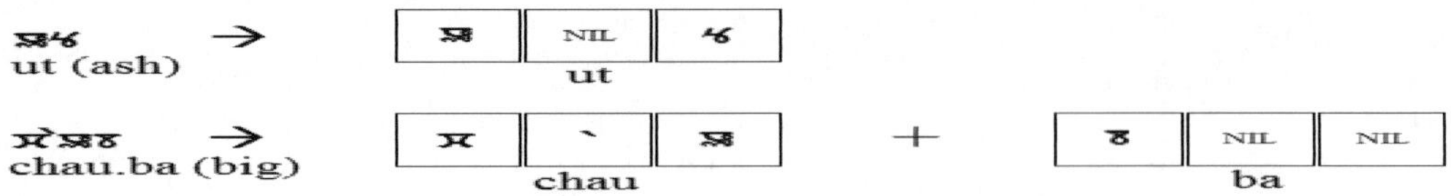

FIGURE 6 – Illustration of Exceptional cases with examples.

3.3 Complex Syllabic Structure

Majority of the syllable are of the basic structure. But occurrence of a slightly complex structure is found if the use of (_) Apun Iyek is found (mostly in close association with ꯋ, ꯌ, ꯔ).

In this case, a syllabic unit is divided into five cells, comprising of initial, final and three intermediate positions.

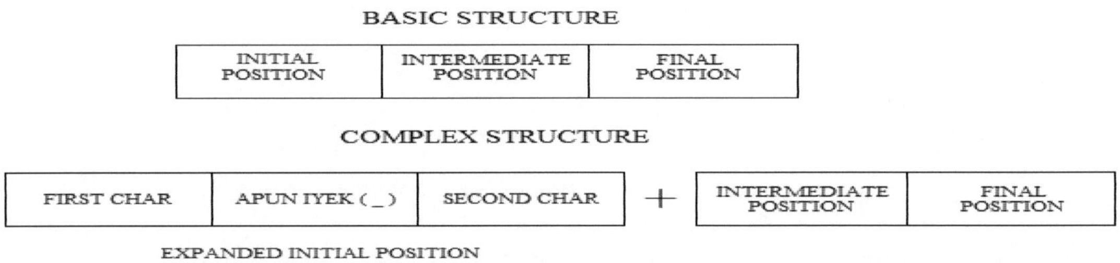

FIGURE 7 – Comparison of Simple and Complex Syllabic Structure.

In another sense, the first three cells can be thought as the expanded form of the initial position in basic structure. The last two cells (4th and 5th) are same as that of basic structure.

The first three cells i.e. expansion of the initial position, the second cell is meant to be occupied by the Apun Iyek (_) and the first and the third cell is filled in by characters from Iyek Ipee character set.

3.4 The Syllabic Pattern

Syllable can be divided into three parts; onset (beginning of a syllable, either a consonant or a semivowel), peak (nucleus of the syllable, vowels) and coda (sound which comes after the peak, generally consonants). In every syllable there must be a peak. But there may not be an onset or coda in Meiteilon syllabic system.

Referring to section 2.4.1 of (Yashawanta, 2000), the syllabic structure, the author has stated that the syllables can be of six forms.

Classification A

1. V
2. VC
3. CV
4. CCV
5. CVC
6. CCVC

where,
V = Syllabic peaks, vowels
C = Syllabic margins, consonants

In this process, syllables are segmented using a script based algorithm and thus the pattern observed also are on the basis of the script (Kishorjit et.al. 2012b). The patterns found are as follows;

Classification B

1. V
2. CV
3. C
4. VVV
5. CVC
6. CC
7. CVV
8. VV
9. VVC
10. VC
11. CCVC

where,
V = vowel characters
C = consonant characters

It must be noted that the previous classification A is based on linguistic approach and the classification B, on computational view.

It may seem like the later classification shows more variety of patterns, but it is not so. Both, classifications are one and same, the only difference lies in the approach. This is elaborated in (Kishorjit et. al., 2012b).

4 System design

The system design of this work can be divided into two parts. The first part is designed in order to identify the syllabic units of a word and the second part is the identification of morphemes from the syllabic units.

4.1 System design for word segmentation

The identification of the syllabic unit follows the same hand craft rule used in the work of (Kishorjit et. al., 2012b). Fig. 8 shows the details of the segmentation system. The first method (segmentor) provides the base foundation in which the Input File is read line by line and every line is tokenized and every tokens or word is provided for syllable extraction. Then from the stack, where the syllables for every word are stored, the unit/mono syllables are again written into the Output File.

The second method (extractor), when called by the first, takes a string parameter (word) and segments the word into unit syllables. Segmentation is done depending on the script based rules and the syllabic structures defined in this chapter. For every syllable extracted it is pushed down into a stack object defined for the particular word. The extraction process starts from the left most syllables, thus suitable for storing in a stack.

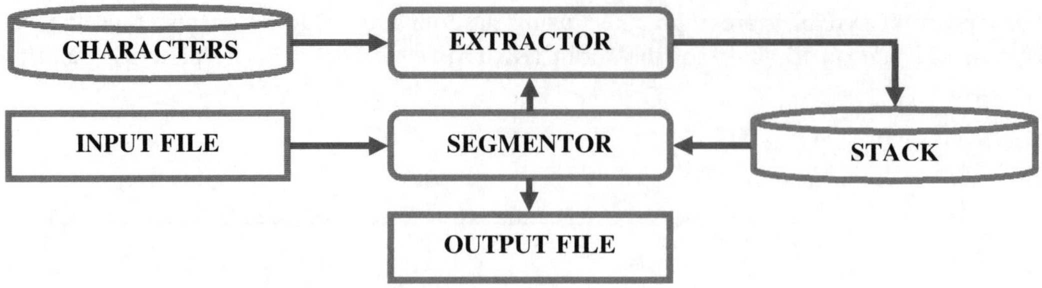

FIGURE 8 – System Diagram of Segmentation

The *Input File* is passed to the segmentation algorithm. The segmentation algorithm tokenizes the string in the file and calls the extractor algorithm passing each word as parameter. The extractor algorithm refers to the character list for checking the various conditions present and pushes down each extracted segment in the stack. A stack is used because the segmentation starts from the end of the word and LIFO (Last In First Out) principle is followed. When extraction is over, control is shifted to segmentation algorithm and it takes the segments from the stack and gives the output.

4.2 Morpheme identification system

With the principle that word consists of syllable or syllables and the syllable can be morpheme but not guaranteed that all the syllables will be a morpheme. For example in the word "unladylike", there are 4 syllables (un-, la-, dy- and like) but only 3 morphemes (un-, lady- and like). Taking a Manipuri word example ꯁꯥꯌꯣꯛꯁꯡ/sa.yok.saŋ/ "*animal rearing place or zoo*", there are three syllables, out of which the first one ꯁꯥ /sa/ "*animal*" is a free root (noun) and the second one is ꯌꯣꯛ /yok/ "*bring up/ rear*" is a bound root (verb) and the last one ꯁꯡ /saŋ/ "*house/shed*" is again a free root (noun). Together these three syllables form the word ꯁꯥꯌꯣꯛꯁꯡ/sa.yok.saŋ/ meaning "*zoo/animal rearing place*" also altogether there are three morphemes.

4.2.1 Pre-processing and segmentation process

The system (Fig. 9) is feed with a text corpus, so pre-processing is very important and the process consists of cleaning of the file. By cleaning it means the correction of spellings, removal of unwanted characters and the grammatical errors. The cleaned file is fed as the input file. The input file is procured from local newspaper Huiyen Lanpao[1] which provides a Meitei Mayek version of the daily news. Approximately some well cleaned 13,045 words are used for the system input file.

The Cleaned file is fed as an input for the segmentation process. The segmentation process follows the same rule mention in section 4.1. The segmented file with syllables as output is used for the next module of morpheme identification.

[1] http://www.hueiyenlanpao.com/meeteilon/

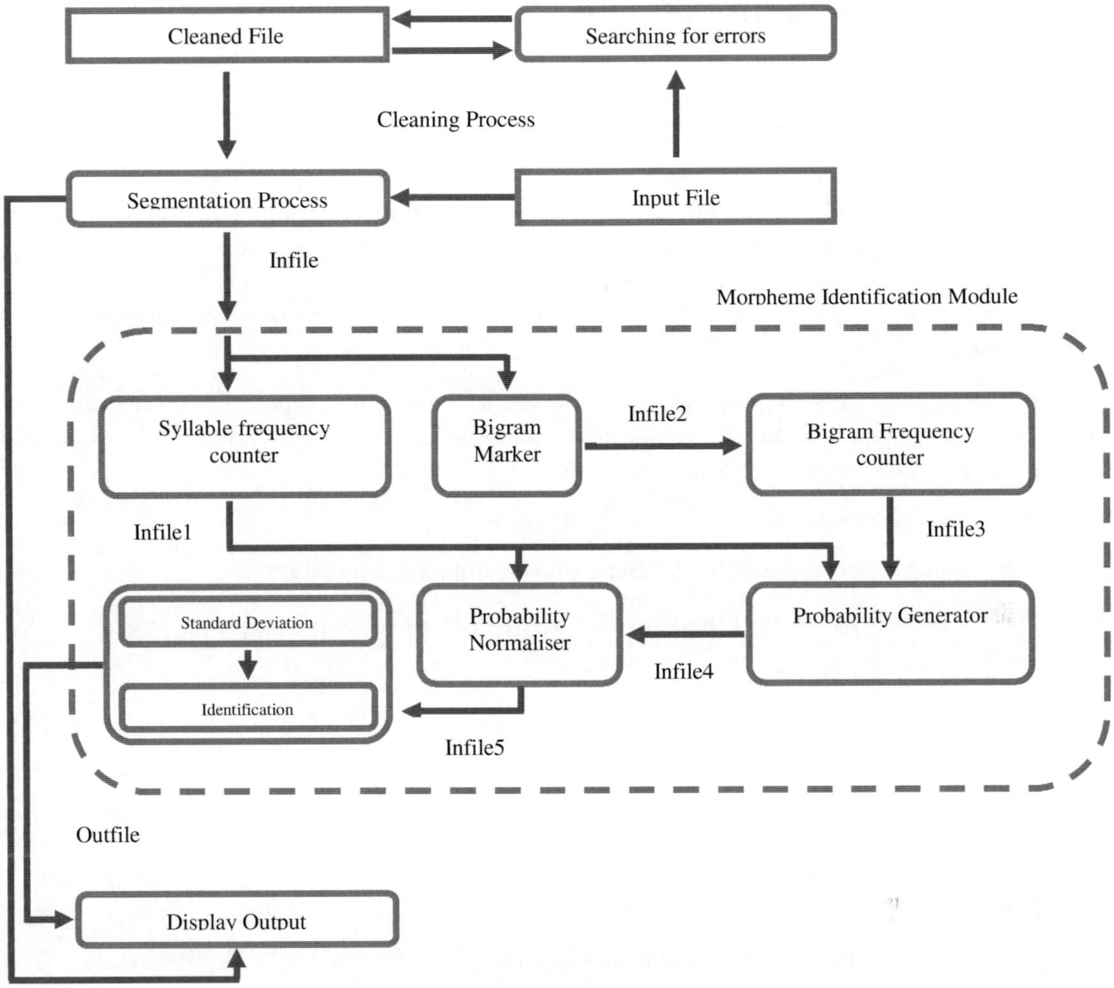

FIGURE 9 – System design

4.3 Morpheme identification module

In the morpheme identification module the syllables are used for frequency finding and other statistical findings. The Bigram model is used in order to measure the relative association between each syllable present in a word and find their corresponding probability values. This probability values are normalized so as to bring uniformity in the data and prevent redundancy and duplication.

The output of Bigram probability is implemented with Standard deviation.

4.3.1 N-gram and Bigram

In order to start a brief discussion of N-gram, the concept of conditional probability is necessary. In probability theory, the **conditional probability** of **A** given **B** is the probability of **A** if **B** is known to occur (or have occurred). It is commonly denoted as $P(A/B)$, and sometime $P_B(A).P(A/B)$ can be visualized as the probability of event **A** when the sample space is restricted to event **B** (Freund et. al., 2006).

Mathematically, it is defined for $P(B) \neq 0$ as :

$$P(A/B) = \frac{P(A \cap B)}{P(B)}$$

An ***n*-gram model** is a type of probabilistic language model for predicting the next item in such a sequence in the form of a **(n-1)** order Markov model.In the fields of computational linguistics and probability, an ***n*-gram** is a contiguous sequence of *n* items from a given sequence of text or speech. The items in question can be phonemes, syllables, letters, words or base pairs according to the application. *n*-grams are collected from a text or speech corpus. Mathemetically, it is defined as :

Given a string of words ($w_1, w_2, w_3, \ldots\ldots, w_n$), we can compute the probability of the complete string using n-gram. If we consider each word occurring in its correct location as an independent event, we can represent this probability as follows:

$P(w_1, w_2, w_3, w_4, \ldots\ldots, w_n)$

This can be further decomposed by the chain rule of probability as follows:

$P(w_1^n) = P(w_1)P(w_2|w_1)P(w_3|w_2)P(w_4|w_3) \ldots\ldots\ldots\ldots\ldots P(w_n|w_1^{n-1})$

$= \prod_{k=1}^{n} P(w_k \mid w_1^{k-1})$

And in order to compute the probability like $P(w_n \mid w_1^{n-1})$, we have to approximate the probability of a word given all previous words.

An *n*-gram of size 1 is referred to as a "unigram"; size 2 is a "bigram", size 3 is a "trigram" and so on. In this system it has restricted to the **bigram** model which approximates the probability of a word given all the previous words $P(w_n \mid w_1^{n-1})$ by the conditional probability of the preceding word $P(w_n \mid w_{n-1})$

As an example, instead of computing the probability

P(rabbit | Just the other day I saw a)

We approximate it with the probability:

***P* (rabbit | a)**

Implementing in the syllabic level, for example for the word ꯁꯌꯣꯛꯁꯪ/sa.yok.saŋ/ "*animal rearing place or zoo*", the three syllables are ꯁ /sa/ "*animal*", ꯌꯣꯛ /yok/ "*bring up/ rear*" and ꯁꯪ /saŋ/ "*house/shed*". And the sample Bigram probability notation is:

***P*(ꯌꯣꯛ|ꯁ), *P*(ꯁ|ꯌꯣꯛ),** etc.

4.3.2 Standard deviation

Standard deviation is the degree of variation in the probability distribution. It expresses the amount of dispersion from the average (mean).

The mean, denoted by μ, of a distribution or set of random variables X is given by:

$$\mu = \frac{\sum_{i=1}^{n} x_i}{n}$$ Where, n = total elements in a population/sample

The standard deviation of a probability distribution is given by the positive square root of its variance. Variance is the square of summation of the difference between the probability values and the mean value divided by the population size.

Variance,

$$\sigma^2 = \frac{\sum_{i=1}^{n} x_i - \mu}{n}$$

Standard Deviation,

$$\sigma = \sqrt{\frac{\sum_{i=1}^{n} x_i - \mu}{n}}$$

Standard deviation (σ) and mean (μ) of the probability distribution is calculated for the given syllables. In Standard Deviation, the domain range is defined as the distance between one σ difference from μ on both negative and positive values. And this range is used to determine whether a syllable is a morpheme or not. In our case only the positive values of μ is considered because negative value is meaningless in our case. It is because the syllabic unit bigram frequency probability outputs do not have negative values.

5 Experiment and evaluation

A total of 13,045 word forms were supplied. The outcome was 35,840 syllables and 972 of them were distinct syllables. In order to evaluate the experiment, the system used the parameter of Recall, Precision and F-score.

Recall,

$$R = \frac{\textit{total no of correct morpheme given by the system}}{\textit{total no of possible correct morpheme in the text}}$$

Precision,

$$P = \frac{\textit{total no of correct morpheme given by the system}}{\textit{total no of morpheme given by the system}}$$

F-measure,

$F = \frac{(\beta^2+1)PR}{\beta^2 P+R}$; where, β is one, which means precision and recall are given equal weight.

The Fig. 10 shows the graph of the syllables with the probability values. It can be observed that the ranges between **0.01** and **0.08** are clustered together. This indicates that there is some consistency in this range and as mention above only these positive values range is considered even though in the standard deviation it has a range both comprises of negative and positive values. It is because negative value is meaningless since it's calculated with the syllabic unit bigram frequency probability outputs which do not have negative values.

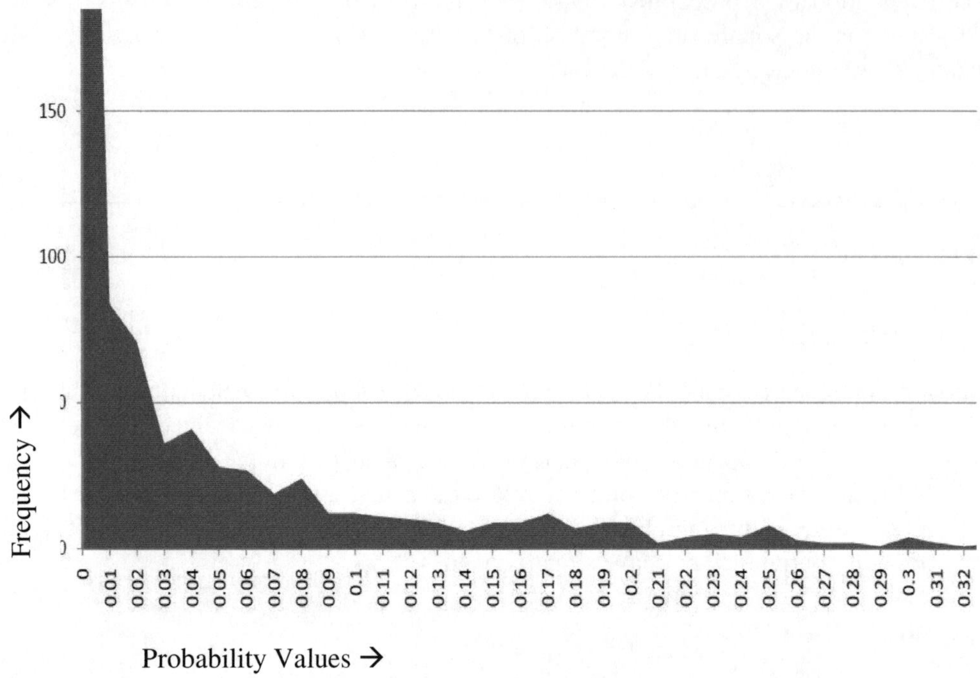

FIGURE 10 – Standard Deviation

The measurement is done using the evaluation method of recall, precision and f-score mention above. So, the system gives a Recall of **59.80%**, Precision of **83.02%**, and F-score of **69.52%.**

6 Conclusion

The system designed is a morpheme identifier not a morphological analyser, so the job of this system is to identify the morpheme from a set of syllables. A syllable segmentation algorithm is applied and the output syllables are verified whether it's a morpheme or not. In the identification, the concept of standard deviation is implemented. There is no such report of identifying Manipuri language morphemes using syllable or syllabic unit inputs.

These could be a boon for this highly agglutinative language since the complexity of Machine translation could be solved up-to a great extend. Other statistical method can also be implemented to improve the output.

References

Bernd Mo¨bius (1998): Word and syllable models for German text-to-speech synthesis, In *Proceedings of the Third International Workshop on Speech Synthesis*, Jenolan Caves, Australia, pages 59–64.

Braschler, M. and Ripplinger, B. (2004): How Effective is Stemming and Decompounding for German Text Retrieval? *Information Retrieval*, Vol. 7, (3-4), pages 291-306.

Daniel Jurafsky, James H. Martin, 2008. *"Speech and Language Processing: An Introduction to Natural Language Processing, Computational Linguistics, and Speech Recognition"*, Dorling Kindersley (India) Pvt. Ltd., licensees of Pearson Education in South Asia.

Freund's E. John, Irwin Miller and Marylees Miller (2006). "*Mathmatical Statistics with Applications*", Dorling Kindersley (India) Pvt. Ltd., licensees of Pearson Education in South Asia.

Rouas, (2007): Automatic prosodic variations modeling for language and dialect discrimination, *IEEE Transaction on Audio, Speech and language Processing*, Vol. 15, 6, pages 1-8.

Kalyani, N. and Sunitha, K.V.N. (2009): Syllable analysis to build a dictation system in Telugu language, *International Journal of Computer Science and Information Security*, Vol.6, No. 3, pp. 171-176.

Kangjia Mangang, Ng. (2003). *"Revival of a closed account; A Brief History of Kanglei Script and the Birth of Phoon (zero) in the World of Arithmetic and Astrology"*, Sanamahi Laining Amasung Punsiron Khupham, Imphal, India.

Kishorjit N., Bishworjit S., Romina M., MayekleimaChanu Ng., Sivaji B., 2011. *"A Light Weight Manipuri Stemmer"*, In: The Proceedings of NCILC, Cochin, India.

Kishorjit N., Vidya Raj RK., Imocha Singh O. and Sivaji B., 2012. *"Automatic Segmentation Of Manipuri(Meiteilon) Word Into Syllabic Units"*, International Journal of Computer Science and Information Technology (IJCSIT). ISSN – 0975 – 3826

Mohanty, S., Santi, P.K. and Adhikary, K.P.D. (2004): Analysis and Design of Oriya Morphological Analyser: Some Tests with OriNet. In: Proceeding of symposium on Indian Morphology, phonology and Language Engineering, IIT Kharagpur.

Nongthombam Nonigopal Singh, 1987. *"A Meitei Grammar of Roots and Affixes"* (Unpublished Thesis), Manipur University, Canchipur, Imphal, India 795003.

Singh, T. D. and Sivaji B. (2008): Morphology driven Manipuri POS tagger, In *Proceedings of IJCNLP-08 workshop on NLP for Less Privilege Languages*, India, pages 91-98.

Sharma, U., Kalita, J. and Das, R. (2002): Unsupervised learning of morphology for building lexicon for a highly inflectional language. In ACL SIGPHON, pages 1–10.

Utpal Sharma, Jugal K. Kalita, and Rajib K. D. (2008): Acquisition of morphology of an Indic language from text corpus, *ACM Transactions on Asian Language Information Processing (TALIP)*, vol. 7, Issue 3, August 2008.

Tomlinson, S. (2003): Lexical and Algorithmic Stemming Compared for 9 European Languages with Hummingbird SearchServerTM, In CLEF 2003, pages 286–300.

Yashawanta Singh, Ch. (2000). "*Manipuri Grammar*", Rajesh Publications New Delhi – 110002.

Domain Based Classification of Punjabi Text Documents using Ontology and Hybrid Based Approach

Nidhi, Vishal Gupta
University Institute of Engineering and Technology, Panjab University
naseeb.nidhi@gmail.com, vishal@pu.ac.in

ABSTRACT

Classification of text documents become a need in today's world due to increase in the availability of electronic data over internet. Till now, no text classifier is available for the classification of Punjabi documents. The objective of the work is to find best Punjabi Text Classifier for Punjabi language. Two new algorithms, Ontology Based Classification and Hybrid Approach (which is the combination of Naïve Bayes and Ontology Based Classification) are proposed for Punjabi Text Classification. A corpus of 180 Punjabi News Articles is used for training and testing purpose of the classifier. The experimental results conclude that Ontology Based Classification (85%) and Hybrid Approach (85%) provide better results in comparison to standard classification algorithms, Centroid Based Classification (71%) and Naïve Bayes Classification (64%).

KEYWORDS: Punjabi Text Classification, Ontology Based Classification, Naive Bayes Classification, Centroid Based Classification.

---

1. Introduction

The amount of electronic data available such as digital libraries, blogs, electronic newspaper, electronic publications, emails, electronic books is increasing rapidly. However, as the volume of electronic data increases the challenge to manage that data also increases. Thus, automatic organization of text documents becomes an important research issue of Text Mining. Manual Text Classification is an expensive and time consuming task, as classifying millions of text documents efficiently and with accuracy is not an easy task. Therefore, automatic text classifier is constructed whose accuracy and time efficiency is much better than manual text classification. There are mainly two machine learning approaches to enhance classification task: supervised approach, where predefined classes are assigned to text documents with the help of labeled documents; and unsupervised approach, that does not require labeled documents to classify the text documents [Chen and Blostein 2006].

So far very little work has been done for text classification with respect to Indian languages, due to the problems faced by many Indian Languages such as: no capitalization, non-availability of large gazetteer lists, lack of standardization and spelling, scarcity of resources and tools. Punjabi is an Indo-Aryan Language, spoken in both western Punjab (Pakistan) and eastern Punjab (India). It is 10th most widely spoken language in the world. Also it is the official language of Indian state of Punjab. In comparison to English language, Punjabi language has rich inflectional morphology. E.g. English verb "Play" has 4 inflectional forms: play, played, playing, plays; whereas same word in Punjabi i.e. "ਖੇਡ" has 47 inflectional forms: ਖੇਡ, ਖੇਡਣਾ, ਖੇਡਣੇ, ਖੇਡਣ, ਖੇਡਦਾ, ਖੇਡਦੇ, ਖੇਡਦੀ, ਖੇਡਦੀਆਂ etc. This depends upon gender, number, person, tense, phase, transitivity values in a sentence. Therefore, using only statistical approaches to classify the Punjabi documents do not provide good classification results, there is a need of linguistic approaches too for the selection of the relevant features that increase the efficiency of the classification.

No work has been done to classify the Punjabi documents due to lack of resources available in electronic format. Therefore, two new approaches are proposed for Punjabi language, Ontology Based Classification and Hybrid Approach. And to compare the results of these classification algorithms, standard classification algorithms, Naïve Bayes and Centroid Based Classification are used.

2. Text Classification for Indian Languages

So far Text Classification Techniques implemented for Indian Languages are: Naïve Bayes classifier has been performed over Telugu News articles in four major classes: Politics, Sports, Business and Cinema; to about 800 documents. In this, normalized TFXIDF is used to extract the features. Without any stopword removal and morphological analysis, at the threshold of 0.03, the classifier gives 93% precision [Murthy 2003].Semantic based classification using Sanskrit wordnet used to classify Sanskrit Text Document, this method is built on lexical chain of linking significant words that are about a particular topic with the help of hypernym relation in WordNet [Mohanty et al. 2006]. Statistical techniques using Naïve Bayes and Support Vector Machine used to classify subjective sentences from objective sentences for Urdu language, in this, language specific preprocessing is done to extract the relevant features. As Urdu language is morphological rich language, this makes the classification task more difficult. The result of this implementation shows that classification results of Support Vector Machines is much better than Naïve Bayes [Ali and Ijaz 2009]. For Bangla Text Classification, n-gram based classification algorithm is used and to analyze the performance of the classifier Prothom-Alo news corpus is used. The result show that as we increase the value of n from 1 to 3, performance of the text classification also increases, but using gram length more than 3 decreases the performance of the classifier [Mansur et al. 2006]. Text classification is done using Vector Space Model and Artificial Neural network on morphological rich Dravidian classical language Tamil. The experimental results show that Artificial Neural network model achieves 93.33% which is better than the performance of Vector Space Model which yields 90.33% on Tamil document classification [Rajan et al. 2009]. A new technique called Sentence level Classification is used for Kannada language; in this, main focus is on sentences as most users' comments, queries, opinions etc are expressed in sentences. This Technique extended further to sentiment classification, Question Answering, Text Summarization and also for customer reviews in Kannada Blogs [Jayashree R. 2011].

3. Problem Description

Manually classifying millions of documents require lots of effort and time. Therefore, automatic Punjabi Text Classifier is constructed to manage these documents efficiently in less time with minimum efforts. In literature review, it has been observed that no work has been done in this context for Punjabi Language.

The problem is to classify large collection of Punjabi Text Documents into one of the predefined classes. These classes are: ਕ੍ਰਿਕਟ (krikaṭ) (Cricket), ਹਾਕੀ (hakı) (Hockey), ਕਬੱਡੀ (kabḍḍī) (Kabaddi), ਫੁਟਬਾਲ (phuṭbāl) (Football), ਟੈਨਿਸ (ṭainis) (Tennis), ਬੈਡਮਿੰਟਨ (baiḍmiṇṭan) (Badminton), ਓਲੰਪਿਕ (ōlmpik) (Olympic).

The tasks that need to do to achieve the objectives are following:

- To develop NER system and language dependent rules to extract names, locations, time/date, designation, abbreviation, numbers/counting from the document.
- To extract the relevant features from the document for better classification results.
- To prepare gazetteer lists for the classification task.
- To create Domain (sports) specific Ontology for the Punjabi language that includes terms related to class.

4. Punjabi Text Classification

For Punjabi Text Classification, initial steps that need to do are following:

- Prepare Training Set for Naïve Bayes and Centroid Based Classifier. The documents in the training set are tokenized and preprocessed. Stopwords, punctuations, special symbols, name entities are extracted from the document.
- For each class, centroid vectors are created so as to calculate the similarity between centroid vectors and unlabelled document vector.

- Create Sports specific Ontology in Punjabi language for Ontology based Classifier that contains terms related to the class e.g. class ਕ੍ਰਿਕਟ (Cricket) contains terms such as ਬੱਲੇਬਾਜ਼ੀ (ballēbāzī) (batting), ਗੇਂਦਬਾਜ਼ੀ (gēndbāzī) (bowling), ਫੀਲਡਿੰਗ (phīlḍiṅg) (fielding), ਵਿਕਟ (vikaṭ) (wicket), ਸਪਿਨ (sapin) (spin), ਆਊਟ (āūṭ), ਵਿਕਟਕੀਪਰ (vikṭakīpar) (wicket-keeper) etc. For the first time such lists are created for Punjabi Language.
- Prepare Gazetteer lists such as list of middle and lastnames (ਸਿੰਘ, ਸੰਧੂ, ਗੁਪਤਾ, (siṅgh, sandhū, guptā)), places (ਬਠਿੰਡਾ, ਚੰਡੀਗੜ੍ਹ, ਪੰਜਾਬ, (baṭhiṇḍā, caṇḍīgaṛh, pañjāb)), date/time (ਕੱਲ (kall), ਸਵੇਰ (savēr)), abbreviations (ਆਈ (āī), ਸੀ (sī), ਐਲ (ail), ਪੀ (pī), ਬੀ (bī)), designations (ਕਪਤਾਨ (kaptān), ਕੋਚ (kōc), ਕੈਪਟਨ (kaipṭan)) etc.

After initial steps, Punjabi Text Classification is implemented into three main phases:

- Preprocessing Phase
- Feature Extraction Phase
- Processing Phase

4.1 Pre-processing Phase

Each Unlabelled Punjabi Text Documents are represented as "Bag of Words". Before processing, stopwords, special symbols, punctuations (<,>, :,{,},[,],^,&,*,(,) etc.) are removed from the documents, as they are irrelevant to the classification task. Stopwords list is manually prepared by analysing the punjabi corpus. Table 1 shows lists of some stopwords that are removed from the document.

ਲਈ (laī)	ਨੇ (nē)	ਆਪਣੇ (āpaṇē)	ਨਹੀਂ (nahīṃ)	ਤਾਂ (tāṃ)
ਇਹ (ih)	ਹੀ (hī)	ਜਾਂ (jāṃ)	ਦਿੱਤਾ (dittā)	ਹੋ (hō)

TABLE 1- Stopwords List

4.2 Feature Extraction Phase

Input document may contain redundant or non-relevant data that increases the computations. Therefore, to reduce the feature space by extracting the relevant features from the document, along with statistical approaches, language dependent rules, gazetteer lists are created by analyzing the Punjabi documents.

4.2.1 Statistical Approaches

For classification of Punjabi Documents TFXIDF is used as statistical approach [Yanbo et al. 2009; Han and Kamber 2001]. TFXIDF weighting is the most common method used for term weighting that takes into account this property. In this approach, the TFXIDF weight of term i in document d assigned proportionally to the number of times the term appears in the document, and in inverse proportion to the number of documents in the corpus in which the term appears.

$$W(i) = tf(i)*\log(N/N_i)$$

TFXIDF weighting approach weights the frequency of a term in a document with a factor that discounts its importance if it appears in most of the documents, as in this case the term is assumed to have little discriminating power.

4.2.2 Linguistic Features

Statistical approach fails to extract language dependent features. Therefore, Hybrid Approach is used which is the combination of Rule Based Approach and List Lookup approach. A number of rules specific for Punjabi language used to extract the language dependent features are following:

1. Name Rule
   a. if word is found, its previous word is checked for middle name.
   b. if middle name is found, its previous word is extracted as first name from the document.
   c. Otherwise, word is extracted from the document.
2. Location Rules
   a. if word is found, it is extracted from the document.
   b. if Punjabi word ਵਿਖੇ (vikhē) is found, its previous word is extracted as location name.
   c. if Punjabi word ਪਿੰਡ (piṇḍ) is found, its next word is extracted as location name.
   d. if Punjabi word ਜ਼ਿਲ੍ਹੇ (zilhē) is found, its previous word is extracted as location name.
3. Date/Time Rules
   a. if month is found, it is extracted.
   b. if week day is found, it is extracted.
   c. if Punjabi words ਅੱਜ (ajj), ਕੱਲ (kall), ਸਵੇਰ (savēr), ਸ਼ਾਂਮ (shāmm), ਦੁਪਹਿਰ (duphir) etc. are found, they are extracted.
4. Numbers/Counting
   a. if any numeric character is found, it is extracted.
   b. if Punjabi words ਇੱਕ (ikk), ਦੂਜਾ (dūjā), ਦੋ (dō), ਪਹਿਲਾ (pahilā), ਛੇਵੀਂ (chēvīṃ) etc. are found, they are extracted.
5. Designation Rule
   c. if designation found e.g. ਕਪਤਾਨ (kaptān), ਕੋਚ (kōc), ਕੈਪਟਨ (kaipṭan), it is extracted.
6. Abbreviation
   d. if words like ਆਈ (āī), ਸੀ (sī), ਐਲ (ail), ਪੀ (pī), ਬੀ (bī) etc. are found, they are extracted.

4.2.3 Gazetteer Lists

Due to limited resources available in electronic format for Punjabi language, gazetteer lists are prepared manually by analyzing the Punjabi Text documents. Each gazetteer list contains 100-150 words in it. These lists are following:

- Middle Names
- Last names
- Location Names
- Month Names
- Day Names
- Designation names
- Number/Counting
- Abbreviations
- Stop words
- Sports Specific Ontology (e.g. preparing list for class ਹਾਕੀ (Hockey) that contain all of its related terms like ਸਟਰਾਈਕਰ (Striker), ਡਰਿਬਲਰ (Dribbler), ਪੈਨਲਟੀ (Penalty) etc.

4.3 Processing Phase

At this phase, apply classification algorithm such as Naïve Bayes, Centroid Based, Ontology Based and Hybrid Approach to relevant features extracted from feature extraction phase in order to classify the unlabelled document into predefined classes.

4.3.1 Naïve Bayes Classification

It is simple probabilistic classifier that considers each term independent of each other. The two common Naïve Bayes Models used for text classification are: Multinomial Event Model and Multi-variate Bernoulli Event Model. For Punjabi Text Classification, Multinomial Event Model is used as it performs better than Multi-variate Bernoulli event model [McCallum and Nigam 1998; Chen et al. 2009]. In this, each document is represented as "bag of words". Following steps are taken to classify the Punjabi text documents using Naïve Bayes Classifier:

Step 1: Training Set
Prepare training set for the classifier in which folders represent class and each folder contains set of documents called labeled documents. Punctuations, special symbols are removed from the document. Then, documents are segmented into meaningful units called words. Stopwords, name entities such as names, locations, date/time, counting etc. are removed from the document as they are irrelevant to the classification task. Calculate probability of each class P(Ci), using equation (1)

$$P(Ci) = (\text{Total docs in } Ci) / (\text{total docs in training set}) \quad (1)$$

Step 2: Test Set
After preprocessing and feature extraction steps, each unlabelled document are represented as list of words i.e. w1, w2 ....wn, where wn is the nth word of the document. Calculate probability of the document to belong to the particular class using equation (2).

$$P(Ci|document) = (P(Ci|w1, w2......wn)/ n \quad (2)$$

Where n is the total word in the input document.
Assign class Ci to the document if it has maximum posterior probability with that class.

$$P(Ci|document) = max (P(Ci)*P(wj|Ci))/ n$$

Where

$$P(wj|Ci) = (1+freq. of wj in class Ci)/(total words in Ci + total words in training set)$$

4.3.2 Centroid Based Classification

Centroid based classifier is simple and efficient method for the classification task. Its basic idea is to construct Centroid vector per class using training set and document vector. And then calculate the distance between each Centroid vector and document vector; assign that class to the document that is having minimum distance from the Centroid vector [Chen et al. 2008]. Following are steps done for classifying Punjabi Text Documents are:

Step 1: Training Set: After preprocessing and feature extraction phase, Centroid vector for each class is calculated using labeled documents in that class. These vectors are: $C_{cricket}$, C_{hockey}, $C_{badminton}$.....etc.
Step 2: Test Set: For each unlabelled document, calculate document vector C_{doc}, where each component of the vector is represented by TFXIDF value i.e.C_{doc}=[$tfidf_1$, $tfidf_2$.......$tfidf_{|V|}$] ;|V| is total dimensions of the collection.
Step 3: Euclidean Distance: Calculate Euclidean distance between C_{doc} and Centroid vector of each class. And assign that class to the document that is having minimum distance from Centroid vector of that class. If d and c are two vectors, Euclidean distance is calculated as in equation (3)

$$Distance(d,c) = sqrt((di- ci) sup 2) \quad where i=1, 2.....7 \quad (3)$$

E.g. assume Euclidean distance between each class and unlabelled document is $C_{cricket,doc}$ = 2.33 and$C_{Hockey,doc}$ =3.15. As $C_{cricket,doc}$ has minimum distance, class Cricket is assigned to the unlabelled document [Chen and Ye 2008].

Input	ਰਾਜਵੰਤ ਸਿੰਘ ਹਾਕੀ ਜਗਤ ਦਾ ਉਹ ਹਸਤਾਖਰ ਹੈ, ਜਿਸ ਨੇ ਬਿਨਾਂ ਕਿਸੇ ਸਰਕਾਰੀ ਮਦਦ ਤੋਂ ਬਠਿੰਡਾ ਜ਼ਿਲ੍ਹੇ 'ਚ ਹਾਕੀ (rājvant siṅgh hākī jagat dā uh hastākhar hai, jis nē bināṃ kisē sarkārī madad tōṃ baṭhiṇḍā zilhē 'c hākī)
Preprocessing Phase & Feature Extraction	ਹਾਕੀ ਜਗਤ ਹਸਤਾਖਰ ਸਰਕਾਰੀ ਮਦਦ ਹਾਕੀ (hākī jagat hastākhar sarkārī madad hākī)
Output	Class: ਹਾਕੀ (hākī)

TABLE 2- An example of Centroid Based Classification

4.3.3 Ontology Based Classification

Traditional Classification methods ignore relationship between words, they consider each term independent of each result. But, in fact, there exist a semantic relation between terms such as synonym, hyponymy etc. [Wu and Liu 2009]. Therefore, for better classification results, there is need to understand the context of the text document. The Ontology has different meaning for different users, in this classification task, Ontology stores words that are related to particular sport. Therefore, with the use of domain specific ontology, it becomes easy to classify the documents even if the document does not contain the class name in it. The ontology is created manually that contains Badminton, Cricket, Football, Hockey, Kabaddi, Olympic and Tennis as their top classes. To create ontology, transliteration and English to Hindi, Hindi to Punjabi translators are used. Each ontology class contain 80-90 terms related to that class. The advantage of using Ontology is that there is no requirement of training set i.e. labeled documents. Hence, no human input is required to create training set. Also this ontology can be used by other researchers for easily classifying Punjabi sports documents with accuracy.

Step 1: Create Domain (i.e. sports) specific ontology, represented as "bag of words".
Step 2: For each unlabeled document, remove stopwords, punctuations, special symbols, and name entities from the document and represent document as "bag of words".
Step 3: To determine in which class unlabelled document belongs, calculate the frequency of document terms matched with class ontology. Assign class cricket to the unlabelled document, if frequency of matching terms with class cricket ontology is maximum.
Step 4: If no match is found or a document shows same results for two or more classes then that document is not classified into any class, and left for manual classification.

Input	ਰਾਜਵੰਤ ਸਿੰਘ ਹਾਕੀ ਜਗਤ ਦਾ ਉਹ ਹਸਤਾਖਰ ਹੈ, ਜਿਸ ਨੇ ਬਿਨਾਂ ਕਿਸੇ ਸਰਕਾਰੀ ਮਦਦ ਤੋਂ ਬਠਿੰਡਾ ਜ਼ਿਲ੍ਹੇ 'ਚ ਹਾਕੀ (rājvant siṅgh hākī jagat dā uh hastākhar hai, jis nē bināṃ kisē sarkārī madad tōṃ baṭhiṇḍā zilhē 'c hākī)
Preprocessing Phase & Feature Extraction	ਹਾਕੀ ਜਗਤ ਹਸਤਾਖਰ ਸਰਕਾਰੀ ਮਦਦ ਹਾਕੀ (hākī jagat hastākhar sarkārī madad hākī)
Output	Class: ਹਾਕੀ (hākī)

TABLE 3- An example of Ontology Based Classification

4.3.4 Hybrid Approach

In hybrid approach, the two algorithms Naïve Bayes and Ontology based Classifier are combined for better results of classification. Using TFXIDF, Information Gain (IG) as feature selection method, results in some features that are still irrelevant. Therefore, Class Discriminating Measure (CDM), a feature evaluation metric for Naïve Bayes that calculates the effectiveness of the feature using probabilities, is used. The results shown in [Chen et al. 2009], indicate that CDM is best feature selection approach than IG. Therefore, instead of using TFXIDF as feature selection method, CDM is used. The term having CDM value less than defined threshold value is ignored. It has been observed that fewer features are left for the computations, this simplifies and speedup the classification task with accuracy. And the remaining terms are used to represent the input unlabelled document; and to match the terms with domain specific ontology, to determine the class of the unlabelled document.

Step 1: For each unlabelled document, remove stopwords, punctuations, special symbols, and name entities from the document and represent document as "bag of words".
Step 2: For each term in the unlabelled document, calculate CDM for that term using equation (4).

$$CDM(w) = |\log P(w|Ci) - \log P(w|\overline{Ci})| \quad (4)$$

Where P(w|Ci) = probability that word w occurs if class value is i
P(w|$\overline{Ci}$) = probability that word w occurs when class value is not i
i=1 to 7
Step 3: Term having CDM value less than threshold value is ignored. Remaining terms are represented as input document, are used to determine the class of the document.
Step 4: Calculate the frequency of document terms matched with class ontology. Assign class cricket to the unlabelled document, if frequency of matching terms with class cricket ontology is maximum.
Step 5: If no match is found or a document shows same results for two or more classes then that document is not classified into any class, and left for manual classification.

Input	ਰਾਜਵੰਤ ਸਿੰਘ ਹਾਕੀ ਜਗਤ ਦਾ ਉਹ ਹਸਤਾਖਰ ਹੈ, ਜਿਸ ਨੇ ਬਿਨਾਂ ਕਿਸੇ ਸਰਕਾਰੀ ਮਦਦ ਤੋਂ ਬਠਿੰਡਾ ਜ਼ਿਲ੍ਹੇ 'ਚ ਹਾਕੀ (rājvant siṅgh hākī jagat dā uh hastākhar hai, jis nē bināṃ kisē sarkārī madad tōṃ baṭhiṇḍā zilhē 'c hākī)
Preprocessing Phase	ਹਾਕੀ ਜਗਤ ਹਸਤਾਖਰ ਸਰਕਾਰੀ ਮਦਦ ਹਾਕੀ (hākī jagat hastākhar sarkārī madad hākī)
Feature Extraction (Naive Bayes)	ਹਾਕੀ ਹਾਕੀ (hākī hākī)
Output	Class: ਹਾਕੀ (hākī), means input text belongs to class Hockey

TABLE 4- An example of Hybrid Based Classification

4.4 Performance Measure

In this phase, the performances of the each classifier is evaluated using standard evaluation measures such as Precision, Recall, F-Score, Fallout, Macro averaged Precision, Recall and F-score.

5. Results and Discussions

5.1 Dataset

The corpus used for Punjabi Text Classification contains 180 Punjabi text documents, 45 files are used as Training Data and rest of the files are used as Test Data. Training set contains total 3313 words that are used to train the Punjabi Text Classifier based on Naïve Bayes and Centroid Based Classification techniques. All the documents in the corpus are sports related and taken from the Punjabi News Web Sources such as likhari.org, jagbani.com, ajitweekly.com. Then, classify unlabelled documents into seven classes: ਕ੍ਰਿਕਟ (krikaṭ), ਹਾਕੀ (hākī), ਕਬੱਡੀ (kabḍḍī), ਫੁਟਬਾਲ (phuṭbāl), ਟੈਨਿਸ (ṭainis), ਬੈਡਮਿੰਟਨ (baiḍmiṇṭan), ਓਲੰਪਿਕ (ōlmpik). The system has been implemented using C#.net platform. The stopword list that is prepared manually for the classification task contains 2319 words.

The data structures used for Punjabi Text Classification are files and arrays. Stopwords list, gazetteer lists and sports specific ontology is stored in text file. During the implementation, these lists are stored in arrays to access the contents fast, otherwise, accessing contents directly from the files increase computational time. Even training set documents and test set document are also stored into files. Test Set contains 154 documents that are distributed among seven classes as shown in figure 1.

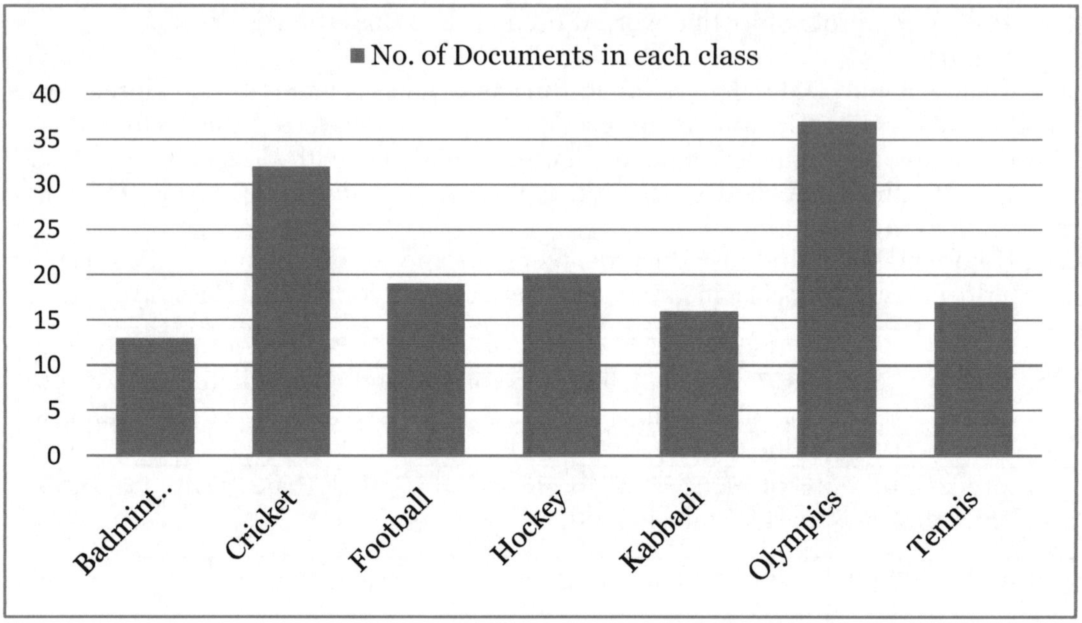

FIGURE 1- Distribution of test set documents

5.2 Screenshot of the system

For classification of Punjabi Text Documents, the dataset of 180 documents are arranged in four sets: Set 1, Set 2, Set 3 and Set 4. Each set contains 40 documents on average. Figure 2 shows main page of the classification system that consists two menu bar items "HELP" and "ABOUT US". In this, there are two buttons "BROWSE" and "APPLY".

"BROWSE" button is used for browsing Punjabi Text Documents that is to be classified. "APPLY" button is used to implement classification algorithm chosen from "COMBOBOX". "COMBOBOX" consists of following items:

1. Ontology Based Classification
2. Naïve Bayes Classification
3. Centroid Based Classification
4. Hybrid Approach

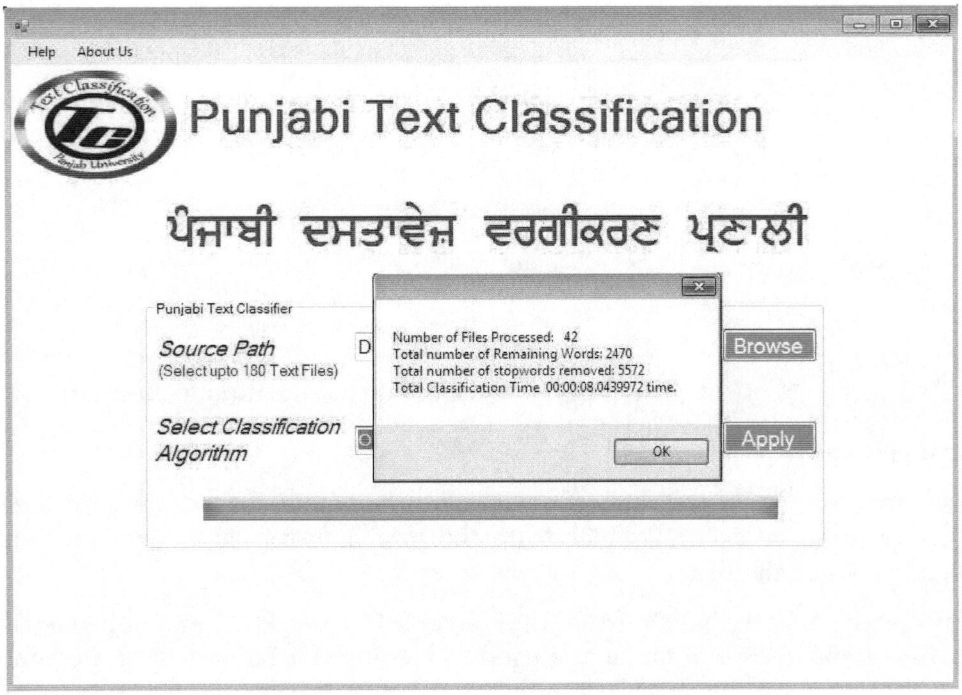

FIGURE 2- Punjabi Text Classifier System

Figure 2 shows the system takes 8 secs 04 ms to classify 42 Punjabi Text Documents. It also gives information about number of stopwords removed and number of words that are left after preprocessing phase.

5.3 Experimental Results

5.3.1 Experiment 1

In experiment 1, F-score for each class is calculated for each classifier using equation (5)

F-Score = (2*Precision*Recall)/ (Precision + Recall) (5)

Precision = (docs correctly classified in class Ci)/ (total docs retrieved in class Ci)

Recall = (docs correctly classified in class Ci)/ (total relevant docs in test set that belong to class Ci)

	Badminton	Cricket	Football	Hockey	Kabaddi	Olympic	Tennis
Ontology Based Classification	0.84	0.89	0.89	0.81	0.88	0.82	0.8
Hybrid	0.83	0.91	0.88	0.84	0.8	0.82	0.88

Classification							
Centroid Based Classification	0.64	0.85	0.8	0.64	0.67	0.56	0.81
Naïve Bayes Classification	0.87	0.77	0.46	0.63	0.42	0.55	0.75

TABLE 5- F-Score of each class using different classification techniques

5.3.2 Experiment 2

In Experiment 2, comparison between classifiers is done, based on non-relevant documents retrieved by each classifier from the total non-relevant documents in the collection as shown in figure 4.

The results show that only 2% from the retrieved documents are non-relevant if Ontology based and Hybrid approach is used to classify the Punjabi Text Documents. Where, in case of Centroid based classifier and Naïve Bayes, 5% and 6% from the retrieved documents are irrelevant, respectively.

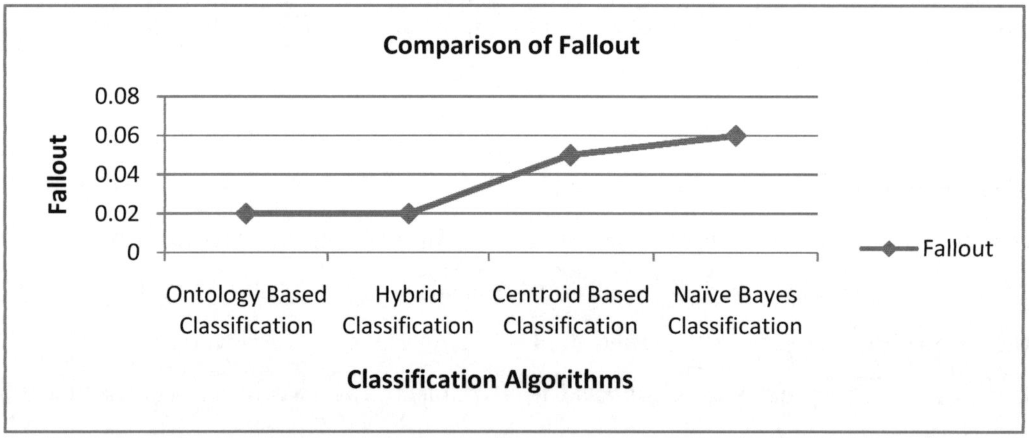

FIGURE 3- Fallout results of each classifier

5.3.3 Experiment 3

The experiment 3 shows the average value of Precision, Recall and F1 for each classifier. From table 6, it can be observed that in comparison with others classifiers, Ontology Based Classification has better averaged Precision (89%) and Recall (85%).

	Ontology Based Classification	Hybrid Classification	Centroid Based Classification	Naïve Bayes Classification
Macro-averaged Precision	0.89	0.88	0.73	0.77
Macro-averaged Recall	0.85	0.84	0.76	0.66

TABLE 6- Macro-averaged Precision and Recall of each classifier

Conclusions

- As of our knowledge, it is first time that we have proposed and implemented two new algorithms for classification of Punjabi documents as previously no other Punjabi document classifier is available in the world.
- Two new algorithms proposed by us are Ontology Based Classification and Hybrid Approach (which is the combination of Naïve Bayes and Ontology Based Classification) for Punjabi documents classification.
- The experimental results conclude that Ontology Based Classification and Hybrid Classification provide better results in comparison to standard classification algorithms Naïve Bayes and Centroid Based for Punjabi documents.
- It is for the first time that sports specific ontology for Punjabi has been developed manually by us, as no such ontology was previously available and it can be beneficial for developing other NLP applications in Punjabi.
- An in depth analysis of Punjabi Corpus is done to prepare gazetteer lists such as middle names, last names, abbreviations, numbers/counting etc. and language dependent rules for Punjabi NER.

References

ALI, ABBAS RAZA AND IJAZ MALIHA (2009). Urdu Text Classification. In: *FIT '09 Proceedings of the 7th International Conference on Frontiers of Information Technology*, ACM New York, USA. ISBN: 978-1-60558-642-7 DOI= 10.1145/1838002.1838025.

CHEN JINGNIAN, HUANG HOUKUAN, TIAN SHENGFENG AND QU YOULI (2009). Feature selection for text classification with Naïve Bayes. In: *Expert Systems with Applications: An International Journal*, Volume 36 Issue 3, Elsevier.

CHEN LIFEI, YE YANFANG AND JIANG QINGSHAN (2008). A New Centroid-Based Classifier for Text Categorization. In: *Proceedings of IEEE 22nd International Conference on Advanced Information Networking and Applications*, DOI= 10.1109/WAINA.2008.12.

CHEN NAWEI AND BLOSTEIN DOROTHEA (2006). A survey of document image classification: problem statement, classifier architecture and performance evaluation. In *Springer-Verlag*, DOI=10.1007/s10032-006-0020-2.

HAN JIAWEI AND KAMBER MICHELIN (2006). *Data Mining: Concepts and Techniques*. Morgan Kaufmann Publishers, 2nd edition, USA, 70-181.

JAYASHREE, R. (2011). An analysis of sentence level text classification for the Kannada language. In: *Proceedings of IEEE International Conference of Soft Computing and Pattern Recognition (SoCPaR)*, 147-151, DOI=10.1109/SoCPaR.2011.6089130.

MANSUR MUNIRUL, UZZAMAN NAUSHAD AND KHAN MUMIT. Analysis of N-Gram Based Text Categorization for Bangla in a Newspaper Corpus. *Center for Research on Bangla Language Processing*, BRAC University, Dhaka, Bangladesh.

McCALLUM, A. AND NIGAM, K. (1998). A comparison of event models for naive Bayes text classification. In: *AAAI-98 workshop on learning for text categorization*. 41-48. Technical Report WS-98-05. AAAI Press.

MOHANTY, S., SANTI, P.K., MISHRA RAJNEETA, MOHAPATRA, R.N. AND SWAIN SABYASACHI . Semantic Based Text Classification Using WordNets: Indian Language Perspective. In: *Proceedings of 3rd International Global Wordnet Conference (GWC 06)*, 321-324, DOI=10.1.1.134.866.

MURTHY, KAVI NARAYANA (2003). Automatic Categorization of Telugu News Articles. In: *Department of Computer and Information Sciences*, University of Hyderabad, Hyderabad, DOI= 202.41.85.68.

PUNJABI LANGUAGE (2012). In: http://en.wikipedia.org/wiki/Punjabi_language.

PUNJABI NEWS CORPUS

RAJAN, K., RAMALINGAM, V., GANESAN, M., PALANIVEL, S. AND PALANIAPPAN, B. (2009). Automatic Classification of Tamil documents using Vector Space Model and Artificial Neural Network. In: *Expert Systems with Applications*, Elsevier, Volume 36 Issue 8, DOI= 10.1016/j.eswa.2009.02.010.

SUN AIXIN AND LIM Ee-PENG (2001). Hierarchical Text Classification and Evaluation. In: *Proceedings of the 2001 IEEE International Conference on Data Mining(ICDM 2001)*, Pages 521-528, California, USA, November 2001.

VERMA, RAJESH KUMAR AND LEHAL, GURPREET SINGH. Gurmukhi-Roman Transliterator GTrans version 1.0, http://www.learnpunjabi.org/gtrans/index.asp.

WANG, YANBO J., COENEN FRANS AND SANDERSON ROBERT (2009). A Hybrid Statistical Data Pre-processing Approach for Language-Independent Text Classification. In: Proceedings of ADMA 5th International Conference on Advanced Data Mining and Applications. 338-349, DOI=10.1.1.157.6558.

WU GUOSHI AND LIU KAIPING (2009). Research on Text Classification Algorithm by Combining Statistical and Ontology Methods. In: *International Conference on Computational Intelligence and Software Engineering*, IEEE. DOI= 10.1109/CISE.2009.5363406.

Using English Acoustic Models for Hindi Automatic Speech Recognition

Anik DEY[1] *Ying Li*[1] *Pascale FUNG*[1]
(1) Human Language Technology Center
Department of Engineering and Computer Engineering
The Hong Kong University of Science and Technology, Clear Water Bay, Hong Kong
adey@ust.hk, eewing@ust.hk, pascale@ee.ust.hk

ABSTRACT

Bilingual speakers of Hindi and English often mix English and Hindi together in their everyday conversations. This motivates us to build a mix language Hindi-English recognizer. For this purpose, we need well-trained English and Hindi recognizers. For training our English recognizer we have at our disposal many hours of annotated English speech data. For Hindi, however, we have very limited resources. Therefore, in this paper we are proposing methods for rapid development of a Hindi speech recognizer using (i) trained English acoustic models to replace Hindi acoustic models; and (ii) adapting Hindi acoustic models from English acoustic models using Maximum Likelihood Linear Regression. We propose using data-driven methods for both substitution and adaptation. Our proposed recognizer has an accuracy of 96% for recognizing isolated Hindi words.

KEYWORDS : English, Hindi, Recognizer, Maximum Likelihood Linear Regression, Adaptation, Substituiton, Data-driven

1. INTRODUCTION

Hindi is one of the most widely spoken languages in the world. It is the major language of India and linguistically speaking, in its everyday spoken form, it is identical to Urdu, the major language spoken in Pakistan. Approximately 405 million people speak Hindi and Urdu worldwide (Sil, 1999). This makes research on Hindi automatic speech recognition systems very interesting due to the high utility of the languages. Hindi is written left to right in a script called Devangari, which we will discuss more in detail in section 1.1.

The last two decades have a seen a gradual progression in the development and fine tuning of automatic speech recognition systems. A few commercial automatic speech recognition (ASR) systems in Hindi have been in use for the last couple of years. The most prevalent ASR systems among them are IBM Via voice and Microsoft SAPI.

In (Kumar and Agarwal, 2011) we see a Hindi ASR being tested and evaluated on a small vocabulary for isolated word recognition. Other recognition systems we have seen so far have been tailor made for certain domains. The Centre for Development of Advanced Computing has developed a speaker independent Hindi ASR which makes use of the Julius recognition engine (Mathur et al., 2010). We have also seen significant work to deal with different accents of Hindi in (Malhotra and Khosla, 2008).

So far the most comprehensive Hindi ASR system we have come across is from the IBM Research Laboratory of India. They have developed a Hindi ASR where the acoustic models are trained with training data that is composed of 40 hours of audio data, and their language model has been trained with 3 million words. The IBM Research group has also worked on large-vocabulary continuous Hindi speech recognition in (Neti, Rajput and Verma, 2004).

However, significant research work has not been done to build a mixed language Hindi-English recognizer. To build such a recognizer we face a low-resource problem, because annotated Hindi speech data is very sparse. Hence, we propose to use well-trained English acoustic models to represent Hindi acoustic models for Hindi speech recognition. In this paper, we have discussed the MLRR adaptation technique, which we have used to map English to Hindi acoustic models using a data-driven approach, in Section 3. We have evaluated the performance of our Hindi ASR system in Section 4.

2. THE DEVANGARI SCRIPT

The Devangari script employed by Hindi contains both vowels and consonants just like in English. However, in contrast to English, Hindi is a highly phonetic language. This means that the pronunciation of any word can be very accurately predicted from the written form of the word.

In comparison with English, Hindi has half as many vowels and twice as many consonants. This usually leads to pronunciation problems. This problem is also encountered while modelling of Hindi phones using English phones is performed. This is because some phones in Hindi may not be present in English at all. For this reason, we propose the data-driven approach. As a result of this approach we can approximate the English phone/s that is most closely matched to such a Hindi phone. The result of this approach is elaborated in the following sections.

In Hindi, consonants can be classified depending on which place within the mouth that they are pronounced.

To pronounce -

- *Velar* consonants: the back of the tongue touches the soft palate.
- *Palatal* consonants: the tongue touches the hard palate.
- *Retroflex* consonants: the tongue is curled slightly backward and touches the front portion of the hard palate. There are no retroflex consonants in English.
- *Dental* consonants: the tip of the tongue touches the back of the upper front teeth.
- *Labial* consonants: lips are used.

The consonants can also be classified according to their manner of articulation, as shown in Table 1 (Shapiro, 2008).

- *Unvoiced* consonants are when the vocal cords are not vibrated during their pronounciation.
- *Voiced* consonants are when the vocal cords are vibrated during pronounciation.
- *Unaspirated* consonants are when consonants are pronounced without a breath of air following the pronounciations. Example in English: "p" in "spit.
- *Aspirated* consonants are when a strong breath of air follows the consonant. Example in English: "p" in "pit".
- *Nasal* consonants are pronounced when some air flows through the nose during pronounciation.

The vowels in Hindi are ordered in similar ways, as shown in Table 2 (Shapiro, 2008)

The manner of articulation of vowels can be classified into two particular categories:

- *Short* vowels are articulated for a comparatively shorter duration of time.
- *Long* vowels are articulated for a comparatively longer duration of time.

Monophthongs are vowels pronounced as a single sound, whereas *diphthongs* are vowels pronounced as a syllable comprising of two adjacent sounds glided together.

	STOPS				
	UNVOICED		VOICED		NASALS
	Unaspirated	Aspirated	Unaspirated	Aspirated	
Velar	क	ख	ग	घ	ङ
Palatal	च	छ	ज	झ	ञ
Retroflex	ट	ठ	ड (ड़)	ढ (ढ़)	ण
Dental	त	थ	द	ध	न
Labial	प	फ (फ़)	ब	भ	म

Table 1: Hindi Consonants

ARTICULATION	VOWELS		
	MONOPHTHONGS		DIPHTHONGS
	SHORT	LONG	
Guttural	अ	आ	
Palatal	इ	ई	
Labial	उ	ऊ	
Retroflex	ऋ	-	
Palato-Guttural		ए	ऐ
Labio-Guttural		ओ	औ

Table 2 : Hindi Vowels

The main difference between vowel pairs in Hindi (such as इ ई) is the vowel length. इ is pronounced like "i" in "bit" whereas ई is pronounced like "ee" in "feet", and उ is pronounced like "u" in "put" whereas ऊ is pronounced like "oo" in "boot".

The final consonants in the Devanagari script are organized into three categories: semivowels/approximants (य र ल व), sibilants (श ष स), and a glottal (ह).

Table 1 and Table 2 shows an in-depth categorization of Hindi alphabets. Since the distinction between manners of articulation is more prominent than from where within the mouth the alphabet is pronounced, we chose to classify the Hindi consonants into two classes, nasals and other consonants and Hindi vowels into two classes, monophthongs and diphthongs.

The distinction between voiced and unvoiced consonants is not as prominent as the difference between nasals and all other consonants, hence we chose to keep all voiced and unvoiced consonants within the same class.

For obtaining the phonetic transcription of English, we are using Arpabet where every English phoneme is represented by one or two capital letters.

In Arpabet, English vowels are classified into three classes : monophthongs, diphthongs and R-colored vowels (The CMU Pronounciation Dictionary, 2007).

Consonants are classified into 6 classes : stops, affricates, fricatives, nasals, liquids and semivowels (The CMU Pronounciation Dictionary, 2007).

By comparing English phonemes with Hindi alphabets, we notice that both languages have nasal consonants and monophthongs and diphthongs vowels. Hence we are also classifying the English phonemes into 4 classes : monophthongs (M), diphthongs (D), nasals (N) and all other consonants (C).

In English Arpabet we have an extra vowel which is neither a monophthong nor a diphthong. This extra vowel, ER, we label into a separate class V.

3. DATA DRIVEN PHONE MAPPING

One of the first steps to map Hindi phones to English phones is to obtain English phoneme transcriptions of Hindi characters. As an intermediate step all the Hindi characters can be transliterated to English using Google Transliteration which uses the International Alphabet of Sanskrit Transliteration (IAST) scheme.

One can use the English recognizer in free form to search through Hindi speech to obtain English phonemes to represent each Hindi characters.

This method yields very poor results when the Hindi acoustic data is limited, and is comparable to randomly searching the Hindi data with an English recognizer with no constraints.

This free form phoneme network of the recognizer allows every phoneme to be followed by every other phoneme including itself just as shown in figure 1.

$phone = all consonants and vowels
(sil <$phone> sil)

Figure 1: Free Form phonetic network

To improve English-phoneme labeling of Hindi speech, we propose to use the linguistic knowledge of Hindi and English as discussed in section 2 to classify all Hindi syllables and English phonemes into four different classes based on their articulation properties.

The four classes we selected are monophthongs (class M), dipthongs (class D), nasals (class N) and consonants (class C).

Each Hindi syllable and English phoneme is labeled to be one of these classes. The classification is shown in table on page.

By using linguistic knowledge of Hindi, we then modify our recognizer into a constrained form network where one phone from one class of the target language, Hindi, is mapped to one phone from the same class of the source language, English.

$phone = class M or class D or class N or class C
(sil <$phone> sil)

Figure 2: Constrained Form phonetic network

For adaptation, we have made use of the Maximum Likelihood Linear Regression (MLRR) technique which is a popular Expectation-Maximisation technique used for speech adaptations.

MLRR adaptation is performed to minimize the mismatch between the English acoustic models and the Hindi acoustic data which is used as the adaptation data. MLLR will compute a set of transformations which will alter the means and variances of Gaussian mixture HMM English acoustic models so that each state of the HMM model is more likely to generate the Hindi adaptation data.

The transformation matrix used to give a new estimate of the adapted mean is given by

$$\hat{\mu} = W \xi,$$

where W is the $n \times (n + 1)$ transformation matrix (where n is the dimensionality of the data) and ξ is the extended mean vector,

$$\xi=[w \mu 1 \mu 2 \ldots \mu n]^T$$

where w represents a bias offset whose value is fixed (within HTK, the Hidden Markov Model Toolkit) at 1.

Hence W can be decomposed into

$$W=[bA]$$

where A represents a $n \times n$ transformation matrix and b represents a bias vector.

After adaptation we can use the Hindi-English phonème mapping (shown in table on page) to construct a pronunciation dictionary for Hindi syllables. Adding linguistic knowledge to enhance the recognizer improves the Hindi ASR.

4. EXPERIMENT

We collected 1 hour of Hindi acoustic data from 9 native Hindi speakers. We asked each speaker a set of questions regarding their university life, likes, dislikes, hobbies and about their career ambitions.

The complete set of Hindi data collected was divided into development and test sets. The test set of data consists of 50 Hindi phrases from one of the 9 speakers. The development set consists of 45 minutes of Hindi acoustic data from 8 different speakers.

After collecting the data, we hired a native speaker of Hindi to transcribe the data for us. Most of the speakers used both English and Hindi while answering the questions on the questionairre. Hence, the transcribed data was a mix of English and Hindi written using the Devangari script.

We used the Carnegie Mellon University (CMU) Pronouncing Dictionary to obtain the phone level transcriptions of all English words in the above transcription. The CMU dictionary uses a phoneme set that consists of 39 phonemes. Each phoneme is represented by one or two capital ASCII letters (ARPAbet).

For all the words written using the Devangari script, we made use of Google's Phonetic Typing service to obtain phone level transcription for all Hindi words. The list of phone level transcription for each Hindi alphabet is shown in table 3 on page 10.

After obtaining the transcriptions, we labelled each phoneme in the transcriptions as one of the 4 classes, discussed in section 3.

For training the English acoustic models 65 hours of native English speech was used, which was kindly shared to us by the guys at the Wall Street Journal.

Using adaptation by reconstruction, we can now obtain the mapping of Hindi phonemes to English. This is shown in table 4 on page 11.

By using English acoustic models, the recognition accuracy to recognize Hindi phrases in the test set, discussed above, is 96%.

CONCLUSION AND DISCUSSION

In this paper, we have proposed steps to rapidly develop a Hindi speech recognizer: (1) by substituting Hindi acoustic models with trained English acoustic models; and (2) by adapting these models using MLRR. We have shown how data-driven methods and linguistic knowledge can be used to map English phonemes to Hindi syllables. With the pronunciation dictionary we constructed we can easily find the phone level transcriptions of any new Hindi word given in written form.

Given a small set of training data, our proposed Hindi constrained-form recognizer has shown promising results. However, there is a lot of room for improvements. Provided that we can collect more Hindi acoustic data, to increase the size of training data drastically, we will be able to better model the Hindi syllables with more than one phoneme transcription.

We also plant to further study multilingual speech recognition since Hindi and English are spoken together by virtually all bilingual speakers of English and Hindi. Also we think better modeling is needed for Hindi phonetic units that do not exist in English.

We are collecting more Hindi acoustic data every month and fine-tuning our Hindi acoustic models. We hope that this can enhance our Hindi acoustic models and improve recognition accuracy.

We are also exploring asymmetric acoustic modelling using selective decision tree merging between a bilingual model and an accented embedded speech model for Hindi and English multilingual speech recognition since this method has shown to improve recognition results for mixed language speech consisting of English and Chinese (Ying et al., 2011). For English and Chinese this method works because English phrases are generally pronounced by a Chinese speaker with varying degrees of accent. The same is true for English and Hindi.

Acknowledgments

We will like to thank Abhilash Veeragouni of IIT Bombay for helping us collect and transcribe Hindi acoustic data which we used as training and test data for our experiments.

References

K. Kumar and R. K. Agarwal (2011). Hindi Speech Recognition System Using HTK. *International Journal of Computing and Business Research*, Vol. 2, No. 2, 2011, ISSN (On- line): 2229-6166.

R. Mathur, Babita and A. Kansal (2010). Domain Specific Speaker Independent Continuous Speech Recognition Using Julius. ASCNT 2010.

K. Malhotra and A. Khosla (2008). Automatic Identification of Gender & Accent in Spoken Hindi Utterances with Re- gional Indian Accents. *IEEE Spoken Language Tech- nology Workshop*, Goa, 15-19 December 2008, pp. 309- 312.

C. Neti, N. Rajput and A. Verma (2004). A Large Vocabulary Continuous Speech Recognition System for Hindi. *IBM Research and Development Journal*, September 2004.

L. Ying, P. Fung, P. Xu, Y. Liu (2011). Asymmetric Acoustic Modeling of Mixed Language Speech. ICASSP 2011.

Michael C. Shapiro (2008). A Primer of Modern Standard Hindi. *Motilal Banarsidass Publishers Private Limited*, 2008 Reprint

Carnegie Mellon University (2007). The CMU Pronounciation Dictionary. < http://www.speech.cs.cmu.edu/cgi-bin/cmudict > (visited 23, October, 2012)

H. Sil (1999). Ethnologue: Languages of the World. < http://www.ethnologue.com/web.asp > (visited 23, October, 2012)

APPENDIX

अ	A
आ	Ā
इ	I
ई	Ī
उ	U
ऊ	Ū
ऋ	R̥
ए	Ē
ऐ	Ai
ओ	Ō
औ	Au
क	Ka

ख	Kha
ग	Ga
घ	Gha
च	Ca
छ	Cha
ज	Ja
झ	Jha
ञ	Ña
ट	Ṭa
ठ	Ṭha
ड	Ḍa
ढ	Ḍha

ण	Ṇa
त	Ta
थ	Tha
द	Da
ध	Dha
न	Na
प	Pa
फ	Pha
ब	Ba
भ	Bha
म	Ma
य	Ya

र	Ra
ल	La
व	Va
श	Śa
ष	Ṣa
स	Sa
ह	Ha

Table 3: IAST Transliteration of Hindi alphabets

kh	k
ai	ey
ch	t
au	ow ey
gh	l
th	l
ph	f
bh	l r
jh	d
a	ah
c	t

b	b
e	ih
d	v
g	l
i	iy
h	l
k	k
j	d
m	m
l	l
o	ah

n	n
p	p
s	s
r	d
u	ah
t	t
v	l
y	hh

Table 4: Hindi to English Phoneme Mapping

Tagger Voting for Urdu

Bushra Jawaid Ondřej Bojar
Charles University in Prague, Faculty of Mathematics and Physics
Institute of Formal and Applied Linguistics
Malostranské nám. 25, Praha 1, CZ-118 00, Czech Republic
{jawaid,bojar}@ufal.mff.cuni.cz

Abstract

In this paper, we focus on improving part-of-speech (POS) tagging for Urdu by using existing tools and data for the language. In our experiments, we use Humayoun's morphological analyzer, the POS tagging module of an Urdu Shallow Parser and our own SVM Tool tagger trained on CRULP manually annotated data. We convert the output of the taggers to a common format and more importantly unify their tagsets. On an independent test set, our tagger outperforms the other tools by far. We gain some further improvement by implementing a voting strategy that allows us to consider not only our tagger but also include suggestions by the other tools. The final tagger reaches the accuracy of 87.98%.

Keywords: Urdu language, Parts-of-speech tagging, Tagger voting, Tagset unification.

1 Introduction

Urdu belongs to the Indo-Aryan language family, a subclass of the Indo-European languages. Urdu is the official language of Pakistan and one of the 23 official languages (including English) spoken in India. It is the native language of at least 65.6 million speakers with another 40 million or more who speak it as a second language[1].

Urdu has borrowed its writing script from Persian, which is a modified form of the Arabic script, the Urdu script is thus called Perso-Arabic. Urdu is written from right to left with numbers written from left to right. The morphology of Urdu is similar to other Indo-European languages, e.g. by having concatenative inflective morphological system.

Urdu is a low-resource language with respect to even the core processing tasks like POS tagging or morphological analysis. Existing taggers for Urdu do not reach sufficient coverage and accuracy.

In this paper, we demonstrate how an ensemble of available tools and data can be joined to achieve a better performance. First, we convert the output of the existing morphological tools to a common representation and more importantly, we unify the different tagsets. Second, we train and evaluate a new tagger on the available annotated data (in our unified tagset) and finally, we implement and evaluate a "voting" scheme that combines the outputs of all available taggers.

2 Resources for Urdu morphology

In this section we briefly list existing morphological tools and POS tagged data for Urdu.

Apart from the available works, there are also some relevant research papers: Anwar et al. (2007a) developed POS tagger for Urdu based on Hidded Markov Models (HMM). They tried to combine several smoothing techniques with HMM model to reduce data sparseness problem. They achieved maximum of 96% accuracy using Good Turing smoothing method when trained on a 70K-token corpus by (Hardie, 2003). The size of the test data is not mentioned.

Anwar et al. (2007b) improve a simple unigram and bigram tagger for unknown and ambiguous words by considering word endings.

2.1 Tools

To the best of our knowledge, only two morphological analyzers for Urdu are freely available: Hussain (2004) and Humayoun (2006). The former is an implementation of a finite-state transducer whereas later is based on a functional morphology toolkit for morphology development in Haskell (Forsberg and Ranta, 2004). Because the tool published by Hussain (2004) requires Windows and its word coverage is rather low, we use only the tool by Humayoun (2006) and call it HUM analyzer in the following.

Language Technologies Research Center of IIIT Hyderabad has developed a shallow parser for Urdu[2] (called SH parser in the following) which analyses Urdu at various levels: tokenization, morphological analysis, POS tagging, chunking, etc. Our main interest is to get the morphologically disambiguated output, which can be extracted from the final output

[1] `http://en.wikipedia.org/wiki/Urdu`

[2] `http://ltrc.iiit.ac.in/showfile.php?filename=downloads/shallow_parser.php`

represented in Shakti Standard Format (SSF)[3]. Detailed description of SSF and a brief overview of tagset is available online[4].

2.2 Data

Besides the tools mentioned above, there is a freely available POS tagged corpus developed by CRULP (Center for Research in Urdu Language Processing)[5]. The underlying tagset is also available online[6]. The actual text of the corpus is a translation of portion of the Wall Street Journal's section of the Penn Treebank. We use this data to train our tagger, see Section 4.

Sajjad and Schmid (2009) manually tagged 110K tokens from a news corpus (www.jang.com.pk) but their data is not freely available[7]. In addition to 110K tokens, they also tagged 8K tokens[8] from BBC News (www.bbc.co.uk/urdu/) and made it freely available online[9]. Sajjad and Schmid (2009) have designed their own tagset[10]. that is purely syntactic in nature, we call this tagset *Sajjad's tagset.*

Note that Sajjad's tagset is more coarse-grained than the one used by CRULP. For instance, Sajjad tags proper noun by PN whereas CRULP distinguishes between the first proper noun in a multi-word name (NNP) and the following ones (NNPC - Proper Noun Continued). For instance, "Saudia Arabia" is tagged as "Saudia|NNP Arabia|NNPC" in CRULP data.

Table 1 summarizes the data we use in our experiments. We see that 1315 of the test tokens (about 15% of the test set) are never seen in the training data.

	Train (CRULP)	Test (Sajjad)	Total
Sentences	4320	404	4724
Tokens	123843	8670	132513
Out-of-vocabulary	–	1315	–

Table 1: Statistics of our training and test data.

3 Format and tagset unification

Due to the low coverage of existing morphological tools for Urdu, it is hard to get an entire corpus tagged with a reasonable accuracy using any of the available linguistic tools alone. To join the forces of the CRULP tagged data and the two analyzers, we need to unify their formats and tagsets.

3.1 Conversion of CRULP's data and output of tools to a common format

The first step in the conversion is a technical mapping of the file formats to a common one.

[3]SSF is a highly readable representation for storing language analysis.

[4]`http://ltrc.iiit.ac.in/analyzer/urdu/shallow-parser-urd-3.0.fc8/doc/ssf-guide-4oct07.pdf`

[5]`http://www.crulp.org/software/ling_resources/UrduNepaliEnglishParallelCorpus.htm`

[6]`http://www.crulp.org/Downloads/ling_resources/parallelcorpus/Urdu%20POS%20Tagset.pdf`

[7]They have used this data for training the taggers in their experiments.

[8]Small dataset is used for taggers evaluation in their work, we also use it for same purpose.

[9]`http://www.ims.uni-stuttgart.de/~sajjad/resources.html`

[10]`http://www.cle.org.pk/Downloads/langproc/UrduPOStagger/UrduPOStagset.pdf`

Table 2 illustrates the common format of the morphological analysis of word "cloths" by both tools. Starting from right, each position in a token represents: word, lemma and tag, separated by the "|" symbol. HUM analyzer, in most cases, provides an ambiguous morphological analysis for the word. All the possible tags are joined using the "-" sign. Each predicted tag has also a simple internal structure (reading left to right): the main part of speech is followed by revelant morphological features. The tag and morphological features are delimited with the "+" symbol.

We also convert the CRULP annotated data from the original format "<CD>اکسٹھ" to "CD|اکسٹھ".

	HUM Analyzer	SH Parser
Output	N+NF+Pl+Nom+Masc|کپڑا|کپڑے	NN+n+m+pl++|کپڑا|کپڑے
	N+NF+Sg+Voc+Masc-	
	N+NF+Sg+Obl+Masc-	

Table 2: The output of HUM Analyzer and SH Parser converted to the common format.

3.2 Unification of tagsets

The second step is the tagset unification. We selected Sajjad's tagset as the target one because it fits our long-term goal of improving English-Urdu phrase-based translation. We manually map each of the tagsets (CRULP data, HUM analyzer and SH parser outputs) to the Sajjad's tagset. The mapping is shown in Table 3.

The symbol "—" indicates that there is no tag in the given tagset that would correspond to the Sajjad's one. In some cases, the Sajjad's tagset is less detailed and we map several tags to a single one, e.g. RB and I in CRULP tagset map to ADV.

When designing the mapping rules, we considered available documentation and also data tagged with the tagset.

3.3 Mapping HUM analyzer and SH parser outputs

Before mapping test set tagged by HUM analyzer and SH parser on Sajjad's tagset, we drop all the morphological information and preserve only the set of proposed POS tags.

A sample test sentence tagged by HUM analyzer and SH parser is shown in Table 4. Again, "|" delimits words from their tags. The mapping to Sajjad's tagset can again introduce ambiguity. We delimit ambiguous tags with "-".

4 Our tagger

Giménez and Màrquez (2004) introduced and made publicly available a multi-purpose tagger called SVM Tool. SVM Tool performed better than state-of-the-art taggers and Sajjad and Schmid (2009) confirmed this for Urdu.

We follow up on this work and train SVM Tool on CRULP manually tagged data (Section 2.2). SVM Tool offers five different kind of models for training a learner. We use 'model 4' with tagging direction from right-to-left. Model 4 boosts identification of unkown words during the learning time by artificially marking some of the words as unknown

Sajjad's Tagset	CRULP	HUM Analyzer	SH Parser
A	JJRP	PostP, Part	PSP
AA	AUXA	—	VAUX
AD	—	RelPron2	DEM
ADJ	JJ	Adj, Adj1, Adj2, Adj3, AdjD	JJ, XC
ADV	RB, I	Adv	RB, INTF, NST
AKP	—	InterPron1, InterPron2, InterPron3	—
AP	—	RelPron2	NST
CA	CD	Num	QC, ECH
CC	CC	Conj	CC
DATE	DATE	—	—
EXP	SYM	—	SYM
FR	FR	—	—
G	PRP$	PossPron	PRP
GR	PRRFP$	—	PRP
I	ITRP	Part	RP
INT	INJ	Intjunc	JJ
KD	—	InterPron	WQ
KER	KER	PossPostPos	PSP
KP	—	InterPron	WQ
MUL	MUL	Verb, Verb1	VM
NEG	NEG	Neg	NEG
NN	NN, NNCM, NNC, NNCR, MOPE, MOPO, NNL	N	NN, XC
OR	OD	RelPron2, N	QO
P	CM	PossPostPos	—
PD	DM	DemPron	PRP
PM	PM	—	SYM
PN	NNP, NNPC	PN	NNP, XC
PP	PR	PersPron, RelPron1	DEM
Q	Q	IndefPron1, IndefPron2, RelPron2, IndefPron, RelPron3	QF
QW	QW	Quest	WQ
RD	DMRL	RelPron	—
REP	PRRL	RelPron	PRP
RP	PRRF	RefPron	PRP
SC	SC	Conj	CC
SE	SE, RBRP	PostP	PSP
SM	SM	—	SYM
TA	AUXT	—	VAUX
U	U	—	—
UNK	UNK	UNK, Verb3, Verb_Aux	UNK
VB	VB, VBL, VBI, VBLI, VBT	Verb, Verb1, Verb2	VM
WALA	WALA	—	—

Table 3: Tagset mapping of Humayoun Morphological Analyzer, Urdu Shallow Parser and CRULP tagset to a common Sajjad's tagset.

words. This feature enhances the capabilities of the learning model and makes it more realistic and refine. Sajjad and Schmid (2009) used the similar model in their work.

Remember that we want to evaluate our tagger using Sajjad's tagset and the mapping described in Section 3.2. This gives rise to two approaches: either we could train the tagger on CRULP manually tagged data and map its output to Sajjad's tagset afterwards, or we could map the training data from CRULP to Sajjad's tagset and train the tagger on this modified training data. We opted for the latter approach, because a deterministic mapping after a statistical classifier in general increases the risk of error cumulation.

We measure the accuracy of the tagger as the percentage of correctly tagged tokens of all the tokens in the Sajjad's test set, see Section 2.2.

With default settings, our SVM Tool tagger achieves the accuracy of only 63.71%. After

HUM Before Mapping	UNK|۔ Verb_Aux|تھا Verb|ہوا Verb1|پڑھا N|جماعت Num|N|سات UNK|چھ
HUM After Mapping	UNK|۔ UNK|تھا VB-MUL|ہوا VB-MUL|پڑھا NN-OR|جماعت NN-OR-CA|سات UNK|چھ
SH Before Mapping	SYM|۔ VAux|تھا VAUX|ہوا VM|پڑھا NN|جماعت ECH|سات QC|چھ
SH After Mapping	SM-PM-EXP|۔ AA-TA|تھا AA-TA|ہوا VB-MUL|پڑھا NN|جماعت CA|سات CA|چھ

Table 4: Mapping HUM Analyzer and SH Parser outputs to the Sajjad's tagset

analyzing the output, we found a few types of errors caused by ambiguous mappings, i.e. when a tag X in CRULP tagset maps to tags Y and Z in Sajjad's tagset. To reduce the risk of wrong or ambiguous mappings, we modified training data prior to training the tagger as follows:

1. We initially mapped PR (Pronoun) to PP (Personal Pronoun) and KP (Kaf Pronoun) and DM (Demonstratives) to PD (Personal Demonstratives) and KD (Kaf Demonstratives). This mapping introduced substantial ambiguities in the training data apparently due to the large number of occurrences of pronouns and demonstratives. To overcome this problem, PM and DM mappings to the Sajjad's tags KP and KD, respectively are removed from the mapping table and we introduce them directly to the training data. All words starting with the the character "ک" (Kaf) get the tag KP (Kaf pronoun) if they were annotated as PR in the CRULP original annotation and the tag KD (Kaf demonstrative) if the original annotation was DM.

2. In the training data, the word "سے" is annotated with the tag "CM" if it is used as a semantic marker. However, in Sajjad's tagset, a special tag "SE" should be used for the word, if it has the characteristics of a semantic marker. To avoid the ambiguous mapping of CM to SE and P (the tag used for marking other semantic markers in Sajjad's tagset) for this word, we remove the mapping CM→SE from the table and apply it to the training data directly: if "سے" is annotated with CM, it gets the Sajjad's tag SE.

3. Negation markers "نہیں" and "نہ" are annotated using RB (Adverb) in the training data. However, in Sajjad's tagset, "NEG" is used to annotate negation markers. Again, we remove the general mapping of RB to NEG and mark these negation markers as NEG explicitly.

Table 5 lists our gradual improvement of accuracy. The column "MOD" shows the accuracy after the above refinement of ambiguous tags, 20% absolute higher than the baseline. On top of that, we created a list of some closed-class words with a fixed tag. The words in the list receive the tag from the list, not from the mapping. Similarly hard-coded list is later added for cardinals, reaching the the accuracy to 85.75%. The "*Best*" tagger uses all the previous modifications and also adds new features for SVM tool: the prefixes of 1 and 2 characters for the current token, the suffixes of 1, 2, 3 and 4 characters of the current token and also the bigram and trigram of preceding word forms and preceding tags. We use only the "Best" tagger in the following experiments.

	Baseline	MOD	CCW	CD	Best
Accuracy	63.71%	84.48%	85.40%	85.75%	**86.18%**

Table 5: Gradual improvements of the baseline tagger: modified training data (MOD), closed-class words (CCW), cardinals (CD), and two new features for the SVM Tool (Best)

In Table 6 we have shown the output of our best accuracy tagger with the reference sentence from the test set.

Tagger output	جس|REP کی|P تفصیل|NN درج|ADJ ذیل|NN ہے|VB ۔|SM
Reference	جس|REP کی|P تفصیل|NN درج|NN ذیل|NN ہے|VB ۔|SM

Table 6: Test set sentence tagged by the best accuracy SVM Tool tagger.

5 Tagger voting

In this section, we evaluate the individual performance of each of the taggers[11]. Then we describe our voting strategy, the resolution of cases where more than one tag get the same score in the voting, and also evaluate the examined configurations of tagger voting.

5.1 Performance of individual taggers

Due to the unavailability of a hand-tagged data using original tagset of each tagger, we originally wanted to measure the accuracy after mapping the output of the taggers on Sajjad's tagset. The mapping can however lead to ambiguity, e.g. the tag PRP by SH parser corresponds to G, GR, PD, REP or RP in Sajjad's tagset, see Table 3. To avoid the need of manual disambiguation of these cases, we collapse all such ambiguities to a common tag for the purposes of this section. The resulting 'coarse tagset' is much less informative than all other ones and would not be very useful in practice. It has only 15 tags instead of the 40 in Sajjad's tagset and lumps e.g. nouns, proper nouns, adjectives and adverbs into one tag, AD-PP-AP-Q-OR-NN-PN-ADJ-INT-ADV.

We map Sajjad's test set and the output of the taggers to the coarse tagset and calculate the accuracy of each of the taggers, see Table 7. HUM analyzer and SH parser sometimes tag a word as unknown (UNK). We see that unknown words amount to one third of the test set for HUM analyzer. Our SVM tagger performs best, reaching 97%. Remember though, that the accuracies in Table 7 are based on the very coarse tagset and they are not comparable with accuracies reported in other tables.

	HUM Analyzer	SH Parser	SVM Tagger
Accuracy (Coarse Tagset)	45.49%	81.51%	97.02%
UNK Tokens	2898 (33.4%)	233 (2.68%)	0 (0%)

Table 7: Taggers accuracies and UNK (unknown) tokens count as observed on Sajjad's test set using a comparable but very coarse-grained tagset.

5.2 Voting

As shown in Table 7, the accuracy of the HUM analyzer and SH parser appears to be surprisingly low even in the coarse tagset. Still, we believe these tools could contribute and propose a simple voting scheme to merge the suggestions from all the three taggers.

Our voting strategy implements the conventional voting style: each tagger has the power of 1 vote. If the tagger emits more than one tags for a token, this one vote is split uniformly (except SVM tagger, see below) among all the suggested tags. Votes for the unknown tag (UNK) are discarded and the tag that receives the highest sum of votes is selected. In case of a voting conflict, i.e. two or more tags receive the same score, we keep them all and

[11] We call HUM analyzer, SH parser and our tagger based on SVM Tool simply "taggers" in the following.

resolve the ambiguity later in Section 5.3. Table 8 illustrates a test sentence before and after voting. Tags in bold are the winners of the voting.

HUM A.	ٹرک|UNK ویسے|**PP** کا|KER-**P** ویسا|**PP** ہی|**I**-A الٹا|**VB-MUL** پڑا|UNK تھا|UNK ۔|UNK
SH P.	ٹرک|**NN**-PN-ADJ ویسے|NN کا|A-KER-SE ویسا|NN ہی|**I** الٹا|**VB-MUL** پڑا|AA-TA تھا|AA-TA ۔|**SM**-PM-EXP
SVM T.	ٹرک|**NN** ویسے|**ADJ** کا|**P** ویسا|**ADV** ہی|**I** الٹا|**PN** پڑا|**VB** تھا|**VB** ۔|**SM**
After Voting	ٹرک|NN ویسے|PP-ADJ کا|P ویسا|ADV-PP ہی|I الٹا|PN-MUL-VB پڑا|VB تھا|VB ۔|SM

Table 8: Output of HUM analyzer, SH parser and SVM tagger before and after voting.

By default, SVM tagger returns its single-best suggestion and always has the power of 1 vote, taking precedence over the other tools too often. To facilitate a smoother merge, we also consider taking more than just the single-best scoring tag from SVM based on its internal probabilities assigned to individual tag options. Taking all the options would not work either, because SVM returns on average more than 5 candidates which would make its votes to these tags too weak.

We thus resort to a fixed number (one, two or three) of considered tags from SVM tagger and we normalize probabilities of these tags to sum to 1, the total power of SVM's vote.

We apply one more hack to tackle the unreliability of SH parser when tagging nouns. Whenever the SH parser proposes NN among the set of suggested tags, we cut its vote for NN by half. An example of this is in Table 8 where the word ویسا received only the tags ADV-PP, despite SH parser was suggesting unambiguous NN.

5.3 Resolving outstanding ambiguities

As seen in Table 8, the word "زیادہ" had more tags reaching the highest score. We use two approaches to resolve such remaining ambiguities: either we use a static preference list, or a list based on the overall frequency of the tags in the training. Of the ambiguous tags, we pick the one that appears highest in the given list.

Table 9 illustrates the sentence from Table 8 with preference-based or frequency-based resolution as well as the reference annotation.

Preference-based	ٹرک|NN ویسے|ADJ کا|P ویسا|ADV ہی|I الٹا|VB پڑا|VB تھا|VB ۔|SM
Frequency-based	ٹرک|NN ویسے|ADJ کا|P ویسا|PP ہی|I الٹا|VB پڑا|VB تھا|VB ۔|SM
Reference	ٹرک|NN ویسے|ADV کا|P ویسا|ADV ہی|I الٹا|ADJ پڑا|VB تھا|TA ۔|SM

Table 9: Voted sentence from Table 8 after applying different fall back options.

5.4 Evaluation

We establish SVM tagger's (individual) accuracy as the baseline for our voting experiments. Table 10 provides the results. SVM-Tag-1, 2, and 3 are our voting setups where we used the top 1, 2, or 3 options from SVM before normalizing their probabilities to sum to the one vote of SVM. The final ambiguity resolution strategy is indicated in the column label.

"Voted Only" means that the ambiguous final output is produced, which has no chance to score well in comparison with the fully disambiguated test set.

A preliminary analysis of SVM Tag-2 and 3 voted output revealed that we make errors in cases where SVM tagger predicts only one tag (so this tag gets the vote of 1) but it is still not selected because it is considered less probable by the remaining two taggers. For such cases, i.e. when SVM had the chance to express its uncertainty but still decided unambiguously, we give it a preference. As indicated in the lines labeled "SVM Preferred If Sure", this gives again a little improvement.

		Voted Only	Voted & Static Fall Back	Voted & Freq. Based Fall Back
Baseline	–	86.18%		
SVM Tag-1	–	85.15%	86.93%	86.85%
SVM Tag-2	Default	86.48%	87.72%	87.64%
	SVM Preferred If Sure	87.65%	87.76%	87.72%
SVM Tag-3	Default	86.66%	87.94%	87.84%
	SVM Preferred If Sure	87.84%	**87.98%**	87.68%

Table 10: Accuracy of test corpus after Voting and applying fall back option.

6 Conclusions and future work

This paper investigated available data and tools for Urdu POS tagging. We unified their respective tagsets and trained our own tagger on the available training data. A comparison on an independent test set documented that our tagger clearly outperforms the other tools.

Additionally, we devised a simple voting scheme and obtained improvement by considering the suggestions of other taggers. The combined tagger reaches the accuracy of 87.98%.

In future, we would like to refine the voting strategy, making it more context-dependent, e.g. by adding one more custom tagger trained to pick the best tag. Also, we are aware that the current ensemble of taggers is somewhat impractical: three taggers have to be run and the final answer is available only after their voting. We plan to run this complex ensemble on a large monolingual corpus and use this data to train a single, standalone tagger. We also plan to release the standalone tagger.

As a separate future goal, we would like to add back the detailed morphological information we are now stripping off.

Acknowledgments

We thank Hassan Sajjad for discussions on characterstics of different taggers and also, Muhammad Humayoun for helpling us with the addition of extra lexicon in his tool, which unfortunately we couldn't add due to time constraints and manual labour involved in it.

This work has been using language resources developed and/or stored and/or distributed by the LINDAT-Clarin project of the Ministry of Education of the Czech Republic (project LM2010013) and it was also partially supported by the grant P406/10/P259 of the Czech Science Foundation.

References

Anwar, W., Wang, X., Lu-Li, and Wang, X.-l. (2007a). Hidden markov model based part of speech tagger for urdu. pages 1190–1198.

Anwar, W., Wang, X., Lu-Li, and Wang, X.-l. (2007b). Morphological ending – based strategies of unknown word estimation for statistical pos urdu tagger. pages 167–173.

Forsberg, M. and Ranta, A. (2004). Functional morphology. In *Proceedings of the Ninth ACM SIGPLAN International Conference on Functional Programming*, pages 213–223. ACM Press.

Giménez, J. and Màrquez, L. (2004). Svmtool: A general pos tagger generator based on support vector machines. In *Proceedings of the 4th LREC*, Lisbon, Portugal.

Hardie, A. (2003). Developing a tagset for automated part-of-speech tagging in urdu. Department of Linguistics, Lancaster University.

Humayoun, M. (2006). Urdu morphology, orthography and lexicon extraction. In *Master's Thesis*. Department of Computing Science, Chalmers University of Technology.

Hussain, S. (2004). Finite-state morphological analyzer for urdu. In *Master's Thesis*. National University of Computer & Emerging Sciences.

Sajjad, H. and Schmid, H. (2009). Tagging urdu text with parts of speech: a tagger comparison. In *Proceedings of the 12th Conference of the European Chapter of the Association for Computational Linguistics*, EACL '09, pages 692–700, Stroudsburg, PA, USA. Association for Computational Linguistics.

BIS Annotation Standards With Reference to Konkani Language

Edna Vaz [1], *Shantaram V. Walawalikar* [2], *Dr.Jyoti Pawar* [3], *Dr.Madhavi Sardesai* [4]
(1) Goa University, Taleigao-Goa.
edna.vaz22@gmail.com, goembab@hotmail.com, jyotidpawar@gmail.com,
madhavikonkani@gmail.com

ABSTRACT

The Bureau of Indian Standards (BIS) Part Of Speech (POS) tagset has been prepared for the Indian Languages by the POS Tag Standardization Committee of Department of Information Technology (DIT), New Delhi, India. The BIS POS tagset aims to ensure standardization in the POS tagging of all the Indian Languages. It has been used for POS tagging in the Indian Languages Corpora Initiative (ILCI) project which has developed parallel annotated corpora consisting of 25000 sentences each from the tourism and the health domain for 11 Indian Languages.

In this paper we present some challenges encountered while using the BIS POS tagset for Konkani, a morphologically rich Indian Language, along with the possible solutions to overcome these challenges.

KEYWORDS: Part Of Speech Tagging, POS, Department of Information Technology, DIT, Bureau of Indian Standards tagset, BIS tagset, Indian Languages Corpora Initiative, ILCI, Konkani, Natural Language Processing, NLP.

1. Introduction

Annotated text corpora are a basic and a very useful resource for researchers in Natural Language Processing (NLP) for developing various language technologies. The annotation of corpora is done using a set of tags defined for this purpose. The BIS tagset is a set of tags evolved by the POS Tag Standardization committee appointed by the DIT to standardize and streamline the process of POS tagging in Indian languages.

A need for standard tagset along with guidelines for using it arose because a lot of researchers were working independently following the tags of their own choice to mark the POS within and across languages. This affected the reusability of the tagged data amongst researchers. Hence, in order to facilitate interoperability an exercise was made to have a consensus on the style and characteristics of POS tagging, so as to arrive at a common standard for tagging in Indian Languages. This led to the standardized BIS tagset for POS tagging for Indian Languages. Several meetings of experts in the field were held to decide on the tagset and all groups engaged in research in NLP were given standard guidelines for annotation. This paper aims at shedding light on the peculiarities of the Konkani language that have posed challenges in tagging corpora using the standard BIS tagset. The paper is organized as follows – section 2 briefly introduces the BIS tagset and the Konkani Language and the challenges encountered while tagging using the BIS POS tagset for Konkani are presented in section 3 which is followed by section on conclusion and future work.

2. BIS tagset and Konkani Language

The BIS POS tagset is prepared keeping in view the comments of experts in the area of NLP and Language Technology (LT) for Indian languages. This tagset is an important step taken by DIT to ensure that NLP practitioners involved in tagging follow a common tagset while tagging various corpora. The tagset initially consisted of 38 tags. These tags were then modified after taking inputs from linguists, computer scientists and language experts. More details of the BIS tagset can be found in Chaudhary, 2010. The BIS tagset is a commendable effort. But the process of tagging was, at times, quite challenging as it was different from the conventional style of tagging (for example, the case of marking adverbs of place and location as NSTs (locative nouns) .

Konkani is an Indo-European (Indo-Aryan) language evolved from Sanskrit. It is a morphologically rich Indian language (Almeida, 1989). It is one of the twenty two languages included in the Eighth Schedule of the Indian Constitution. It is spoken by the people of the state of Goa, in some parts of Maharashtra, Karnataka and in some pockets of Kerala. It is influenced and enriched by various other languages like Marathi, Kannada, Malayalam, Hindi, Arabic, Persian, Portuguese and English. It is the official language of Goa with Devanagari as the officially recognized script. It is also written in Roman, Kannada, and Malayalam scripts (Walawalikar, et.al. 2010).

2.1 BIS POS tagset for Konkani

The BIS tagset was used for tagging the Konkani ILCI corpus consisting of a total of 50000 sentences (730330 tokens). The main objective of the ILCI project was to develop standard quality parallel annotated corpora for 11 Indian languages including English language to promote NLP research for Indian Languages (Chaudhary, 2010).

The following is the tagset for Konkani prepared in line with the BIS tagset.

SI	Category			Label	Annotation Convention		
	Top Level	Subtype (level1)	Subtype (Level2)			Hindi	Konkani
1	**Noun**			N	N	संज्ञा	नाम
1.1		Common		NN	N__NN	जातिवाचक संज्ञा	जातीवाचक नाम
1.2		Proper		NNP	N__NNP	व्यक्तिवाचक संज्ञा	व्यक्तीवाचक नाम
1.3		Nloc		NST	N__NST	देश-काल-सापेक्ष संज्ञा	थळ-काळ-सापेक्ष नाम
2	**Pronoun**			PR	PR	सर्वनाम	सर्वनाम
2.1		Personal		PRP	PR__PRP	पुरूषवाचक सर्वनाम	पुरूश सर्वनाम
2.2		Reflexive		PRF	PR__PRF	निजवाचक सर्वनाम	आत्मवाचक सर्वनाम
2.3		Relative		PRL	PR PRL	संबंधवाचक सर्वनाम	संबंदी सर्वनाम
2.4		Reciprocal		PRC	PR__PRC	पारस्परिक रार्वजाग	एकमेकी रार्वजाग
2.5		Wh-word		PRQ	PR__PRQ	प्रश्नवाचक सर्वनाम	प्रस्नार्थी सर्वनाम
2.6		Indefinite		PRI	PR_PRI		अनिश्चीत सर्वनाम
3	**Demonstrative**			DM	DM	संकेतवाची	दर्शक
3.1		Deictic		DMD	DM__DMD		
3.2		Relative		DMR	DM__DMR	संबंधवाचक संकेतवाची	संबंदी दर्शक
3.3		Wh-word		DMQ	DM__DMQ	प्रश्नसूचक संकेतवाची	प्रस्नार्थी दर्शक
		Indefinite		DMI	DM_DMI		अनिश्चीत दर्शक

4	**Verb**			V	V	क्रिया	क्रियापद
4.1		Main		VM	V__VM	मुख्य क्रिया	मुखेल क्रियापद
4.1.1			Finite	VF	V_VM_VF	परिमित क्रिया	पूर्ण क्रियापद
4.1.2			Non-finite	VNF	V_VM_VNF		अपूर्ण क्रियापद
4.1.3			Infinitive	VINF	V_VM_VINF	अपरिमित क्रिया	सादारण रूप
4.2		Gerund		VNG	V_VM_VNG	क्रियावाचक संज्ञा	क्रियावाचक नाम
4.4		Auxiliary		VAUX			
4.4.1			Finite		V_VAUX_VF	पालवी क्रिया	पालवी पूर्ण क्रियापद
4.4.2			Non-Finite		V_VAUX_VNF		पालवी अपूर्ण क्रियापद
5	**Adjective**			JJ		विशेषण	विशेशण
6	**Adverb**			RB		क्रियाविशेषण	क्रियाविशेशण
7	**Postposition**			PSP		परसर्ग	संबंदी अव्यय
8	**Conjunction**			CC	CC	योजक शब्द	जोड अव्यय
8.1		Co-ordinator		CCD	CC_CCD	समानाधिकरण	समानाधीकरण जोड अव्यय
8.2		Subordinator		CCS	CC_CCS	आश्रित	आश्रीत जोड अव्यय
9	**Particles**			RP	RP	अव्यय	अव्यय
9.1		Default		RPD	RP_RPD	सामान्य	सरभरस अव्यय
9.2		Classifier		CL	RP_CL	वर्गक	वर्गक
9.3		Interjection		INJ	RP_INJ	विस्मयादि बोधक	उमाळी अव्यय

9.4		Intensifier		INTF	RP__INTF	तीव्रता-बोधक	तिव्रकारी अव्यय
9.5		Negation		NEG	RP__NEG	नकारात्मक	न्हयकारी अव्यय
10	**Quantifiers**			QT	QT	संख्यावाची	संख्यादर्शक
10.1		General		QTF	QT__QTF	सामान्य	सामान्य
10.2		Cardinals		QTC	QT__QTC	गणनावाची	संख्यावाचक
10.3		Ordinals		QTO	QT__QTO	क्रमवाची	क्रमवाचक
11	**Residuals**			RD	RD	अवशिष्ट	हेर
11.1		Foreign word		RDF	RD_RDF	विदेशज	विदेशी
11.2		Symbol		SYM	RD_SYM	चिह्न	कूरू
11.3		Punctuation		PUNC	RD_PUNC		विरामकूरू
11.4		Unknown		UNK	RD__UNK	अज्ञात	अनवळखी
11.5		Echowords		ECH	RD__ECH	प्रतिध्वनि-शब्द	पडसादी उतरां

TABLE 1 – The BIS tagset for Konkani

3. Issues in tagging using the standardized BIS tagset

POS tagging is an ongoing process and we may need to modify the tagset to accommodate newer findings, etc. Some tags have been modified whereas some are still being discussed. For example, in the initial stages of BIS POS discussions, it was decided that names of cities, institutions, organizations, people and months were to be tagged as Proper Nouns (NNP) whereas names of medicines, diseases, flowers, animals and seasons were to be taken as Common Nouns (NN). This decision was later refined. Blood Cancer (a specific type of a Cancer) was tagged as NNP and Cancer (a general category of diseases) was tagged as NN. Decisions taken may have to be modified and documenting these will help us trace the line of our path. So also this documentation will help newcomers in this area to foresee problems which may arise in tagging corpora using this tagset. It is important to remember that flexibility in the tagset is for the purpose of refinement and accuracy in the tagging process and not for disclosing our earlier 'inappropriate' decisions. We know that words in a language have the capacity to function differently when they appear in a sentence. For example, in रांदिल्लें जेवण (rAMdilleM jevaNa) '**cooked food**', रांदिल्लें functions as a modifier whereas रांदिल्लें in हांवें दनपारां जेवण रांदिल्लें (hAveM danapArAM jevaNa rAMdilleM) ('I had **cooked** food in the afternoon') functions as a verb. The present tagset is used to tag words according to their lexical rather than syntactic function. The lacunae if any in this practice may come to light only when we move to higher levels of NLP.

Some of the minor challenges arising from the usage of the proposed BIS tagset while POS tagging the ILCI Corpora for Konkani language could be placed under the following main heads:

3.1 **Word Sense Disambiguation Challenges**

The hyphen is marked as punctuation in the BIS tagset, but in Konkani it conveys different information on different occasions. In some cases, a pair of two words joined by a hyphen is a compound word whereas in other cases it may be just a noun phrase. Various senses conveyed by the hyphen need to be separated and structurally identified as specific compounds. This would facilitate word sense disambiguation.

Examples:

- बरें-वायट bareM-vAyaT ('good-bad'). In this example, the hyphen marks a pair of antonyms. In isolation, the words in this pair function as adjectives whereas the pair as a whole functions as a noun.
  For example, in तें एक बरें चली teM eka bareM chalI ('she is a good girl'), and तें एक वायट चली teM eka vAyaT chalI ('she is a bad girl', बरें bareM 'good' and वायट vAyaT 'bad' both function as adjectives. However, in ताका बरें-वायट समजना tAkA bareM-vAyaT samajanA ('he does not know what is good and what is bad' i.e. 'he does not know his good'), the pair बरें-वायट bareM-vAyaT functions as noun.
- The hyphen in the pair बायल-मनीस bAyal manIsa ('woman-human') marks a specifier-specified relationship. In Konkani, मनीस manIsa 'human being' is a gender neutral term. The following sentences illustrate this point:
  1. तो एक बरो मनीस to ek baro manIs ('he is a good human being')
  2. ती एक बरी मनीस tI ek barI manIs ('she is a good human being')

We see that in both the above sentences मनीस 'human being' remains the same. However, the term can be specified by other gender specific nouns such as दादलो dAdlo (masculine) 'man', चली chalI (feminine/neuter) 'girl/daughter', बायल bAyl (feminine) 'woman' when it occurs in compounds such as दादलो मनीस ('man-human'), बायल मनीस ('woman-human'), चली मनीस ('girl-human'). For example, in दादल्या मनशाक तें कळचेंना dAdlya manashAka teM kaLacheMnA ('a male human (i.e. a man) will not understand this'), dAdlo 'man' specifies the masculine gender of मनीस manIsa 'human being'. Thus the role of hyphen cannot be ignored in the compounds of the above type.

- In भाट-बेंस bhAT- beMsa ('property-assets'), the hyphen is used to mark a 'synonymic compound'. Such an occurrence of a hyphen is very common in Konkani. For example, भांगर-शिंगर, धन-दौलत etc. These synonymous pairs are mostly a combination of a native and a foreign language word. For example, in भाट-बेंस, the first word is a native word whereas the second one is a word from Portuguese.
- The hyphen in किताब-ए-हिंद kitAba-e-hiMda ('kitab-e-hind') is used to highlight a foreign title.
- The hyphen in 10-20 means 'to' (i.e. it conveys the inclusion of numerals from 10 to 20). The hyphen does occur in other expressions containing numerals. However, it conveys a different sense. For example in the Konkani sentence ताका मारपाक सात-आठ मनीस आशिल्ले (tAkA mArapAka sAta-ATh manIs Ashille) 'to hit him seven-eight people were there' (i.e. 'around seven to eight people were present to hit him'), the phrase सात-आठ is joined by the hyphen. Here, the hyphen expresses a sense of 'unsurety' within the mind of the speaker about number of people that were present before him.

- The phrase साडे-सात sADe-sAta means 'half past seven'. Such an usage of the hyphen can be found in other **temporal expressions** such as in सवाय-आठ savAya-ATh (quarter past eight), etc. It is the hyphen that helps to mark this phrase.

3.2 Punctuation

Marking an inverted comma as punctuation is misleading in some cases. For example, in 'कॉंग्रेस पार्टी' चो kA.Ngresa pArTI cha.o ('of Congress Party'), चो is a suffix of the noun phrase 'Congress Party'. This phrase is put in inverted commas as it is a foreign language phrase. Thus marking inverted commas in such cases as punctuation is not proper.

3.3 Tagging of spatio-temporal adverbs as NST

All nouns in Konkani undergo oblique formation before they take a case suffix.

राम rAm becomes रामा rAmA before it takes any suffix like -क ka, -न na, -चो cho, etc. However, the spatio-temporal adverbs take suffixes before undergoing oblique formation. E.g. भायर+लो bhAyara + lo> भायलो bhAyalo 'of outside', सकयल +च्यान sakayala +chyAna > सकयल्यान sakayalyAna 'from below'.

Moreover, these adverbs take only the above mentioned suffixes. Combinations like भायर +क bhAyara +ka 'to the one outside' भायर +आंत bhAyara+AMta 'in the one outside' are not permitted in the language. If these adverbs are tagged as nouns (NSTs) then they must be treated as a special category of nouns.

3.4 Recognition of frozen expressions

Some expressions in language function in a certain way. खरें म्हणल्यार khareM mhaNalyAra (Truly/Really speaking) खरें KhareM in Konkani means 'truth' whereas म्हणल्यार mhaNalyAra means 'having told' which is a quotative.

However, when these two words come together, they always function like an adverb. Tagging these words individually would serve no purpose. Some more examples in the same category are listed below -

सांगपाचें म्हणल्यार sAMgapAcheM mhaNalyAra "Of-telling if told" means 'actually'.

तशें पळेल्यार tasheM paLayalyAra "that way if seen" also means 'actually'.

3.5 Negation

One has to be careful in the treatment of negation in Konkani. Negation found in Hindi is not all the same in Konkani. In Hindi, negation is mainly a syntactic process whereas in Konkani, it is a morphological one. Examples illustrating this point are given below:

Hindi:

3.5.1 a नहीं. मैं नहीं आउंगा nahIM. maiM nahI AuMgA ('**No**. I will not come')

3.5.1 b नहीं. हम नहीं आयेंगे nahIM. hama nahIM AyeMge ('**No**. We will not come')

Konkani:

3.5.2 a ना. हांव येवंचो ना nA. hAMva yevaMcho nA ('**No**. I will **not** come')

3.5.2 b ना. आमी येवंचे नात nA. AmI yevaMche nAt ('**No**. We will **not** come')

So also in Hindi, negation occurs at all places as a particle (in the sentences 3.5.1 a and 3.5.1 b), whereas in Konkani the first word in 3.5.2 a and 3.5.2 b is a particle and the second one in 3.5.2b is a finite verb.

Conclusion and Future Work

A fruitful comparison between languages (for example between different grammatical categories) has been possible because of the BIS tagset. The tagset has helped in bringing to our minds the differences existing between Indian Languages. For example, Konkani words marked as NSTs (a subcategory of nouns) under the BIS tagset do not have an oblique form whereas other subcategories of nouns in Konkani always have an oblique form. However, the tag NST seems to work fairly well in other Indian languages.

Differences between languages which may pose **challenges in Indian Language–Indian Language translation can be predicted** to a fair extent with this tagset. For example, postpositions like Hindi का never occur separately in Konkani. One may be tempted to translate राम का rAm kA (of Ram) as राम चो rAm -cho which actually should be रामाचो rAmAcho.

- **solutions proposed for the issues faced:**

The BIS tagset has no doubt prepared the ground for fruitful annotations. It is up to the experts of each language to examine this tagset closely and suggest necessary refinements pertaining to their language. It may not be possible to include new tags to handle current issues but we could deal with them keeping the standardized tagset intact. We propose following suggestions to deal with some of the above mentioned issues.

The hyphen sometimes functions as an integral part of compounds and phrases. Marking it as a punctuation mark will mean ignoring the subtle information that it conveys in these occurrences. We feel that the role of the hyphen has to be recognized as it would not only help in word sense disambiguation (as in the case of बरें-वायट bareM-vAyaT 'good-bad') but also bring to light certain peculiarities of Konkani (as in the case of भाट-बेंस bhAT- beMsa 'property-assets' where the synonymic compound is formed with a word from Portuguese).

Frozen expressions, for example can be marked with a special tag at POS level itself so that there is no wastage of time in unnecessary work, later. For example, in खरें म्हणल्यार KhareM mhaNalyAra 'really/truly speaking' tagging individual words would serve no purpose. Instead the token **'खरें म्हणल्यार'** could be marked as **FE** i.e. frozen expression. The appropriate category (i.e. adverb) could be marked at the next level of NLP.

While recognizing the importance of standardization in the POS tagging of all the Indian Languages, we also feel that we should be careful in not to lose on the grammatical peculiarities of individual languages as it may have an adverse effect on the later stages of NLP.

References

Almeida, Matthew. (1989). *A Description of Konkani.* Miramar, Goa: Thomas Stephens Konkani Center.

Chaudhary. Narayan et.al. (2010). *ILCI Parts of Speech guidelines document.*

Jawaharlal Nehru University.

Walawalikar et.al. (2010) *Experiences in Building the Konkani Wordnet using the Expansion Approach* in Proceedings of the 5th Global Wordnet Conference.

Automatic Extraction of Compound Verbs from Bangla Corpora

Sibansu Mukhopadhyay[1] *Tirthankar Dasgupta*[2] *Manjira Sinha*[2] *Anupam Basu*[2]
(1) Society for Natural Language Technology Research, Kolkata 700091
(2) Indian Institute of Technology Kharagpur, Kharagpur 721302
{sibansu, iamtirthankar, manjira87, anupambas}@gmail.com

ABSTRACT

In this paper we present a rule-based technique for the automatic extraction of Bangla compound verbs from raw text corpora. In our work we have (a) proposed rules through which a system could automatically identify Bangla CVs from texts. These rules will be established on the basis of syntactic interpretation of sentences, (b) we shall explain problems of CV identification subject to the semantics and pragmatics of Bangla language, (c) finally, we have applied these rules on two different Bangla corpuses to extract CVs. The extracted CVs were manually evaluated by linguistic experts where our system and achieved an accuracy of around 70%.

KEYWORDS: COMPOUND VERBS, AUTOMATIC EXTRACTION, VECTOR VERBS

1 Introduction

Compound verbs (henceforth CV) are special type of complex predicates consisting of a sequence of two or more verbs acting as a single verb and express a single expression of meaning. However, not all verb sequences are considered as compound verbs. A compound verb consists of a sequence of two verbs, V1 and V2 such that V1 is a common verb with /-e/ [non-finite] inflection marker and V2 is a finite verb that indicates orientation or manner of the action or process expressed by V1 (Dasgupta, 1977). The verb V1 is known as pole and V2 is called as vector. For example, in the sentence রুটিগুলো খেয়ে ফেলো *(/ruTigulo kheYe phela/) "bread-plural-the eat and drop-pres. Imp"* "Eat the breads", the verb sequence "kheYe phela" is an example of CV.

Identification of compound verbs from sentences is useful in many NLP applications including Wordnet development, Information Retrieval, and Machine Translation. However, automatic identification of compound verbs from a given text document is not a trivial task. As mentioned in (Dasgupta, 1977), a sequence of two or more verbs does not always guarantees to be a compound verb. Depending on the context a verb sequence may or may not act as CV. Thus, automatic identification of compound verbs is extremely important and a challenging task.

This paper deals with the rule-based automatic identification of these types of Bangla CV, where V1 is a pole and V2 is a vector. In our work (a) we shall propose rules through which a system could automatically identify Bangla CVs from texts and these rules will be established on the basis of syntactic interpretation of sentences, (b) we shall explain problems of CV identification subject to the semantics and pragmatics of Bangla language, (c) finally we shall make a statistical evaluation of our rules.

The rest of the paper is organized as follows: In section 2 we first perform the linguistic study and the related concepts of the compound verb and different issues related to the automatic extraction of CVs. Section 3 briefly discuss about the different related works done in this area. Section 4 discuss about the different linguistic rules that can be applied to extract CVs from text corpuses. Section 5 presents the experimentations, evaluations and results of our work.

2 Background

An important feature of CV is that the vector verb has no independent meaning. The Vector verb only can affect/support the pole to express some certain pragmatic expression. Linguists call this process of semantic nullification, *process of grammaticalization*. Considering the previous example, if we have a CV like 'খেয়ে ফেলো', we, or any native speaker of Bangla, must not differentiate those two verbs to comprehend the meaning for the each. Bangla native speakers have the sense that the combination 'খেয়ে ফেলো' produces a common meaning which is almost but not really same to the central meaning of the verb 'খা' [*khaa*: 'eat']. And the meaning of the 2nd verb, 'ফেল্' [*phel*: 'drop'] is being bleached out. This second or the vector verb is functionally attached to the pole and grammatically subservient and both the two verbs produce a single meaning.

This is true that each of the verbs of this phrase can be used as a pole or as an independent verb in different contexts. Native speakers are pragmatically competent to understand the phrase duly depending on the certain contexts. If one says in Bangla, "রুটিগুলোর কয়েকটা খেয়ে ফেলে দাও।" (*/ruTigulor kaYekaTaa kheYe phele daao/*), it means "Eat some of the breads and reject the rest of breads." The same combination of the root verbs, "খা" (eat) and "ফেল্", (drop) plays a different role. The interesting thing can be pointed out that there is another one verb 'দাও' is being attached on the right side of the combination 'খেয়ে ফেলে' and the 'ফেলে' is containing an infinite inflection /-e/. It means 'ফেলে' (phele) is no more playing role of a vector. There the combination of CV is being shifted from 'খা' (eat) and 'ফেল' (drop) to 'ফেল্' (drop) and 'দে' (give). The new CV has a new vector 'দে' (give), which has lost its meaning. There about twenty two verbs are used as vectors which support poles to describe its action in CVs.

2.1 Why Compound Verbs Occur?

Now a psycho-cognitive question arises. Why do the speakers intend to speak a half-hearted semantically bliched out vector verb with a main verb, when she has an option to manage her expression with a pole? We have to say that the poles always do nothing in such cases where speakers need to realize specific genres of daily speech, though it is a question of natural language survey. We have to consider some examples [(8) to (11)], where the poles cannot cover up the specification necessary for the conversation.

(8) তুমি কি কাল টাকাটা অমলের হাতে দিতে পেরেছো?
Expression: "Could you give the money to Amal yesterday?"

(9) তুমি কি কাল টাকাটা অমলের হাতে দিয়ে উঠতে পেরেছো?
Expression: "Could you at last give the money to Amal yesterday? Or something like: "Had you managed your time to give the money to Amal yesterday?"

(10) তুমি কাজটা করেছো।
Expression: You have done the job.

(11) তুমি কাজটা করে ফেলেছো।
Expression: You have finished the job.

(8)-(9) and (10)-(11) are the pairs of sentences, where (9) and (11) have CVs, whereas (8) and (10) have not. The expressions are indicating the differences between CV and non-CV. Some verbs feel lonely. They cannot take the risks of such expressions, which go beyond the physical property of the language. Hook (1974) shows that, a CV can tackle sometimes aspectual or modal expressions in Hindi.

The speech act of vector can be discussed under the area of pragmatics. Ancient Indian tradition of grammar proposed more than one way of understanding meaning of speech. According to such Indian grammatical discourse, native speakers have the potential to under meaning depending on some *lakshans* (indication) of the components. A word or a speech unit has this power of concieving intended meaning (*lakshana shakti*). Vectors also have the power. Let us consider again some examples below.

(12) অমল গান গাইলো।
"Amal sang song."

(13) অমল গান গেয়ে উঠলো।
"Amal started to sing song."

(14) অমল এমন সময় হঠাৎ গান গাইলো।
"At that time, suddenly Amal sang song."

(15) অমল এমন সময় হঠাৎ গান গেয়ে উঠলো।
"At that time, suddenly Amal started to sing the song."

(16) অমল কাল সন্ধ্যেবেলা জলসায় গান গাইবে।
"Amal will sing song in a function tomorrow evening."

(17) *অমল কাল সন্ধ্যেবেলা জলসায় গান গেয়ে উঠবে।
"Amal will start to sing (suddenly) song in a function tomorrow evening."

Now we need to focus on the above sentence (12) which is a simple sentence. Speaker states that "Amal sang song". Sentence (13) has a complex predicate */geYe uThalo/*. Sentence like (13) expresses that there is a reason for which Amal started to sing song. This sentence also deserves sentential extension with such words like "emana samaYa haThat.h" (at that time suddenly) to relate the reason for which Amal started to sing song [(15)]. Therefore, we see there is a question of appropriateness we have to face regarding understanding the semantics of the vectors. As "*uThalo*" refer to the *sudden* reason behind fact of Amal's singing in past, it cannot be appear in future. That is why the sentence (17) is unacceptable to Bengali speakers. So CV is very specific for its use in the social discourses.

2.2 Challenges in Automatic CV Extraction

Now allow us to turn to the question of identification. We have understood that a couple of verbs (V1+V2) can be considered as a CV when the second verb helps to express some pragmatic specification of the first verb (pole) and when the second verb has no independent meaning. We recognize a CV as we have the pragmatic competence. But how do we *refer* that pragmatic sense which is beyond the physical property? How does a machine understand that these compound components are CV and these are not? After POS-tagger describes a sentence, how can a machine annotate CV, as there are so many possibilities where more than one verb occurs immediately in a syntagmatic order?
This paper tries to reveal such syntactic conditions for the identification of CV without applying pragmatics. And we have targeted to fix certain properties for the CV that a system can easily identify. This has to be said that these conditions will work well to a trained or supervised data but not for the all. However, the easiest way to identify a CV is to mark the vectors in a language first. Let us consider following non-semantic or non-pragmatic conditions to identify a CV in Bangla:

(18) (a) Verb (V1) + verb (V2).
(b) V1 ends with an inflection /-e/ (not –te of course).
(c) V2 is a marked vector.

But these conditions (18) do not properly handle the situations. We have discussed little earlier that all the verb plus verb is not CV. V1 with /-e/-ending is also a common form of infinitive in Bangla. For example, consider (19).

(19) রবি ভাত খেয়ে বলবে।
/rabi bhaata kheYe balabe/
"Eating rice Rabi will say."

"*kheYe balabe*" in this sentence (19) is not a CV, though there V1 ends with /-e/. And for (18)/(c), this is said that the vectors, usually, are poles (normal verbs). This is very difficult to identify a verb as a vector, if we do not have the idea of context or the information about its position in a V+V sequence. If a machine understands that the second position in a V+V is for the vectors and if such a vector, machine finds from the list it may identify that this V+V is a CV. But, even in Bangla, there are many options, where a vector-listed verb plays a role of pole. In those cases, V+V are to be sub-categorized as Pole + Pole, not as Pole + Vector. Table 1 describes a list of 16 vector verbs as proposed by (Paul, 2003).

Table 1: Bangla Vector Verb List

Sl. No.	**Vector Verb**	**Transliteration**	**General Meaning**	**Example**
1	যা	*/yaa/*	Go	সকাল থেকে বৃষ্টি পড়ে যাচ্ছে।
2	আস্	*/aas.h/*	Come	বহুদিন ধরে রবি কাজ ক'রে আসছে।
3	পড়্	*/pa.D.h/*	Fall	রবি আজ সকাল সকাল ঘুম থেকে উঠে পড়ল।
4	ফেল্	*/phel.h/*	Drop	রবি কথাটা বলে ফেলল।
5	দে	*/de/*	Give	রবি বিস্কুটটা খেলো না ফেলে দিলো।
6	নে	*/ne/*	Take	রবি তাড়াতাড়ি হাতের কাজ ক'টা সেরে নিল।
7	মর্	*/mar.h/*	Die	তুমি শ্যামলের জন্য মিথ্যে ভেবে মরছো।
8	বস্	*/bas.h/*	Seat	রবি সকলের সামনে কথাটা বলে বসলো।
9	উঠ্	*/uTh.h/*	Get up	তুমি কি তোমার বাবাকে কথাটা বলে উঠতে পারলে?
10	তুল	*/tul/*	Lift	তুমি কি মানুষকে জাগিয়ে তুলবে ভাবছো?
11	ছাড়্	*/chhaa.D.h/*	Leave	রবি কাজটা করে ছাড়লো।
12	রাখ্	*/raakh.h/*	Put down	মোহর সকাল সকাল কাজ গুছিয়ে রেখেছে।
13	আন্	*/aan.h/*	Bring	কাজটা প্রায় শেষ করে এনেছি।
14	পাঠা	*/paaThaa/*	Send	তিনি বলে পাঠিয়েছেন।

3 Related works

Recent trends in computational linguistics revisit several old issues from hardcore linguistics or traditional grammar. CV is one such issue, natural language scientists have the scope to use it in the computational aspect and experiment through a large linguistic corpus. CV issues in Indian language perspective have been reviewed by many Indian researchers, such as (Alsena, 1991; Abbi, 1991, 1992; Gopalkrishnan and Abbi, 1992; Butt, 1993; Butt, 1995) with a special focus to Hindi (Burton-Page, 1957; Hook, 1974), Urdu (Butt, 1995), Bangla (Sarkar, 1975; Paul, 2003, 2004, 2010), Kashmiri (Kaul, 1985) and Oriya (Mohanty, 1992, 2010).

Paul (2004) has attempted to work on a *constraint-based* and *semantically-grounded* account of Bangla CV within the HPSG (Head-Driven Phrase Structure Grammar) framework (Paul, 2010). An automatic extraction of Hindi CV was presented in (Chakrabarty et al., 2008). They analyses the Hindi complex predicate system and provides scope of linguist test for identification of Hindi CV. Chakrabarty and Paul, both have conceptualized vector and used an incomplete list of those vectors. An automatic extraction of Bangla complex predicates have been performed by (Das et.al, 2010). The system uses the vectors as proposed in the literature of (Paul, 2003). To the best of our knowledge, this is the only attempt made to extract Bangla CV from the text corpuses.

4 Compound Verb Identification Grammar and Formal Rules

Apart from all and keeping (18) in our mind we can certify some more rules for the identification of CV in Bangla. This section is basically an overall revisit of our entire dialogues. To identify a CV we can follow the following condition:

(I) The common identification of a CV: Verb + Verb [V1 (+ /-e/) + V2 (-so many inflectional endings according to the tense, aspect, modality and so on)].

(II) Noun + Verb combination is not a Compound Verb, it may be considered as Composite Verb (For Example, হাসি পেল, রাগ করলো, ঘুম পেল.)

(III) V1+V2 = CV and v2 has no meaning. V2 is grammatically subservient, i.e., v2 serves or acts in a subordinate capacity and formally attached to the v1. On the other hand v1 is grammatically central. (Hook, 1974; Dasgupta, 1977)

(IV) As V2 plays a role of an essentially subordinate of V1, it cannot even take a modifier.

(V) V1, i.e., a pole must not immediately be followed by a V2, i.e. a vector. For example, কাজটা করে(v1) তুমি ঠিক ফেলবে(v2)। This implies possibilities of such following combinations too:
N+P+N+V = CV
N+P+V+N = CV

(VI) CV collapses if there is an adverb in between V1 and V2. For example, *বইটা পড়ে (v1) তাড়াতাড়ি (adv) ফেল (v2) ।

(VII) If there is a sequence like V+V+V, then first two verbs should be (normally) poles. <v1+v2+v3 = pole + pole + vector>.

(VIII) Direct question to a vector is not allowed. Consider an example,

অমল গল্পের বইটা পড়ে ফেলবে।
Amal story book-sing-the read (inf) drop-future
Amal will finish the story book.

One cannot ask question to the vector of the combination, 'পড়ে ফেলবে';

* অমল কি ফেলবে?
One must ask completely;
অমল কি পড়ে ফেলবে?

This proves CV (V1 + V2) is a single entity and as V2 is subservient, it cannot take a question directly.

(IX) Bangla CV does not allow double negation like English

5 Experimentation and Results

Based on the CV extraction technique discussed in the earlier section, we try to identify Bangla CVs from the Rabindra-Rachanabali [1] and Bankim Rachanabali [2] corpus. The Rabindra-Rachanabali corpus has a collection of 176000 Bangla sentences and the Bankim-Rachanabali corpus has a collection of 34000 sentences. These sentences were POS (part of Speech) tagged using the Bangla POS tagger[3]. From the POS tagged corpus, we have identified all possible sentences containing multiple verbs. We consider the verb + verb combinations within these sentences, as potential CVs. Altogether 26500 sentences containing the potential CVs are identified from the corpus (see Table 1).

Table 1: Corpus Statistics

Total No. of Sentence in Corpus	2,10,000
Total Number of V+V sequence	26500
Total No. of CV Annotated Sentence	6500
Total No. of CVs (identified manually)	895

Table 2: Results of the Compound Verb Extraction Module

	Before POS Modification	After POS Modification
No. of V+V correctly identified as CV by the system (True Positive)	313	427
No. of V+V correctly identified as Not-CV by the system (True Negative)	197	197
No. of V+V falsely identified as CV by the system (False Positive)	201	160
No. of V+V falsely identified as non-CV by the system (False Negative)	184	111
Precision (%)	61	72
Recall (%)	63	79
F-Measure (%)	62	75
Accuracy (%)	57	70

Out of these 26500 Bangla sentences, we have manually annotated 6500 sentences using a Linguist. We then applied the CV extraction rules, mentioned in the previous section. The extracted CVs are then compared with the manually evaluated gold standard data. The summary of the results obtained are depicted in table 2.

---

1 www.rabindra-rachanabali.nltr.org

2 www.bankim-rachanabali.nltr.org

3 www.nltr.org/downloades/

The result from table 2 implies that, we have a precision of around 61% and a recall value of 63%. The F-measure is coming out to be 62% whereas the overall accuracy of the system comes to be 57%.

The results of table 2 imply that a lot of anomalous verb sequences have been incorrectly identified as CV by the present system. A close observation over the result reveals some interesting findings that may play some crucial role during the extraction of Bangla CV. Our result shows that, whenever a pole is attached with a suffix "-te" the V1+V2 sequence does not belongs to the CV group irrespective of whether V2 belongs to the pre-defined list of vectors. Thus, we have incorporated an additional rule on the system that checks whether a pole verb contains a suffix "-te" along with its vector counterpart. We further observe that, the loss in precision was also caused due to high error in POS tagging. We identified around 30% of errors are generated due to incorrect POS tags. Thus, when measures were taken to eliminate these errors we reached an accuracy of around 70%.

Further, we perform the analysis for each of the individual vector verbs. The result shows that not all vector verbs are equally responsible to form compound verbs. It has been observed that in most of the cases, vector verbs like, তোলা, বেড়ানো, and মরা have a higher tendency of forming compound verbs as compared to vectors like, আসা, থাকা and দেখা. Figure 1 presents the graph that shows the percentage of cases for which different vectors form the compound verb structure.

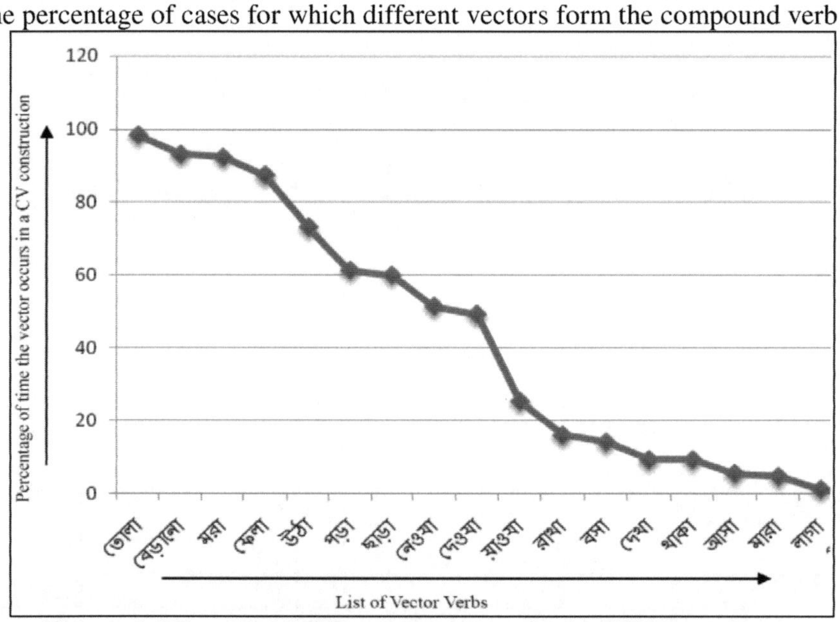

Figure 1: The role of different vector verbs in CV formation

We further classify the vector verbs according to their frequencies. Depending on the frequency, we categorize the list of vectors into the following four different classes:

- Class-I: Frequently occurring vectors with high precision like, ফেলা and উঠা.
- Class-II: Less frequent vectors with high precision like, তোলা and বেড়ানো.
- Class-III: Frequently occurring vectors with low precision like, যাওয়া and আসা
- Class-IV: Less frequent vectors with low precision like, আনা and রাখা.

We have considered the low frequency vectors to be those for which the frequency is below the average frequency. We observe that, the vectors belonging to class-III are very frequent but have a very low probability of being a CV. Similar effects have been found for vectors belonging to class-IV. We also observed that low frequency vectors have a higher tendency to construct the CV where as high frequency words do not tend to construct CVs.

Conclusion

In the present work we try to automatically extract the Bangla Compound verbs from the literary documents belonging to Rabindra Rachanabali and Bankim Rachanabali. These corpuses have been chosen because of the varied type of text contents. In order to extract the CV we have used the vector verb list as provided by (Paul, 2003). We observe that vector verbs cannot identify the occurrence of compound verbs alone. There are several other features responsible for a verb + verb combination to be a CV. We also saw that, frequencies as well as the type of a vector are very much responsible in order to classify a V+V combination as CV.

In the next stage of our work, we will try to enhance the existing model of CV identification and try to apply the information content measures to identify the degree of compositionality of a given CV.

Acknowledgement

We thank Prof. Probal Dasgupta for providing us useful linguistic insight about the problem and Society for Natural Language Technology Research Kolkata for providing us with the Bangla corpus and partially sponsoring us to conduct the research work.

References

Abbi, Anvita. 1991. Semantics of Explicator Compound Verbs. *In South Asian Languages, Language Sciences*, 13(2): 161-180.

Alsina, Alex. 1996. Complex Predicates: Structure and Theory. *Center for the Study of Language and Information Publications*, Stanford, CA.

Butt, Miriam. 1995. The Structure of Complex Predicates in Urdu. Doctoral Dissertation, Stanford University.

Burton-Page, John. 1957. Compound and conjunct verbs in Hindi. *Bulletin of the School of Oriental and African Studies,* 19: 469-78.

Chakrabarti, Debasri, Mandalia Hemang, Priya Ritwik, Sarma Vaijayanthi, Bhattacharyya Pushpak. 2008. Hindi Compound Verbs and their Automatic Extraction. *International Conference on Computational Linguistics –2008*, pp. 27-30.

Das, D., Pal, S., Mondal, T., Chakraborty, T., Bandyopadhyay, S., "Automatic Extraction of Complex Predicates in Bengali", Proceedings of the Multiword Expressions: From Theory to Applications (MWE 2010), pages 37–45, Beijing, August 2010

Dasgupta, Probal. 1977. The internal grammar of Bangla compound verbs. Indian Linguistics 38:2.68-85.

Hook, Peter. 1974. The Compound Verbs in Hindi. *The Michigan Series in South and South-east Asian Language and Linguistics*. The University of Michigan.

Kaul, Vijay Kumar. 1985. The Compound Verb in Kashmiri. Unpublished Ph.D. dissertation. Kurukshetra University.

Mohanty, Panchanan. 2010. WordNets for Indian Languages: Some Issues. *Global WordNet Conference-2010*, pp. 57-64.

Mohanty, Gopabandhu. 1992. The Compound Verbs in Oriya. Ph. D. dissertation, Deccan College Post-Graduate and Research Institute, Pune.

Paul, Soma. 2010. Representing Compound Verbs in Indo WordNet. *Golbal Wordnet Conference- 2010*, pp. 84-91.

Paul, Soma. 2004. An HPSG Account of Bangla Compound Verbs with LKB Implementation. Ph.D dissertation, University of Hyderabad, Hyderabad.

Paul, Soma. 2003. Composition of Compound Verbs in Bangla. *Multi-Verb constructions*. Trondheim Summer School.

Sarkar, Pabitra. 1975. Aspects of Compound Verbs in Bengali. Unpublished M.A. dissertation, Chicago University.

Influences of particles on Vietnamese tonal Co-articulation

Thị Lan NGUYỄN[1] *Đỗ Đạt TRẦN*[1]
(1) International Research MICA, 1 Dai Co Viet, Hanoi, VIETNAM
thi-lan.nguyen@mica.edu.vn, Do-Dat.Tran@mica.edu.vn

ABSTRACT

In continuous speech, the pitch contour exhibits variable patterns and it is strongly influenced by its tone context. Although several effective models have been proposed to improve the accuracy for tonal syllables, the quality of Vietnamese synthesis system is poor by lack of lexical parameters corresponding to each syllable in modelling of fundamental frequency. This problem will be clarified by our experiment in this study.

This paper presents our study on tonal co-articulation of particles which are frequently used in Vietnamese language. The obtained results show that tonal co-articulation phenomenon always takes place at the transition between two adjacent syllables, the progressive co-articulation is the basic tonal co-articulation and there is an influence of the function of particles on form of F0 contour of Vietnamese tones.

KEYWORDS : tonal co-articulation; Vietnamese tones; F0 generation ; lexical category; particles

1 Introduction

Vietnamese is a monosyllabic and tonal language. Each Vietnamese character corresponds to a syllable which is associated with a lexical tone. Syllables with different tone have different meanings, so the tone plays an important role in distinguishing lexical meaning for a family of syllables. As is well known, for a tonal language, like Vietnamese, Chinese (Mandarin or Cantonese) or Thai, fundamental frequency (F0) contours of utterances are always composed of tonal local features (tones and the co-articulation between adjacent tones) and the sentential intonation (corresponding to higher-level structures). This makes F0 variations of sentence more complicated than non-tonal languages such as English or French.

Recently, Vietnamese has been the subject of much linguistic research. Most of studies have concentrated on analyzing the characteristics of isolated word [2][3] or some on tonal features [1][4]. Researches on tonal co-articulation in Vietnamese were also presented in studies [1][4][5].

Tonal co-articulation phenomena are specific co-articulation phenomena for languages using tones. In Thai language [6], there are two types of tonal co-articulation: anticipatory and carryover co-articulation. The F0 contour shape of a syllable that is influenced by the succeeding syllable is called "anticipatory co-articulation". The carryover co-articulation occurs when the preceding syllable influences the succeeding syllable. Gandour [6] reported that the co-articulation effect of Thai tones is asymmetric. Thai tones were more influenced by carryover than by anticipatory co-articulation. The tonal co-articulation in Mandarin is also classified into both types: anticipatory and carryover co-articulation [7][8]. In Shen's study [7], nonsense strings of syllables were used as reading list, whereas Shir and Sproat [8] used real words and phrases. In Shir's study speakers were instructed to produce the utterances as naturally as possible. In order to study phenomena involved in co-articulation of tones in Mandarin, Xu Y [9] provided 4 theoretically possible transitional patterns between two tones. Similar to the results of [8], two in four possible tonal transitions (Exclusive Assimilation and Exclusive Carryover) were found for Mandarin language.

In Vietnamese, the studies [1][4] and [5] show that the progressive tonal co-articulation is stronger than the regressive tonal co-articulation. In these studies, authors focused on analysis of tonal co-articulation between two adjacent syllables, they have not take into account information about lexical category (or part of speech) of considered words.

In order to study the influence of lexical category in phenomena of tonal co-articulation, this paper presents our study on tonal co-articulation of particles (such as 'ạ', 'dạ', 'chứ', 'đi' ...) which are frequently used in Vietnamese language. The paper is organized as follows. Section II introduces the speech corpus which is used in the analysis process. Section III gives the analysis results on the tonal co-articulation phenomenona which occur at the considered particles. Section IV gives some conclusions and perspectives.

2 Bi-tone speech corpus

A speech corpus of bi-tone pairs of two adjacent syllables was prepared in our experiment. In addition, each sentence in the text corpus is constructed of an affirmative sentence and a particle at the last position of the sentence, for instance: "*Lâu lâu mới gặp lại, chị vào nhà tôi chơi / nhé!*"(We haven't met each other for a long time, let's come to my house). In the sentence the word "*nhé*" is a particle and "*Lâu lâu mới gặp lại, chị vào nhà tôi chơi*" is an affirmative sentence. The bi-tone pairs in these sentences are the last two syllables. For example, in the sentence *"Trước mẹ con vẫn gắp cho con kia!"* (Figure 1) the last two syllables *"con kia"* are analyzed. The corpus of these bi-tone pairs help to clarify the effects which the tonal context or the lexical context causes.

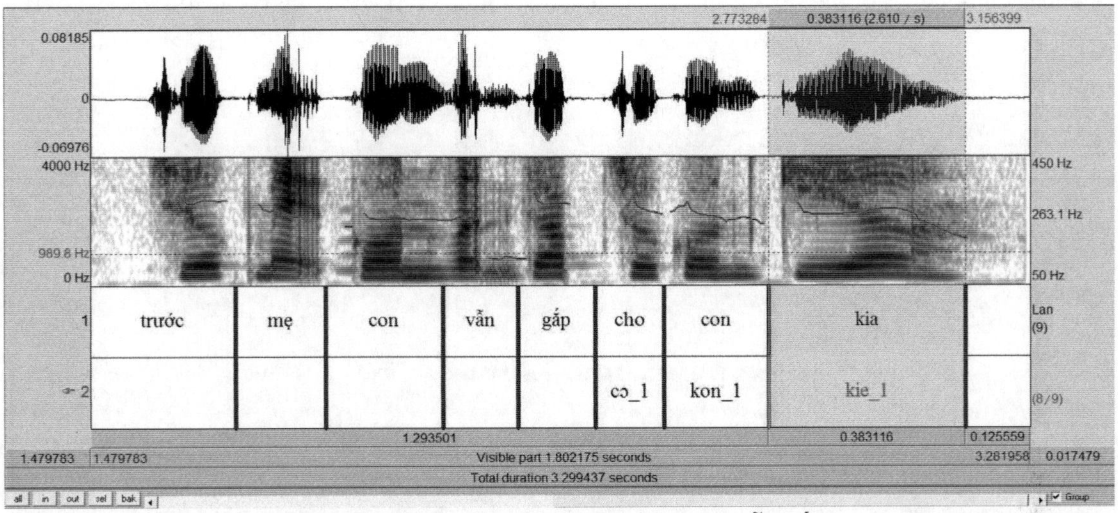

Figure 1: F0 contour of the sentence *"Trước mẹ con vẫn gắp cho con kia!"*

Therefore, a text corpus including 144 sentences in dialogs which were extracted from 6 Vietnamese famous short stories *"Bóng mây chiều", "Dế mèn", "Tuyển tập truyện ngắn Hồ Dzếnh", "Kính vạn hoa", "Tuyển tập truyện ngắn Thạch Lam" và "Tuổi 20 yêu dấu"* was collected.

These 144 sentences are divided into 6 groups as follows:

- *Group 1*: 24 sentences contain particles carrying the level tone (Tone 1).
- *Group 2*: 24 sentences contain particles carrying the falling tone (Tone 2).
- *Group 3*: 24 sentences contain particles carrying the broken tone (Tone 3).
- *Group 4*: 24 sentences contain particles carrying curve tone (Tone 4).
- *Group 5*: 24 sentences contain particles carrying the rising tone (Tone 5).
- *Group 6*: 24 sentences contain particles carrying the drop tone (Tone 6).

Each group is divided into 6 subgroups based on the tone (6 tones) which is carried by the preceding syllable of the particle. Each subgroup contains 4 sentences. For example:

Group 1 is composed of 6 subgroups: S1-1, S1-2, S1-3, S1-4, S1-5 and S1-6. In the subgroup S1-1, the sentences have particles carrying level tone and the preceding syllable also carrying level tone.

- *"Trước mẹ con vẫn gắp cho* ***con / kia****!"(In meal my mother used to pick food for me)*
- *"Có một việc quan trọng phải nhờ cậu mới* ***xong / đây****!"(There is an important work that we must need your help)*

The text corpus is then used to build a speech corpus. The recording progress was taken place in a quite environment at a quiet studio. A male and female who have Hanoi voice were asked to read each sentence two times at a normal speaking rate. The speech corpus was then labeled manually using the PRAAT program.

3 Analysis

We carry out an analysis of the variation of fundamental frequency for every subgroup of sentences. F0 values of the sentences are extracted automatically by using Praat software.

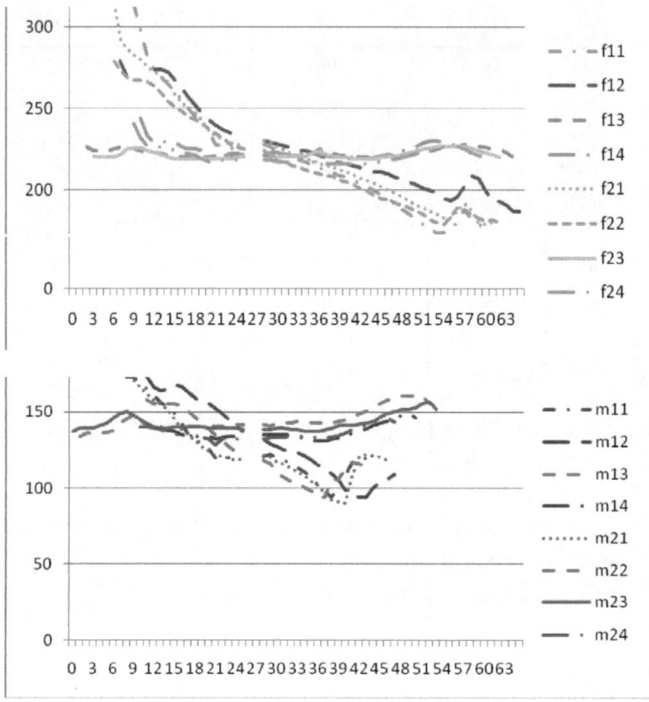

Figure 2: F0 contours in subgroup 2-2

Figure 2 presents evolution of F0 contours in subgroup S2-2 (which has a pair of tones: falling – falling). In the figure *m* and *f* refer consequently "male" and "female"; m*ij* denotes the i*th* recorded sample of the j*th* sentence of the male speaker in the group; and f*ij* denotes the i*th* recorded sample of the j*th* sentence of the female speaker.

We can see in Figure 2, the F0 contours of the preceding falling tones fall slowly and converge at the ending position. However, values of F0 at the beginning positions of these syllables are quite different. By carrying a larger analysis, we found that the difference is caused by an effect of tonal co-articulation. The tones of the syllables that stand just before the analyzed syllables are different. For example, concerning f11 and f14 sentences, the three last syllables of these sentences are "có tiền à" (*/kɔ_5 tien_2 a_2/*) and "nhiều tiền mà" (*/ɲiew_2 tien_2 ma_2/*) consequently. It is easy to see that the last two syllables have the same pair of tones (falling – falling), but the tone of the 1st syllable in case of f14 is the falling tone (Tone 2), while the tone of the 1st syllable in case of f11 is the rising tone (Tone 5). Thus, F0 values of the beginning positions in sentence f11 are higher than that of sentence f14.

Concerning the falling tone carried by the particle words, in Figure 2 we found that, the shape of F0 contours of this tone has a little difference in comparison to that in the static mode. The F0 contours of these syllables fall slowly at the start positions and then rise to the ending positions. This can be explained as follows: a particle is also the last syllable of an imperative or a question, so its F0 contour usually rises up, like the results of studies [10][11].

To observe the tonal co-articulation more clearly, similar to the research of Brunelle [1], we carried out comparing an effect of the preceding syllable's tone on the succeeding syllable's tone. In order to facilitate the analysis, the values of the extracted F0 are normalized into a sequence of six points. Each syllable is divided into 6 parts and the average value of F0 is calculated for each part. Therefore, for a syllable pair, points from 0 to 5 are belong to the first syllable (the last syllable of the affirmative sentence), and points from 6 to 11 are belong to the second syllable (a particle).

4 The results

The normalized F0 contours of the subgroups of sentences are presented in figures 3, 4, 5, 6, 7, 8. In these figures:

- t1 presents the average normalized F0 contour of the set of sentences that have the preceding syllable (the syllable stands before the particle) porting the level tone (Tone 1).
- Similar to t1, t2 – t6 present the average normalized F0 contours of sets of sentences that have the preceding syllable carrying tones 2, 3, 4, 5 and 6 consequently.

From these figures, the first result can be easily seen that: tonal co-articulation phenomenon always happens at the transition between two adjacent syllables, and the progressive co-articulation seems the basic tonal co-articulation, like the results presented in [1][4][5].

We pay more attention to representations of Tone 1 and Tone 2 which are presented in the figures 3 and 4.

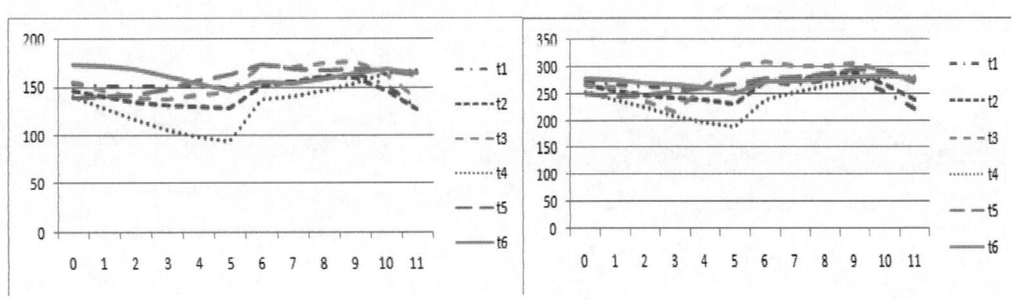

Figure 3: F0 contours of tone pairs in Group 1 (particle carries level tone) with male (left) and female (right) speakers

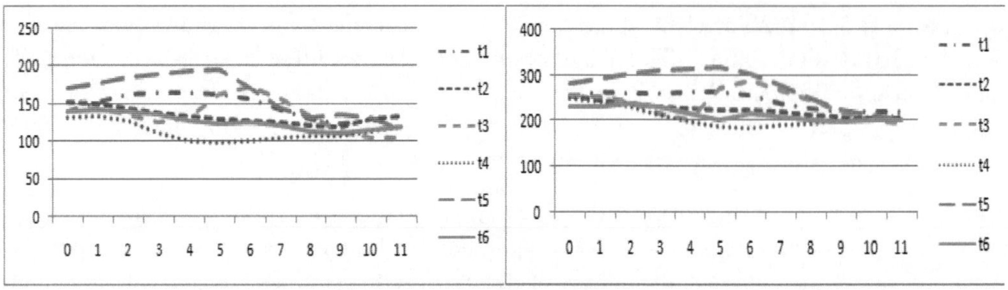

Figure 4: F0 contours of tone pairs in Group 2 (particle carries falling tone) with male (left) and female (right) speakers

In Figure 3, after ending the preceding syllable, F0 contours of Tone 1 (level tone) tend to rise to the end of succeeding syllables and it only fall lightly at the last point. Whereas, in studies [1][11], the F0 contour of Tone 1 is quite stable and falls lightly down to the end of the succeeding syllable (same as Tone 1 in isolated syllable).

Like the particles carrying Tone 1, we can see clearly the same result in case of the particles porting Tone 2 (falling tone). In Figure 4, F0 contour of this tone can start at either low or high register. At the last half of syllable F0 contour either is stable or rises slightly. Whereas, in static mode, Tone 2 starts lower than the level tone then falls slowly and its slope is never goes up. In the studies of [1][11], in dynamic mode (continuous speech), F0 contours of Tone 2 falls slowly. This results shows that there is an affect of the function of particles on evolution of F0. The result seems logic, because the particles in our corpus stand at the last position of sentence. The function of these words is to make the sentence become either an interrogative or an imperative sentence. According to studies [10][11], in Vietnamese interrogative and imperative sentences, the contour of the last syllable or of its second half tends to increase.

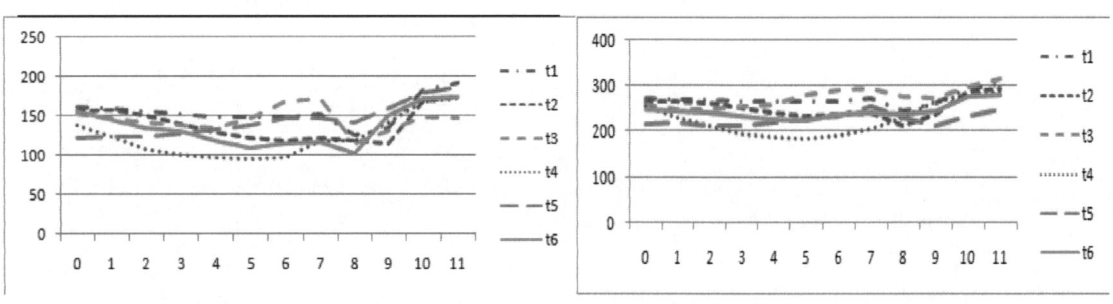

Figure 5: F0 contours of tone pairs in Group 3 (particle carries broken tone) with male (left) and female (right) speakers

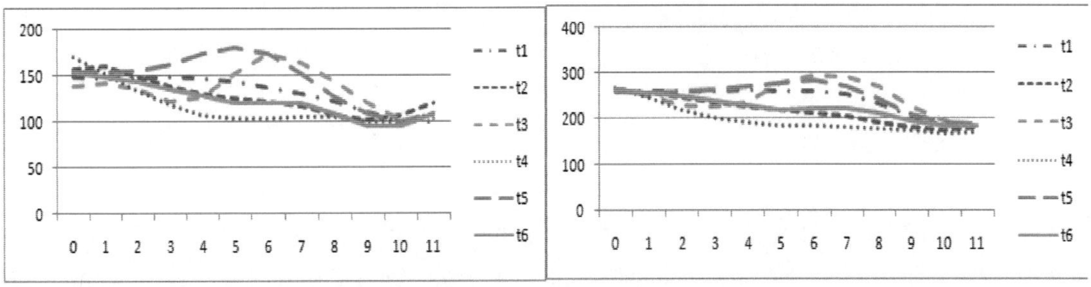

Figure 6: F0 contours of tone pairs in Group 4 (particle carries curve tone) with male (left) and female (right) speakers

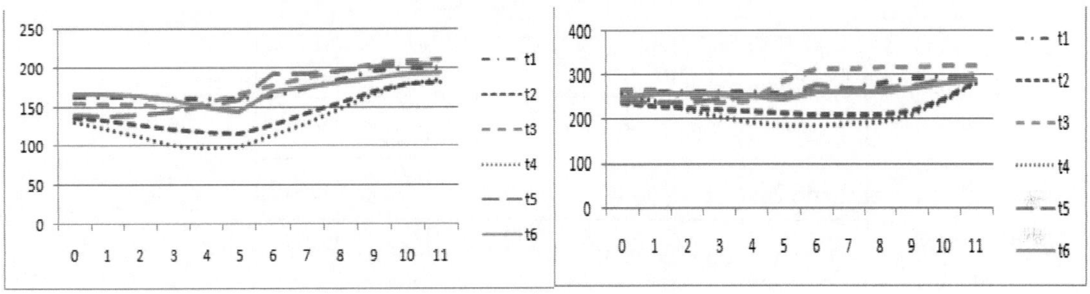

Figure 7: F0 contours of tone pairs in Group 5 (particle carries rising tone) with male (left) and female (right) speakers

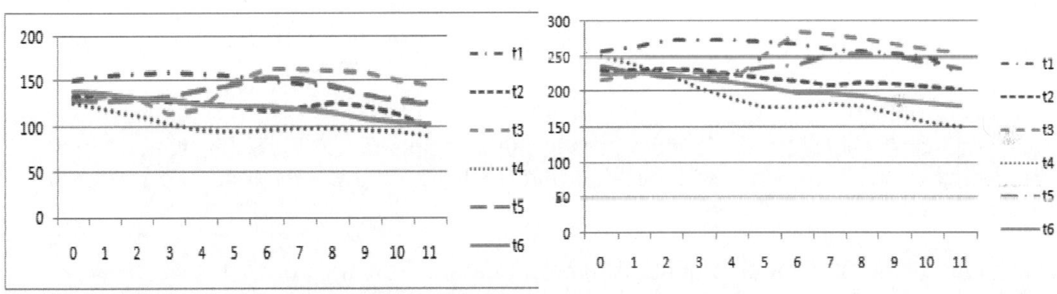

Figure 8: F0 contours of tone pairs in Group 6 (particle carries drop tone) with male (left) and female (right) speakers

In remaining tones, the phenomenon in which F0 contour of the last half of particle rises up also takes place. However, phenomenon is caused not only by the function of particles but also by the evolution of F0 contour of the tone that syllables carry. These tones (Tone 3, Tone 4 and Tone 5) have the F0 contour rising at the last half of syllable.

The standard deviation of 6 tones at 6 points is presented in following tables:

Table 1: Standard deviation (%) of tones at 6 points (male)

Point	P1	P2	P3	P4	P5	P6
Tone 1	8.1	6.6	5.6	4.5	5.5	11.5

Point	P1	P2	P3	P4	P5	P6
Tone 2	18.0	12.9	8.1	7.6	7.8	8.5
Tone 3	18.0	14.9	9.6	10.4	6.2	7.8
Tone 4	19.1	15.4	12.1	7.6	3.7	5.2
Tone 5	18.0	14.1	10.5	7.7	6.0	5.3
Tone 6	17.7	17.3	16.2	16.2	15.3	17.2

Table 2 : Standard deviation (%) of tones at 6 points (female)

Point	P1	P2	P3	P4	P5	P6
Tone 1	7.6	5.3	4.3	3.85	5.26	8.73
Tone 2	17	13	9.1	4.66	3.22	4.09
Tone 3	12	11	8.2	8.04	7.03	7.12
Tone 4	16	16	14	9.12	5.08	2.56
Tone 5	17	16	16	14.6	10	4.55
Tone 6	17	16	16	16.5	17.1	16.7

We can see that the standard deviation values at initial points (P1, P2 and P3) which are close to the preceding syllable are almost higher than that's of the final points (P4, P5 and P6). This is entirely consistent with above results.

The variation of F0 of Tone 6 is quite different in comparison with other tones. Because of the glottalization phenomenon at ending position, F0 contour at the second last syllable of syllables porting this tone changes in large range and this can make a non precise measurement of F0 by Praat. Therefore, value of standard deviations is quite high.

Conclusion and perspectives

The paper presents our research on phenomena of tonal co-articulation on particles in Vietnamese. The obtained results show that tonal co-articulation phenomena always take place at the transition between two adjacent syllables, and the progressive co-articulation is the basic tonal co-articulation. And *there is an influence of the function of particles on form of F0 contour of Vietnamese tones.* Therefore, it has to take into account this information when doing an analysis variation of fundamental frequency, especially on modeling Vietnamese intonation for Vietnamese text to speech synthesis.

In our study, the corpus is still limited. There are only two speakers and the particles always stand at the last position of sentences. These limitations will be studied more deeply in next researches with more speakers and other specific words at different positions.

Acknowledgments

The research leading in the paper was supported by the Vietnamese National Key Project KC03.07/11-15. We would like to thank the project and people involved in this project

References

[1] Brunelle M. "Co-articulation effects in Northern Vietnamese tones", Proc. ICPhS, Barcelona, pp. 2673 – 2676, 2003.

[2] Nguyen, Q.C, "Reconnaissance de la parole en langue Vietnamienne", PhD. thesis INP-Grenoble, France, June 2002.

[3] Tran D.D, Castelli E., Serignat JF., Le X.H., Trinh V.L., "Influence of F0 on Vietnamese syllable perception", Proc. of Interspeech2005, Lisbon, pp. 1697-1700, 2005.

[4] Han M.S. and Kim K., "Phonetic variation of Vietnamese tones in disyllabic utterances", Journal of Phonetics April 1974, pp.223-232, 1974.

[5] Tran D.D, Castelli E., "Generation of F0 contours for Vietnamese speech synthesis", Third International Conference on Communications and Electronics (ICCE), Nha Trang, 2010.

[6] Gandour, J., Potisuk, S., & Dechangkit, S. (1994). "Tone co-articulation in Thai,Journal of Phonetics", 22, 477-492.

[7] Shen, X. S. (1990). "Tonal co-articulation in Mandarin. Journal of Phonetics", 18,281-295.

[8] Shih, C., & Sproat, R (1992). "Variations of the Mandarin rising tone". In Proceedings of the IRCS Workshop on Prosody in Natural Speech No. 92-37, (pp. 193-200). Philadelphia: The Institute for Research in Cognitive Science, University of Pennsylvania.

[9] Xu Y., "Contextual tonal Variations in Mandarin", Journal of Phonetics 25, 61-83, 1997.

[10] Nguyen, T. T. H. 2004, Contribution à l'étude de la prosodie du vietnamien. Variations de l'intonation dans les modalités: assertive, interrogative et impérative, PhD. thèses, Doctorat de Linguistique Théorique, Formelle et Automatique, Paris.

[11] Vu M.Q., Tran D. D., Castelli E. 2006, Prosody of Interrogative and Affirmative Sentences in Vietnamese Language: Analysis and Perceptive Results, The Ninth International Conference on Spoken Language Processing – INTERSPEECH 2006 - ICSLP, Pittsburgh, Pennsylvania, USA, September 2006.

[12] Tran D.D. Castelli E., Serignat J.F., Trinh V.L. & Le X.H., "Linear F0 Contour Model for Vietnamese Tones and Vietnamese Syllable Synthesis with TD-PSOLA", Proc. TAL2006, La Rochelle, April 2006.

Toward an amazigh language processing

Fatima Zahra NEJME[1] *Siham BOULAKNADEL*[2] *Driss ABOUTAJDINE*[1]
(1) GSCM-LRIT, Université Mohamed V, BP 1014 Agdal-Rabat, Maroc
(2) IRCAM, Avenue Allal El Fassi, Madinat Al Irfane, Rabat-Instituts, Maroc
Fatimazahra.nejme@gmail.com, Boulaknadel@ircam.ma,
aboutaj@fsr.ac.ma

ABSTRACT

Since antiquity, the Amazigh heritage is expanding from generation to generation. In the aim of safeguarding it from being threatened of disappearance, it seems opportune to equip this language of necessary means to confront the stakes of access to the domain of New Information and Communication Technologies (ICT). In this context, and in the perspective to build tools and linguistic resources for the automatic processing of Amazigh language, we develop a lexicon and morphological rules using finite state technology within the linguistic developmental environment Nooj to parse amazigh texts.

Vers un traitement automatique de la langue Amazighe

Depuis l'antiquité, le patrimoine Amazighe est en expansion de génération en génération. Dans l'objectif de sauvegarder, exploiter ce patrimoine et éviter qu'il soit menacé de disparition, il semble opportun d'équiper cette langue de moyens nécessaires pour affronter les enjeux d'accès au domaine des nouvelles technologies de l'information et de la communication (NTIC) qui s'avère primordial pour promouvoir et informatiser cette langue. Dans ce contexte, et dans les perspectives de développer des outils et des ressources linguistiques pour le traitement automatique de cette langue, nous avons entrepris d'utiliser la plateforme d'ingénierie linguistique NooJ afin de créer un module pour la langue Amazighe standard (Ameur et al., 2004a). Notre premier objectif est l'analyse des textes Amazighe. A cet effet, nous commençons par la formalisation du vocabulaire Amazighe (Nom, Verbe et Particules). Dans cet article nous nous intéresserons à la formalisation de deux catégories, nom et de particules, permettant de générer à partir d'une entrée lexicale son genre (masculin, féminin), son nombre (singulier, pluriel) et son état (libre, annexion). Enfin, nous développons un dictionnaire électronique afin de l'utiliser, d'une part, pour tester nos règles de flexions et d'autre part pour l'analyse lexicale des textes Amazighe.

KEYWORDS: Amazigh language, NooJ, Natural language processing, Less-resourced language, lexical analysis, inflectional morphology, flexional grammar, dictionary.

KEYWORDS IN L_2 : La langue Amazighe, NooJ, Traitement automatique des langues naturelles, langue peu dotée, analyse lexicale, morphologie flexionnelle, grammaire flexionnelle, dictionnaire.

Introduction

The Amazigh language in Morocco is considered as a prominent constituent of the Moroccan culture and this by its richness and originality. However it has been long discarded otherwise neglected as a source of enrichment cultural. Nevertheless, due to the creation of the Royal Institute of Amazigh Culture (IRCAM)[1], this language has been introduced in the public domain including administration, media also in the educational system in collaboration with ministries. It has enjoyed its proper coding in the Unicode Standard (Andries, 2008; Zenkouar, 2008), an official spelling (Ameur et al., 2006a), appropriate standards for keyboard realization and linguistic structures that are being developed with a phased approach (Ameur et al., 2006b; Boukhris et al., 2008). This process was initiated by the standardization, vocabularies construction (Kamel, 2006; Ameur et al., 2009a; Ameur et al., 2006a; Ameur et al., 2009b), Alphabetical Arrangement (Outahajala, 2007), spelling standardization (Ameur et al., 2006a) and development of rules grammar (Boukhris et al., 2008).

However, this not sufficient for a less-resourced language (Berment, 2004) as the Amazigh to join the well-resourced language in information and Communication Technologies, mainly due to the lack of already available language processing resources and tools. Therefore, a set of scientific and linguistic research are undertaken to remedy to the current situation. These researches are divided, on the one hand, on researches that are concentrated on optical character recognition (OCR) (Amrouch et al., 2010; Es Saady et al., 2010; Fakir et al., 2009), and in the other hand, on those that are focused on natural language processing (Iazzi and Outahajala, 2008; Ataa Allah and Jaa, 2009; Boulaknadel, 2009; Ataa Allah and Boulaknadel, 2010; Outahajala et al., 2010; Boulaknadel and Ataa Allah, 2011), which constitute the priority components of researches.

In this context, the present work deals with ongoing research efforts to build tools and linguistic resources for the Amazigh language. Our first main objective is to develop a morphological analyzer to parse amazigh texts. For this purpose, we begin by building a morphological analyzer for Amazigh nouns, implemented using the Finite State Technology within the linguistic developmental environment Nooj.

This paper is structured around five main sections: the first present a description of the Amazigh language particularities. The second expose the automatic Amazigh language processing, which includes an overview of NooJ environment, and the formalization of a set of rules. While the last section is dedicated to the conclusion and perspectives.

Amazigh language particularities

The Amazigh language also known as Berber or Tamazight (ⵜⴰⵎⴰⵣⵉⵖⵜ [tamazight]), is belonged to the African branch of the Afro-Asiatic language family, also referred to as Hamito-Semitic in the literature (Greenberg, 1966; Ouakrim, 1995). It is currently presented in a dozen countries ranging from Morocco, with 50% of the overall population[2] (Boukous, 1995), to Egypt, passing through Algeria with 25%, the Tunisia, Mauritania, Libya, Niger and the Mali (Chaker, 2003).

[1] Institution responsible for the preservation of heritage and the promotion of the Moroccan Amazigh culture and its development (see http://www.ircam.ma/).

[2] It present the Amazigh population largest in number.

In Morocco, we distinguish between three major Amazigh dialects. Tarifit is spoken in northern Morocco, Tamazight in the Middle Atlas and south-eastern Morocco, and Tashelhit in south-western Morocco and the High Atlas.

Today, the current situation of the Amazigh language is at a pivotal point. It holds co-official status in Morocco. Its morphology as lexical standardization process is still underway. At present, it represents the model taught in must schools and used on media and official papers published in Morocco.

Amazigh morphology

The Amazigh language presents a rich and complex morphology whose words can be classified into three morphosyntactic categories which we cite: the noun, the verb and particles (Boukhris et al., 2008; Ameur et al., 2004b). Practically, nouns and verbs are the base of the Amazigh morphology and the more important categories to focus on, as others can be derived from them. In this paper, we are interested in noun morphology.

1. Noun characteristics

The noun in the Amazigh language is always composed of one word between two spaces and formed from a root and a pattern. It is characterized by gender (masculine or feminine), number (singular or plural), and state (free or construct) (Boukhris et al., 2008).

Gender: the Amazigh noun is characterized by one of grammatical gender: masculine or feminine.

- The masculine noun: begins with one of the initial vowels: ⴰ [a], ⵉ [i] or ⵓ [u]. However, there are some exceptions as: ⵉⵎⵎⴰ [imma] "(my) mother".
- The feminine noun: is marked with the circumfix ⵜ .... ⵜ [t....t]. However, there are some exceptions such as nouns which have only the initial ⵜ [t] or the final ⵜ [t] of morpheme of the feminine: ⵜⴰⴷⵍⴰ [tadla] "the sheaf", ⵕⵕⵎⵓⵢⵜ [ṛṛmuyt] "the fatigue".

Number: the noun, masculine or feminine, has a singular and plural. This latter has four forms: the external plural, broken plural, mixed plural and plural in ⵉⴷ [id].

- The external plural: is formed by an alternation of the first vowel ⴰ /ⵉ [a/i] accompanied by a suffixation of ⵏ [n] or one of its variants.
- The broken plural: involves a change in the vowels of the noun.
- The mixed plural: is formed by vowels' change accompanied, sometimes by the use of the suffixation by ⵏ [n].
- The plural in ⵉⴷ [id]: this kind of plural is obtained by ⵉⴷ [id] prefixing. It is applied to a set of nouns including: nouns with an initial consonant, proper nouns, parent nouns, compound nouns, numerals, as well as borrowed nouns.

State: we distinguish between two states: the free state and the construct one.

- The free state: is unmarked. The noun is in free state if it is: a single word isolated from any syntactic context, a direct object, or a complement of the predictive particle ⴷ [d].

- The construct state: involves a variation of the initial vowel. In case of masculine nouns, it takes one of the following forms: initial vowel alternation ⴰ [a] /ⵓ [u] or adding of ⵡ [w]; adding of ⵢ [y] to the nouns of vowel ⵉ [i]. For the feminine nouns, it consists to drop the initial vowel or maintaining of this vowel.

Automatic Amazigh language processing: development and evaluation

Nooj platform

NooJ[3], released in 2002 by Max Silberztein (Silberztein, 2007), is a linguistic development platform that provides a set of tools and methodologies for formalizing and developing a set of Natural Language Processing (NLP) applications. It presents a package of finite state tools that integrates a broad spectrum of computational technology from finite state automata to augmented/recursive transition networks. Thus, it presents a complete platform for formalizing various types of textual phenomena (orthography, lexical and productive morphology, local, structural and transformational syntax). For each of these formalization levels, NooJ propose a methodology, one or more formalisms, tools, software development and a corresponding parser that can be used to test each piece of the linguistic formalization over large corpora.

Given these advantages, we have undertaken to adopt NooJ for formalization, description and analysis of Amazigh language for building a module for that language. We begin our work by the formalization of the Amazigh language vocabulary. This formalization is described and stored into inflectional grammars, and can recognize all the corresponding inflected forms. To test these grammars, we built an electronic dictionary in which the lexical entries are attached to a set of linguistic information automatically generate using inflectional grammars which will be used for lexical analysis of texts.

Development of the lexicon

As part of developing a NooJ module for the Amazigh language, we elaborate our dictionary for Amazigh nouns based on a set of lexicons: Taifi dictionary (Taifi, 1988), amazigh vocabulary (Ameur et al., 2006b), and vocabulary of media (Ameur et al., 2009a).Our dictionary contains, currently, 5210 lexical entries which consist of: 4542 simple nouns, 424 proper nouns, 200 Non-inflected nouns and 44 numerals which are given with their plural form, feminine correspondent and annexation state. Our inflected dictionary, calculated after the compilation of the dictionary, encounters 19,597 entries. Thus, we get from each lexical entry all forms related to it.

Morphological rules implementation

This study presents the formalization of the noun category in the NooJ platform. For this, a set of rules has been defined allowing to generate from a each entry, its inflectional information: gender, number and state.

The formalization is based on the use of certain generic commands predefined such as:

- <LW> move at the beginning of Lemma,
- <RW> move at the end of Lemma,
- <S> delete current character,

[3] See http://www.nooj4nlp.net/ for information of NooJ

- <B> delete last character,
- <L> go left,
- <R> go right,

- Gender

To formalize the gender we built this rule that generates from a masculine entry its feminine correspondent. The rule is to add the discontinuous morpheme ⵜ [t] at the beginning and at the end of the noun.

The rules in Nooj	Explanation	Examples
<LW>ⵜ <RW>ⵜ /f+s	This rule adds "ⵜ " at the beginning and at the end.	ⵉ ⵙⵍ ⵉ [isli] “married” -> ⵜ ⵉ ⵙⵍ ⵉ ⵜ [tislit] “married”.

TABLE 1 – Example of a gender rule.

- Number

For the amazigh plural, we have many plural forms which are generally unpredictable due to Amazigh complex morphology. To formalize these plural types, we have have relied on the works of Boukhris (Boukhris et al., 2008) and those of Oulhaj (Oulhaj, 2000). We searched formal rules to unify the calculation of plural forms. According to these works and to an heuristic study of the nouns in the Taifi dictionary and those of amazigh language vocabulary, we have raised, at this moment, 303 classes which 97 classes is for the external plural, 99 for the broken plural, 104 for the mixed plural and 3 classes for the plural in ⵉ ⴷ [id]. Each word could be associated with, at least, one flexional class. Thereafter, we provided some examples of rules for each of plural types.

- The external plural

The rules in Nooj	Explanation	Examples
<LW>ⵉ <S><RW>ⵜ ⵏ /m+p	The initial vowel is transformed into ⵉ and the suffix ⵜ ⵏ [tn] is add at the end of the noun.	ⴰ ⵙ ⵉ ⵔ ⴰ [asira] “desk” -> ⵉ ⵙ ⵉ ⵔ ⴰ ⵜ ⵏ [isiratn]

TABLE 2 – Plural forms for the masculine nouns beginning and ends with ⴰ [a].

- The broken plural

The rules in Nooj	Explanation	Examples
<LW>ⵉ <S><RW><L>ⴰ /m+p	The rule changes the initial vowel into ⵉ [i] and include ⴰ [a] before the final consonant.	ⴰ ⵣⴳⵣⵍ [azgzl] abbreviation” -> ⵉ ⵣⴳⵣⴰ ⵍ [izgzal]

TABLE 3 – Plural forms for the nouns in VCn form.

- The mixed plural

The rules in Nooj	Explanation	Examples
<LW>ⵉ <S><RW>ⵏ <L2>ⵉ /m+p	The rule change the initial vowel into ⵉ [i], include the vowel ⵉ [i] before the last consonant and add a suffix ⵏ [n] at the end of the noun.	ⴰⵃⵓⴷⵔ [aḥudr] "fait de se pencher" -> ⵉⵃⵓⴷⵉⵔⵏ [iḥudirn]

TABLE 4 – Example of plural forms for the masculine nouns.

- The plural in in ⵉⴷ [id]

The rules in Nooj	Explanation	Examples
<LW>ⵉⴷ " "/m+p	The rule adds ⵉⴷ [id] before the noun.	ⴱⵓⵜⴳⵔⴰ [butgra] "tortoise" -> ⵉⴷ ⴱⵓⵜⴳⵔⴰ [id butgra]

TABLE 5 – Example of plural in ⵉⴷ [id].

- State

The rules in Nooj	Explanation	Examples
<LW><R><B>ⵓ /EA+m	The rule deletes the initial vowel and adds ⵓ [u] at the beginig of the noun.	ⴰⴼⵉⵔⴰⵙ [afiras] "pear" -> ⵓⴼⵉⵔⴰⵙ [ufiras]

- TABLE 6 – Example of plural in ⵉⴷ [id].

Evaluation

We conducted our experimentation on a sample of texts for story children. By applying our morphological grammars and our dictionary on text, we obtained the following results:

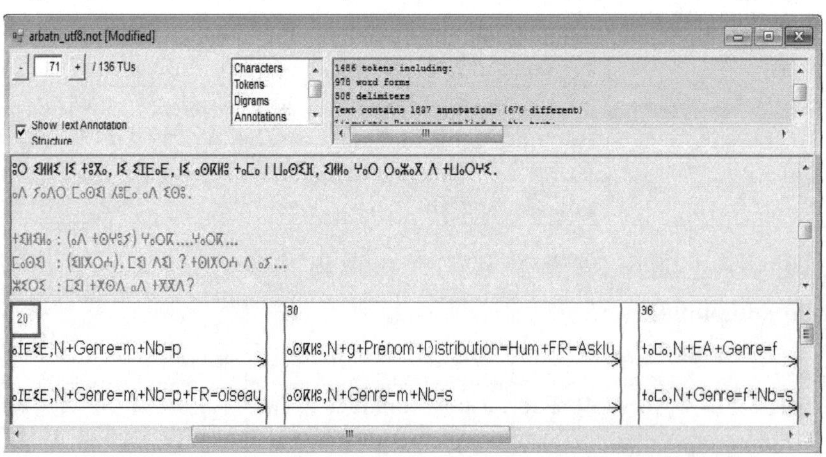

FIGURE 11 – Example of lexical analysis of Amazigh text

The text contains 778 nouns. After performing lexical analysis we identified a total of 686 occurrences of nouns recognized and well annotated (1837 annotations). However, a total of 92 occurrences expressing unknowns nouns. This experiment shows that only 8% of the unknowns nouns that do not belong to our dictionary.

Conclusion and future works

In this paper, we try to restore the Amazigh language and culture and give it more visibility nationally and internationally through developing tools and resources necessary for its computational processing. Our aim to work on a morphological analyzer for Amazigh came from this scarcity of computational framework, a morphological analyzer being one of the fundamental tools in many NLP tasks. However, we build a morphological analyzer for Amazigh nouns, implemented using the Finite State Technology within the linguistic developmental environment Nooj. Amazigh morphological analyzer for nouns is an underway work and further development must be performed to make it a complete one. However, our analyzer achieves over 92% correct results in the analysis of 778 nouns extracted from the corpus.

For future work we planed to:

- Enlarge the lexicon to include nouns from other dialects,
- Include other part of speech in the morphological analyzer,
- Construct a corpus of texts to evaluate the out-of-vocabulary rate of our dictionary.

References

Ameur M., Boumalk A. (DIR) (2004a). *Standardisation de l'amazighe*, Actes du séminaire organisé par le Centre de l'Aménagement Linguistique à Rabat, 8-9 décembre 2003, Publication de l'Institut Royal de la Culture Amazighe, Série : Colloques et séminaires.

Ameur M., Bouhjar A., Boukhris F., Boukouss A., Boumalk A., Elmedlaoui M., Iazzi E., Souifi H. (2004b). *Initiation à la langue amazighe*. Rabat, Maroc: IRCAM.

Ameur M., Bouhjar A., Boukhris F., Boukouss A., Boumalk A., Elmedlaoui M., Iazzi E. (2006a). *Graphie et orthographe de l'amazighe*. Rabat, Maroc : IRCAM.

Ameur M., Bouhjar A., Boukhris F., Elmedlaoui M., Iazzi E. (2006b). *Vocabulaire de la langue amazighe (Français-Amazighe)*. série : Lexiques N°1, IRCAM, Rabat, Maroc.

Ameur M., Bouhjar A., Boumalk A., El Azrak N., Laabdelaoui R. (2009a). *Vocabulaire des médias (Français-Amazighe-Anglais-Arabe)*. série : Lexiques N°3, IRCAM, Rabat, Maroc.

Ameur M., Bouhjar A., Boumalk A., El Azrak N., Laabdelaoui R. (2009b). *Vocabulaire grammatical*. série : Lexiques N°5, IRCAM, Rabat, Maroc.

Amrouch M., Rachidi A., El Yassa M., Mammass D. (2010). *Handwritten Amazigh Character Recognition Based On Hidden Markov Models*. International Journal on Graphics, Vision and Image Processing. 10(5), pp.11--18.

Andries P. (2008). Unicode 5.0 en pratique, *Codage des caractères et internationalisation des logiciels et des documents*. Dunod, France, Collection InfoPro.

Ataa Allah F., Jaa H,. (2009). *Etiquetage morphosyntaxique : Outil d'assistance dédié à la langue amazighe*. In Proceedings of the 1er Symposium international sur le traitement automatique de la culture amazighe, Agadir, Morocco, pp. 110- -119.

Ataa Allah F., Boulaknadel S. (2010). *Online Amazigh Concordancer*. In Proceedings of International Symposium on Image Video Communications and Mobile Networks. Rabat, Maroc.

Berment V. (2004). *Méthodes pour informatiser des langues et des groupes de langues peu dotées*, Thèse de doctorat de l'Université J. Fourier - Grenoble I, France.

Boukhris F., Boumalk A., Elmoujahid E., Souifi H. (2008). *La nouvelle grammaire de l'amazighe*. Rabat, Maroc: IRCAM.

Boukous A. (1995), Société, langues et cultures au Maroc: Enjeux symboliques, Casablanca, Najah El Jadida.

Boulaknadel S. (2009). *Amazigh ConCorde: an appropriate concordance for Amazigh.* In Proceedings of the 1er Symposium international sur le traitement automatique de la culture amazighe, Agadir, Morocco, pp. 176--182.

Boulaknadel S., Ataa Allah F. (2011). *Building a standard Amazigh corpus.* In Proceedings of the International Conference on Intelligent Human Computer Interaction. Prague, Tchec.

Chaker S. (2003), Le berbère, Actes des langues de France, 215-227.

Es Saady Y., Rachidi A., El Yassa M., Mammas D. (2010). *Printed Amazigh Character Recognition by a Syntactic Approach using Finite Automata.* International Journal on Graphics, Vision and Image Processing, 10(2), pp.1--8.

Fakir M., Bouikhalene B., Moro K. (2009). *Skeletonization methods evaluation for the recognition of printed tifinaghe characters.* In Proceedings of the 1er Symposium International sur le Traitement Automatique de la Culture Amazighe. Agadir, Morocco, pp. 33--47.

Greenberg J. (1966). *The Languages of Africa.* The Hague.

Iazzi E., Outahajala M. (2008). *Amazigh Data Base.* In Proceedings of HLT & NLP Workshop within the Arabic world: Arabic language and local languages processing status updates and prospects. Marrakech, Morocco, pp. 36--39.

Kamel S. (2006). *Lexique Amazighe de géologie*. Rabat, Maroc: IRCAM.

Max S. (2007). *An Alternative Approach to Tagging*. NLDB 2007: 1-11

Ouakrim O. (1995). *Fonética y fonología del Bereber*, Survey at the University of Autònoma de Barcelona.

Oulhaj L. (2000). *Grammaire du Tamazight.* Imprimerie Najah El Jadida.

Outahajala M. (2007). *Les normes de tri, Du clavier et Unicode*. La typographie entre les domaines de l'art et de l'informatique. Rabat, Morocco, pp. 223--237.

Outahajala M., Zekouar L., Rosso P., Martí M.A. (2010). *Tagging Amazigh with AnCoraPipe.* In Proceeding of the Workshop on Language Resources and Human Language Technology for Semitic Languages. Valletta, Malta, pp. 52--56.

Taifi M. (1988). *Le lexique berbère (parlers du Maroc central).*

Zenkouar L. (2008). *Normes des technologies de l'information pour l'ancrage de l'écriture amazighe.* Etudes et documents berbères. 27, pp. 159--172.

Bidirectional Bengali Script and Meetei Mayek Transliteration of Web Based Manipuri News Corpus

Thoudam Doren Singh
Centre for Development of Advanced Computing (CDAC)
Gulmohor Cross Road No 9, Juhu
Mumbai-400049, India
thoudam.doren@gmail.com

ABSTRACT

The transliteration has attracted interest of several sections of researchers. Several techniques of transliteration have been developed and used – both statistical based approaches and rule based approaches. In the present method, a simple but effective rule based technique is developed for the transliteration between Bengali script and Meetei Mayek script of written Manipuri text. Typically, transliteration is carried out between two different languages –one as a source and the other as a target. But, for the languages which use more than one script, it becomes essential to introduce transliteration between the scripts. This is the reason why the present task is carried out between Bengali script and Meetei Mayek for Manipuri language. The proposed rule based approach points out the importance of deeper linguistic rule integration in the process by making use of the monosyllabic characteristics of Manipuri language. The Bengali script to Meetei Mayek transliteration system based on the proposed model gives higher precision and recall compared to the statistical model. But, in contrast to that, the statistical based approach gives higher precision and recall compared to the rule based approach for the reverse transliteration.

KEYWORDS : Meetei Mayek, Bengali Script, Transliteration, Monosyllabic

1 Introduction

Manipuri language is in eighth schedule of the constitution of India and spoken approximately by three million people mainly in the state of Manipur in India and in the neighbouring countries namely Bangladesh and Myanmar. It is a less privileged Tibeto-Burman language and highly agglutinative in nature, influenced and enriched by the Indo-Aryan languages of Sanskrit origin and English. The Manipuri or Meeteiron is represented using two different scripts, viz. Bengali script and Meetei Mayek (also known as Meitei Mayek). So, it is essential to produce a Manipuri text both in Bengali script as well as Meetei Mayek. The Meetei Mayek is the original script used to represent Manipuri language. It may be noted that Manipuri is the only Tibeto-Burman language which has its own script. We carry out transliteration to cope up with different writing systems by converting from one writing system to another writing system between Bengali script and Meetei Mayek. Transliteration is used in several applications of natural language processing such as machine translation, named entity transliteration, out of vocabulary transliteration and cross lingual information retrieval etc. The proposed rule based approach points out the importance of deeper linguistic rule integration in the transliteration process by making use of the monosyllabic characteristics. Natural language processing tasks for Manipuri language is at the very initial stage and most of the tools available so far do not perform at the required measure and more importantly, there is not enough digitized Manipuri language resources, be it monolingual or bilingual.

2 Related Work

The transliteration models can be categorized as grapheme based, phoneme-based and hybrid based. The grapheme based model (Li et al, 2004) is the direct orthographic mapping and only uses orthography-related features while phoneme based model (Knight and Graehl, 1998) works on phonetic correspondence to generate the target text. The hybrid method refers to the combination of several different models which may use other knowledge source. The papers by (Gao, 2004), (Knight and Graehl, 1998), (Virga and Khudanpur, 2003) report the attempt to build statistical transliteration model. In this approach, the transliteration model performance is limited by what it sees during the training process from the training data. This approach faces one important challenge to disambiguate the noise introduced during the training process for reverse / backward transliteration. The reason behind is that some of the silent syllable may be lost due to the noisy model as in the case of Chinese-English transliteration (Yang et al, 2008). Some of the researchers devised methods to improve the statistical approach by making use of bilingual resources.

Manipuri is a resource constrained language and a bilingual resource is very limited (Singh and Bandyopadhyay, 2010a). The first Manipuri to English transliteration is reported for the named entities using modified joint source channel model (Ekbal et al., 2006) and is used in the parallel corpora extraction from comparable news corpora (Singh and Bandyopadhyay, 2010b) and reused in the Manipuri to English example based machine translation system (Singh and Bandyopadhyay, 2010c) and Phrase Based Statistical Machine Translation (PBSMT) system development (Singh and Bandyopadhyay, 2011). The performance of the rule based approach is improved by integrating syllable based unit as transliteration unit (TU) in the present grapheme based approach. However, Manipuri being a tonal language, there is loss of accents for the tonal words. There is essence of intonation in Manipuri text; but differentiation between Bengali characters such as ি (i) and ী (ee) or ু (u) and ূ (oo) cannot be made using Meetei Mayek. This increases the lexical ambiguity on the transliterated Manipuri words in Meetei Mayek script. To the best of our knowledge, the present task of transliterating from Meetei Mayek to Bengali is the first attempt so far. This attempt is essential for the generation who are accustomed to Bengali script only prior to full fledged reinstatement of Meetei Mayek at schools, offices and administrative levels.

3 The Manipuri News Corpus

The web walked into the ACL meetings starting in 1999 as a source of linguistic data. In recent times, there are online Manipuri news websites available such as http://www.thesangaiexpress.com/ where the news items are published in both Manipuri and English. Some other websites are http://www.ifp.co.in/ published in English; http://www.poknapham.in/ published in Manipuri and http://www.hueiyenlanpao.com/ is published in both English and Manipuri (in both Bengali script and Meetei Mayek script). However, the Manipuri news is available only in PDF format from these websites. A web based Manipuri news corpus collection is reported (Singh and Bandyopadhyay, 2010a) using the Bengali script in Unicode format. The resource constrained Manipuri language news corpus is collected from http://www.thesangaiexpress.com/. At present, there is a Manipuri news monolingual corpus of 4 million wordforms in Bengali script Unicode format. Our experiment makes use of this corpus on news domain. The news items cover national and international news, brief news, editorial, letter to editor, articles, sports etc. The local news coverage is more than the national and international news in these websites. The corpus is tokenized and cleaned to minimise spelling errors.

4 Manipuri scripts and Linguistic Features

Manipuri uses two different scripts – Bengali Script[1] and Meetei Mayek[2] (Unicode range: ABC0-ABFF of Unicode Standard Version 6.0) also known as Meitei Mayek script to some linguists. The Bengali script has 52 consonants and 12 vowels. The Meetei Mayek has 27 letters (Iyek Ipee), 8 dependent vowel signs (Cheitap Iyek), 8 final consonants (Lonsum Iyek), 10 digits (Cheising Iyek) and 3 punctuation (Cheikhei, Lum Iyek and Apun Iyek). The transliteration models convert source text to target text based on the phonetic equivalent mapping. Though there can be direct one-to-one mapping for the 27 Meetei Mayek letter (Iyek Ipee) to Bengali script, there are some Bengali scripts which does not have a one-to-one direct mapping to Meetei Mayek such as (ঋ, ক্ষ, ঃ, ঞ, ঁ etc.) which has resulted in the loss of target representation. This is the most basic problem with grapheme based transliteration system. An important question is – how do we handle these characters in Manipuri text with Bengali script for the transliteration into Meetei Mayek. An expert level agreement on mapping these characters to Meetei Mayek is the need of the hour in order to improve the rules based transliteration performance between the two scripts.

[1] http://unicode.org/charts/PDF/U0980.pdf
[2] http://unicode.org/charts/PDF/UABC0.pdf

5 Bengali script to Meetei Mayek Transliteration

Our method has two advantages. Firstly, there is a sizable monolingual Manipuri news corpus available to be used. Secondly, our method can be improved by including syllable based transliteration unit to the existing list of TU. Concretely, there are two phases involved in our approach. In the first phase, we split the individual words into syllables, and then a syllable based searching can be employed to revise the result. In the second phase, for any syllable unit or TU match, it is searched from the list of TUs and the corresponding mapping unit is picked up from the mapping table and the syllables are concatenated to form the target word. Two different models are developed – baseline and monosyllabic based model.

5.1 Baseline Model

As a baseline system, a grapheme based – that is character to character and numeral to numeral transliteration is carried out. A hand crafted one-to-one mapping rule between Bengali script and Meetei Mayek is established and transliteration is carried out. However, there is no exact one-to-one correspondence between each phoneme associated with each Bengali script grapheme and Meetei Mayek grapheme. A direct one-to-one grapheme for the conjuncts between Bengali script and Meetei Mayek is not possible based on the order of appearance of each character. This model has several drawbacks including the mishandling of conjuncts. Hence, this model does not give a reasonably good transliteration. So, the several NLP tools developed using the transliterated corpus using this model suffers very badly in terms of performance.

5.2 Syllable Based Model

As a baseline system, a grapheme based – that is character to character and numeral to numeral transliteration is carried out. There is no one-to-one correspondence between phoneme associated with the Bengali script grapheme and Meitei Mayek grapheme. So, a hand crafted rule between this is established and transliteration is carried out. This scheme has several drawbacks including the mishandling of conjuncts. There is no direct one-to-one grapheme for the conjuncts as well. Thus, the injective function behaviour does not suit between the two character sets for transliteration. Hence, this model does not give a reasonably good transliteration.

Bengali Script	Meetei Mayek
ষ, স, শ, ছ	ꯁ (Sam)
ন, ণ	ꯅ (Na)
ট, ত	ꯇ (Til)
থ, ঠ	ꯊ (Thou)
য়, য	ꯌ (Yang)
দ, ড	ꯗ (Dil)
ঢ, ধ	ꯙ (Dhou)
উ, ঊ	ꯎ (Un)
ই, ঈ	ꯏ (Ee)
র, ড়, ঢ়	ꯔ (Rai)
ি, ী	ꯤ (Inap)
ু, ূ	ꯨ (Unap)

TABLE 1 – Many-to-One mapping table.

Based on the above observation, there is no possibility of one-to-one mapping between the two scripts for all the Meitei Mayek scripts as given in table 1, a syllable based transliteration model is developed. One of the most significant shortfalls is that – the conjuncts which are appearing in the Bengali representations need to be addressed as a single transliteration unit. Use of conjuncts using Bengali script of Manipur text is very common and large in numbers. The overall conjunct representation is many-to-many characters in nature for the bilingual transliteration task of Bengali-Manipuri language pair. Some of the example words using the conjuncts are given as:

প্রেসন ←→ ꯄ꯭ꯔꯦꯁꯅ (*press-na*)

ডিষ্ট্রিককি ←→ ꯗꯤꯁ꯭ꯇ꯭ꯔꯤꯛꯀꯤ (*district-ki*)

সেক্রেটরিয়েত্তা ←→ ꯁꯦꯛ꯭ꯔꯦꯇꯔꯤꯌꯦꯇ꯭ꯇꯥ (*secretariate-ta*)

পেট্রোল ← → ꯄꯦꯇ꯭ꯔꯣꯜ (*petrol*)

And the Bengali script conjuncts and its constituents along with the Meetei Mayek notation for the above examples are as given below:

প্রে → প + ্র + ে → ꯄ꯭ꯔꯦ

ষ্ট্রি → ষ + ট + ্র + ি → ꯁ꯭ꯇ꯭ꯔꯤ

ক্রে → ক + র + ে → ꯛ꯭ꯔꯦ

ট্রো → ট + র + ো → ꯇ꯭ꯔꯣ

One of the observations is that vowels presentation of Bengali and Meetei Mayek is not in the same order. Again, the ে (ꯦ–e) is a constituent of ো (ꯣ–o) and ৌ (ꯧ -ou) . This may result in the misinterpretation in case of character by character transliteration. Over and above, the conjuncts need to be fragmented down towards its basic units. In such occurrences the one-to-one mapping fails to work as given in the order. So, a better solution to this problem is addressed in the proposed syllable based model. Since Manipuri is monosyllabic and highly agglutinative, it is essential to analyze at the syllable level for each word. Each syllable can be represented by a group of characters also termed as transliteration unit (TU). Inside this TU, there can be conjuncts such as (ঙ+ক = ঙ্ক) .In this syllable based model, the monosyllabic TU with the highest number of characters are picked from a table, i.e., a many-to-many model. This table maintains the Bengali TU and its corresponding Meetei Mayek representation as shown in table 2. The step is repeated towards the smaller conjuncts up to single character level. This technique is specifically effective for the transliteration of the same language with different scripts.

Bengali Script	Meetei Mayek
ট্রো	ꯇ꯭ꯔꯣ
ক্রে	ꯛ꯭ꯔꯦ
প্রে	ꯄ꯭ꯔꯦ।
ষ্ট্রি	ꯁ꯭ꯇ꯭ꯔꯤ

TABLE 2 – Sample transliteration unit mapping between Bengali and Meitei Mayek scripts

The mapping tables have been prepared at different levels with separate tables for single characters and conjuncts with two or more than two characters. The single character mapping table contains 72 entries and the multiple characters mapping table consists of 738 entries. There are conjuncts of 2, 3 and 4 characters. Sub-tables for each of the conjuncts are prepared. The many-to-many character based syllables are collected from the news corpus based on its occurrence and iterative procedure till it covers the written text in the corpus followed by one-to-one mapping. First of all, we split the transliteration candidate TC_i in the word list into syllables, {s1, s2,…..sn}. Then this syllable sequence is used as a query for syllable-based searching and mapping using the mapping table. An input word can be represented by a vector of syllables {s1, s2,…..sn}. The syllables are the units to construct a word. The algorithm for search and map starts using the mapping table with highest degree of many-to-many mapping table. This reduces the overall complexity still keeping the performance high. Figure 1 shows two examples of convergence due to phonetic similarity of TU from Bengali script to Meetei Mayek.

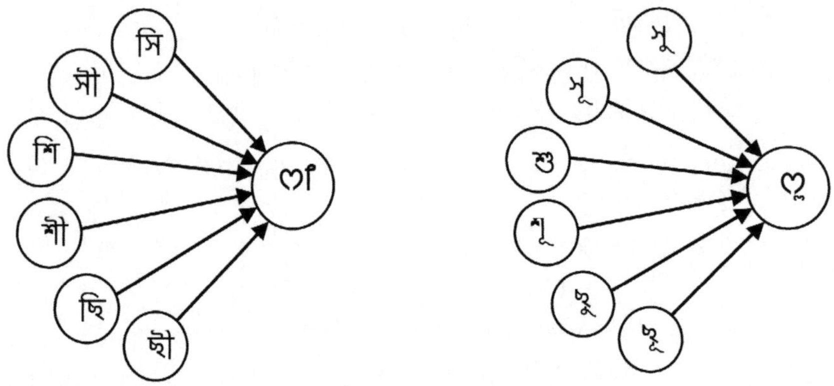

(a) (b)

FIGURE 1 – Two examples of convergence of TU from Bengali Script to Meitei Mayek.

5.3 Modified Joint Source Channel

The problem of machine transliteration has been studied extensively in the paradigm of the noisy channel model. A Bengali script to Meetei Mayek script transliteration of Manipuri news text is developed based on Modified Joint Source Channel Model for transliteration (Ekbal et al, 2006). A bilingual training set of Bengali script and their respective Meetei Mayek transliterations, has been created. This bilingual training set is automatically analyzed to acquire mapping knowledge in order to transliterate new Bengali script to Meetei Mayek. Transliteration units (TUs) are extracted from the Bengali script to Meetei Mayek counterparts. Some examples are given below:

(a) মনিপুর (ꯃꯅꯤꯄꯨꯔ) *[manipur]* → ম । নি । পু । র

ꯃꯅꯤꯄꯨꯔ → ꯃ | ꯅꯤ | ꯄꯨ | ꯔ

রাজকুমার (ꯔꯥꯖꯀꯨꯃꯥꯔ) *[rajkumar]* → রা । জ । কু । মা । র

ꯔꯥꯖꯀꯨꯃꯥꯔ → ꯔꯥ | ꯖ | ꯀꯨ | ꯃꯥ | ꯔ

(b) অভিনন্দন (ꯑꯚꯤꯅꯟꯗꯟ) *[abhinandan]* → অ । ভি । ন । ন্দ । ন

ꯑꯚꯤꯅꯟꯗꯟ → ꯑ | ꯚꯤ | ꯅ | ꯟꯗ | ꯟ

The TUs are the lexical units for machine transliteration. The Bengali script is divided into Transliteration Units (TU) with patterns C+M, where C represents a consonant or a vowel or a conjunct and M represents the vowel modifier or matra. The system learns mappings automatically from the bilingual training set of 20,000 entries. Aligned TUs along with their contexts are automatically derived from this bilingual training set to generate the collocation statistics.Transliteration units (TUs) are extracted from the Bengali script and the corresponding Meetei Mayek words, and Bengali script TUs are associated with their Meetei Mayek counterparts along with the TUs in context.

6 Meetei Mayek to Bengali Script Transliteration

The reverse/backward transliteration of Bengali to Meetei Mayek is carried out using the same mapping tables. This Meetei Mayek to Bengali transliteration faces several challenges using linguistics rules. Based on the table 2, the many-to-one mapping is one-to-many mapping for Meetei Mayek to Bengali script transliteration thus it suffers very badly due to probability distribution based on the number of target characters. A one-to-one map is not feasible option. A step to enhance the performance of the transliteration is to consider the preceding few characters and following few characters of the TU to be transliterated as a context in order to forecast the most likely target TU. This enables to choose the right mapping by a certain factor. However, in case of a single character TU, this approach does not help much.

In the Meetei Mayek to Bengali transliteration, there are certain limitations which are caused by many-to-one character mapping and identification and addressing of the right representation of Bengali. However, this issue can be further addressed using possible language model and its probability parameters. One typical example of many-to-one transliteration such as ষ, স, শ and ছ to ꯁ (as given in the Table 2) which results in the lost of tone that could affect other NLP activities such as various lexical ambiguity of word sense disambiguation, POS tagging etc using the transliterated corpus. The convergence shown in figure 1 has to be resolved for the backward transliteration through a statistical approach since the exploration and establishment of rules is quite difficult for such cases for the Meetei Mayek to Bengali script transliteration process. Similarly, there are several other cases of many-to-one and one-to-many sets in between Bengali script and Meetei Mayek. For such instances, the transliteration deems to face the difficulty to make the right choice of the target TU using the rule based approach.

7 Evaluation

Once the experimental corpus is decided, a metric to measure the system's precision and recall is required. The appropriate metric depends on the scenario in which the transliteration system is to be used. The human evaluation takes enormous time compared to automatic evaluation. In our present task, we used 50,000 wordforms as gold standard reference test set. Table 3 gives the precision and recall of the different transliteration systems.

Transliteration model	Baseline Model		Syllable Based Model		Modified Joint Source Channel Model	
	Precision	Recall	Precision	Recall	Precision	Recall
Bengali to Meetei Mayek	68.31	65.23	96.23	94.57	93.23	92.45
Meetei Mayek to Bengali	59.56	58.87	89.78	88.56	93.43	91.97

TABLE 3 – Precision and Recall of the Transliteration Models

Conclusion and Discussion

A bidirectional transliteration system between Bengali script and Meetei Mayek of Manipuri text is developed exploiting the monosyllabic characteristics of Manipuri language. The system abruptly outperforms compared to the baseline transliteration systems of this language using the given two scripts. Since, the Meetei Mayek script is in the process of induction at different administrative and academic levels, there is a need still for Meetei Mayek to be transliterated back to Bengali script to reach other section of Manipuri speakers who know only the Bengali script. The grapheme based approach works well for the transliteration of the same language using the two different scripts. In future, statistical model for transliteration between Bengali script and Meetei Mayek can be experimented using a decent size of training data collected from different sources. Over and above, the Meetei Mayek to Bengali script transliteration has the shortfall using the same TU list using the linguistics rules and a statistical approach is the alternative to yield a better result.

Acknowledgments

I, sincerely, thank Dr. Zia Saquib, Executive Director, CDAC (Mumbai), Prof. Sivaji Bandyopadhyay, Jadavpur University, Kolkata and the anonymous reviewers for their support and valuable comments.

References

Ekbal, A., Sudip K. N., Bandyopadhyay, S. (2006). A Modified Joint Source-Channel Model for Transliteration, *Proceedings of the COLING/ACL 2006 Main Conference Poster Sessions*, Pages 191–198, Sydney.

Gao, W. (2004). Phoneme-based Statistical Transliteration of Foreign Name for OOV Problem. *A thesis of Master*. The Chinese University of Hong Kong.

Knight, K. and Graehl, J. (1998). Machine Transliteration. *Computational Linguistics* 24(4).

Li, H., Zhang, M., and Su, J. (2004). A joint source-channel model for machine transliteration. *In Proc. 42nd ACL Annual Meeting*, pages 159–166, Barcelona, Spain.

Singh, T. D., Bandyopadhyay, S. (2010a). Web Based Manipuri Corpus for Multiword NER and Reduplicated MWEs Identification using SVM, *Proceedings of the 1st Workshop on South and Southeast Asian Natural Language Processing (WSSANLP)*, the 23rd International Conference on Computational Linguistics (COLING), Pages 35–42, Beijing.

Singh, T. D., Bandyopadhyay, S. (2010b) Semi Automatic Parallel Corpora Extraction from Comparable News Corpora, *In the International Journal of POLIBITS*, Issue 41 (January – June 2010), ISSN 1870-9044, Pages 11-17.

Singh, T. D., Bandyopadhyay, S. (2010c). Manipuri-English Example Based Machine Translation System, *International Journal of Computational Linguistics and Applications* (IJCLA), ISSN 0976-0962, Pages 147-158.

Singh, T. D., Bandyopadhyay, S. (2011). Integration of Reduplicated Multiword Expressions and Named Entities in a Phrase Based Statistical Machine Translation System, *Proceedings of the 5th International Joint Conference on Natural Language Processing*, Pages 1304–1312, Chiang Mai, Thailand, November 8 – 13.

Virga, P., Khudanpur, S. (2003). Transliteration of proper names in cross-lingual information retrieval. *In Proc. of the ACL workshop on Multilingual Named Entity Recognition*.

Yang, F., Zhao, J., Zou, B., Liu, K., Liu, F. (2008). Chinese-English Backward Transliteration Assisted with Mining Monolingual Web Pages, *Proceedings of ACL-08: HLT*, pages 541–549, Columbus, Ohio, USA, June.

Rule-based Machine Translation between Indonesian and Malaysian

Raymond Hendy Susanto[1] *Septina Dian Larasati*[2] *Francis M. Tyers*[3]
(1) Department of Computer Science, National University of Singapore
(2) Institute of Formal and Applied Linguistics, MFF, Charles University in Prague
(3) Dept. Lleng. i Sist. Inform., Universitat d'Alacant
`raymondhs@nus.edu.sg`, `larasati@ufal.mff.cuni.cz`, `ftyers@dlsi.ua.es`

ABSTRACT
We describe the development of a bidirectional rule-based machine translation system between Indonesian and Malaysian (id-ms), two closely related Austronesian languages natively spoken by approximately 35 million people. The system is based on the re-use of free and publicly available resources, such as the Apertium machine translation platform and Wikipedia articles. We also present our approaches to overcome the data scarcity problems in both languages by exploiting the morphology similarities between the two.

KEYWORDS: machine translation, Malay languages, morphology.

---

1 Introduction

In this paper we describe the development of `apertium-id-ms`, a bidirectional Indonesian and Malaysian machine translation system based on the Apertium platform. The paper is laid out as follows: Section 2 gives a brief description of the two languages; Section 3 gives a short review of the previous work in Indonesian-Malaysian language pair; Section 4 describes the system and the creation of the resources; Section 5 presents an evaluation of the system, and finally we describes future work that could be done and some concluding remarks.

2 Languages

Indonesian (*Bahasa Indonesia*) and Malaysian (*Bahasa Malaysia*) are standards of the Malay language and both belong to the Austronesian family. Indonesian is spoken by approximately 35 million people[1], mostly from Indonesia, but also widespread in the Netherlands, the Philippines, Saudi Arabia, Singapore, and the United States. Malaysian has 10 million speakers across the Peninsular Malaysia, and other speakers coming from parts of Sarawak, Indonesia (Sumatra), Singapore, and United States.

Indonesian and Malaysian are closely related; both languages are mutually intelligible to a great extent. The morphology of the two languages are the same, where agglutination is used extensively (by means of affixation, reduplication, and compounding), although some affixes are more frequently used in one language over the other. For instance, the prefix *juru-* is often used in Malaysian to indicate an actor characterized by the stem it is attached to. While this affixation also happens in Indonesian, it is not as frequently found as in Malaysian.

The main difference between Indonesian and Malaysian languages lies in their vocabulary; Indonesian is largely influenced by Dutch and Javanese, whereas Malaysian has many words borrowed from English, e.g. *dokter* vs. *doktor* ('doctor') and *tas* vs. *beg* ('bag'). Moreover, there are frequent minor spelling differences, e.g. *kabar* vs. *khabar* ('news') and *mau* vs. *mahu* ('want').

3 Motivation

The development of this system is motivated by an early prototype Apertium system developed in Larasati and Kubon (2010). Since then, most of the components in the prototype were completely redesigned, and the direction of the development was based on the following rationale:

- Morphological analyser: We wanted to create a morphological analyser which is not only robust, but also does not overgenerate either. Both Indonesian and Malaysian morphology are characterized by rich derivational morphology, but poor inflectional morphology, unlike some other morphologically-complex languages such as Arabic and Turkish. Moreover, each root undergoes an idiosyncratic subset of these derivational processes (i.e. we cannot simply apply the derivational affixes to new words).
- Bidirectional: A new translation direction from Malaysian to Indonesian was added, and used as the starting point instead of the opposite direction, since translating from Indonesian to Malaysian appears to be more ambiguous.
- Evaluation: Finally, we performed a quality evaluation of our system, which has not been done before.

[1] `http://www.lmp.ucla.edu/Profile.aspx?menu=004&LangID=89` Last accessed: October 2012

We have chosen the rule-based approach, instead of the ubiquitous corpus-based statistical approach, due to the dearth of parallel corpora for the two languages. Moreover, the closeness between the two languages makes the rule-based approach favourable. Recent development for closely related languages with the rule-based approach have shown competitive performance with respect to the statistical approach, e.g. the rule-based Swedish→Danish system in Tyers and Nordfalk (2009) and the Italian→Catalan system in Toral et al. (2011), where both systems outperform a rivaling statistical-based system.

4 System

The system is based on the Apertium machine translation platform (Forcada et al., 2011).[2] The platform was originally aimed at the Romance languages of the Iberian peninsula, but has also been adapted for other, more distantly related language pairs. The whole platform, both programs and data, are licensed under the Free Software Foundation's General Public Licence[3] (GPL) and all the software and data for the 33 supported language pairs (and the other pairs being worked on) is available for download from the project website.

4.1 Architecture of the system

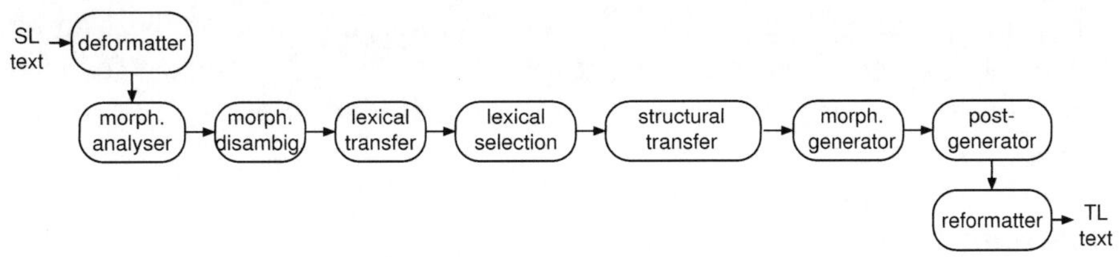

Figure 1: The pipeline architecture of the Apertium system.

The Apertium translation engine consists of a Unix-style *pipeline* or *assembly line* with the following modules (see Fig. 1):

- A *deformatter* which encapsulates the format information in the input as *superblanks* that will then be seen as blanks between words by the other modules.
- A *morphological analyser* which segments the text in surface forms (SF) (*words*, or, where detected, multi-word lexical units or MWLUs) and for each, delivers one or more *lexical forms* (LF) consisting of *lemma*, *lexical category* and morphological information.
- A *morphological disambiguator* (constraint grammar) which chooses, using linguistic rules the most adequate sequence of morphological analyses for an ambiguous sentence.
- A *lexical transfer* module which reads each SL LF and delivers the corresponding target-language (TL) LF by looking it up in a bilingual dictionary encoded as an FST compiled from the corresponding XML file. The lexical transfer module may return more than one TL LF for a single SL LF.
- A *lexical selection* module which chooses, based on context rules the most adequate translation of ambiguous source language LFs.

[2] `http://www.apertium.org/`

[3] `http://www.fsf.org/licensing/licenses/gpl.html`

- A *structural transfer* module which performs local syntactic operations, is compiled from XML files containing rules that associate an *action* to each defined LF *pattern*. Patterns are applied left-to-right, and the longest matching pattern is always selected.

- A *morphological generator* which delivers a TL SF for each TL LF, by suitably inflecting it.

- A *reformatter* which de-encapsulates any format information.

4.2 Morphological transducers

There is one publicly available morphological tool for Indonesian, MorphInd (Larasati et al., 2011). However, MorphInd is only designed for analysis, while we wanted a tool for both morphological analysis and generation. Moreover, there are rarely linguistic resources and tools available for Malaysian. Baldwin (2006) has developed the free/open-source lemmatiser for Malay, but this does not meet our need either since we wanted to include more robust morphological information into our Malaysian transducer, such as part-of-speech and affixes. Thus, we decided to build the morphological transducers from scratch.

Similar to most Apertium language pairs, the morphological transducers for both Indonesian and Malaysian are constructed using *lttoolbox*, a toolbox for morphological analysis and generation that is available under a free/open-source licence. The monolingual dictionary for each language is provided as XML-formatted entries, which is then compiled into a finite state transducers using *lttoolbox*.

4.2.1 Indonesian morphological transducer

A lexicon list was created semi-automatically to the Indonesian morphological analyser based on a words frequency list, with the most frequent words being added first. The frequency list was taken from a database dump of the Indonesian Wikipedia. For each word in the frequency list, we obtained its lemma and part-of-speech information from Kateglo[4], an online Indonesian dictionary with over 70,000 entries licensed under CC BY-SA 3.0.[5]. Since we also wanted to include affix information in our analyser, we wrote a rule-based morpheme segmentor to decompose a given Indonesian surface form into their constituent morphemes, also by making use of the lemma information from Kateglo. Moreover, closed word classes (e.g. pronouns, conjunctions) were added by hand.

4.2.2 Malaysian morphological transducer

A frequency list for Malaysian was also created based on a database dump of the Malaysian Wikipedia. Unlike Indonesian, we did not find a comprehensive Malaysian dictionary with adequate morphological information, such as lemma and part-of-speech. Hence, the Malaysian analyser was built using the two strategies below.

First, Malaysian words that also exist as an Indonesian word were assumed to share the same morphological information (i.e. the same lemma and part-of-speech), and were added automatically to the analyser. Although this method may introduce a number of false friends (e.g. *polisi* means 'policy' in Malay but 'police' in Indonesian), the benefit outweighs the risk

[4]`http://kateglo.bahtera.org/`
[5]`http://creativecommonsorg/licenses/by-sa/3.0/`

since there is huge overlap in the lexicons of the two languages. Moreover, most of these false friends usually belong to the same part-of-speech.

Second, we also added Malaysian words which appear in our bilingual dictionary. Since every entry in a bilingual dictionary is a pair of words with the same meaning, we can assume that these words also belong to the same part-of-speech most of the time. Our approaches to building the bilingual dictionary are presented in the following section.

4.3 Bilingual dictionary

There is no freely available bilingual dictionary between Indonesian and Malaysian, so we had to build the dictionary from scratch. At the moment, the bilingual dictionary contains 12,142 entries, which was developed in several ways described below.

First, most of the entries were added using automatic word alignments. We created an Indonesian-Malaysian parallel corpus by translating many articles taken from Malaysian Wikipedia. The translation process is mostly automatic, with the help of existing Malaysian-Indonesian machine translation systems such as Google Translate.[6]

Next the Wikipedia corpus is tagged using our morphological analyser, and word alignments were created by running `GIZA++` (Och and Ney, 2003) on the tagged corpus. We fed the probabilistic dictionary into the `ReTraTos` toolbox (Caseli et al., 2006), which extracts both phrases and single-word translations from alignments, and converts them into Apertium translation entries. The `ReTraTos` method gave us about 12,000 translation entries, but also required a manual check due the amount of noise in the resulting data.

Finally, some entries were added manually, which included closed word classes and words that frequently appeared in Wikipedia but were not yet added to the bilingual dictionary.

4.4 Disambiguation

The output from the morphological analysis is disambiguated using Apertium's statistical disambiguator module. The module implements a bigram part-of-speech tagger based on hidden Markov models (HMM). To improve the accuracy of our disambiguator, a Constraint Grammar (Karlsson, 1990) could be used as a pre-disambiguator module before feeding the input to the HMM, which is left for future work.

4.5 Lexical selection rules

Given the closeness of the languages, lexical selection is not a large problem between Indonesian and Malaysian. However, a number of rules can be written for ambiguous words; for example, the Malaysian preposition *daripada* 'from (to explain the origin of something), than (comparison)' can be translated into Indonesian as either *dari* 'from' or *daripada* 'than (comparison)', depending on the surrounding context.

Another example is the copulas *adalah* and *ialah* (both meaning 'be'), which exist in both Indonesian and Malaysian, but have a slightly different usage in each language. In Malaysian, *adalah* is used before an adjective phrase or a prepositional phrase, and *ialah* is used only before a noun phrase. In comparison to Indonesian, there are no strict rules governing the use of the two words, and their usage is more interchangeable.

[6] `http://translate.google.com/`

4.6 Transfer rules

There are barely differences between the grammar of Indonesian and Malaysian, in that the structure of words, phrases, clauses, and sentences are almost exactly the same. That said, the lexical transfer between the two languages works by simple word substitution in most cases.

(Malaysian) Input	Cuaca kelmarin amatlah sejuk.
Mor. analysis	^Cuaca/Cuaca<n><sg>$ ^kelmarin/kelmarin<adv>$ ^amatlah/amatlah<adv>$ ^sejuk/sejuk<adj>$ ^./.<sent>$
Mor. disambiguation	^Cuaca<n><sg>$ ^kelmarin<adv>$ ^amatlah<adv>$ ^sejuk<adj>$^.<sent>$
Transfer	^Cuaca<n><sg>$ ^kemarin<adv>$ ^amatlah<adv>$ ^dingin<adj>$^.<sent>$
Mor. generation	Cuaca kemarin amatlah dingin.

Table 1: Translation process for the sentence *Cuaca kelmarin amatlah sejuk.* 'The weather yesterday is very cold'.

5 Evaluation

The system was evaluated in three ways. The first was the coverage[7] of the system. The second was the word error rate (WER) of the translation output for our test data set, together with the error analysis of the translations. Lastly, we did a comparative evaluation with an existing system.

5.1 Coverage

Lexical coverage of the system is calculated over the Indonesian and Malaysian Wikipedia articles, as shown in Table 2. The database dump of the Indonesian Wikipedia[8] was from the 29th April 2012, and that of Malaysian Wikipedia[9] from the 28th April 2012. Both database dumps were stripped of formatting.

Corpus	Tokens	Coverage
Indonesian Wikipedia	19,021,087	80.70%
Malaysian Wikipedia	12,613,364	80.10%

Table 2: Naïve vocabulary coverage over Wikipedia articles.

5.2 Quantitative and Qualitative

We tested our system on a 2,084 word text taken from various articles in Malaysian Wikipedia. The translation quality was measured using Word Error Rate (WER), a metric based on the

[7] Here coverage is defined as *naïve coverage*, that is for any given surface form at least one analysis is returned by our monolingual dictionaries

[8] `http://id.wikipedia.org/`; `idwiki-20120429-pages-articles.xml.bz2`

[9] `http://ms.wikipedia.org/`; `mswiki-20120428-pages-articles.xml.bz2`

Levenshtein distance (Levenshtein, 1966). We calculated the WER for each sentence using the `apertium-eval-translator`[10] tool. The WER metric was preferred to other MT metrics such as BLEU (Papineni et al., 2002) since we want to evaluate the system for the *postedition* task. That is, we want to assess the amount of manual labour needed to improve the machine-generated translation.[11]

For the Malaysian to Indonesian direction, the sentences were translated by the system, and then postedited by a native Indonesian speaker. For the Indonesian to Malaysian direction, we used the reference translation, as postedited by the native speaker and used it as a source of Indonesian to be translated to Malaysian, then the original Malaysian sentence was used as the reference translation.

Corpus	Direction	Tokens	Unknown	WER
Malaysian Wikipedia	id→ms	2,079	211	14.43% (83.89%)
	ms→id	2,084	256	7.58% (69.53%)

Table 3: Word error rate over the Malaysian Wikipedia test data. Number in parentheses gives percentage of unknown words which were free rides.

We consider the WER of our system, as depicted in Table 3 is quite acceptable for postediting. In our system, unknown words are left unprocessed. Nonetheless, many of these unknown words are *free rides*[12], which will not affect the final quality of the translation.

As a direction for future improvement, we did an error analysis by reviewing the translation outputs from our system. Most of the translation errors were due to the mistakes and gaps in our analyser. Specifically, many of the stems do not have the complete set of its derived forms. As a result, it cannot provide analysis for a unknown derived wordform even if the stem already exists in the analyser. Moreover, the analyser cannot handle clitics attached to unknown words (e.g. possessive enclitic *-nya*). These errors can be fixed by a more thorough revision of the morphological analyser. Lastly, the system is often not capable of choosing the most suitable translation given a particular context. A lexical selection module can be written to alleviate this problem.

Dir.	System	WER
id→ms	Apertium	14.43%
	Google	13.90%
ms→id	Apertium	7.58%
	Google	4.07%

Table 4: Accuracy comparison between the two systems.

[10]`https://apertium.svn.sourceforge.net/svnroot/apertium/trunk/apertium-eval-translator/`

[11]BLEU is not used in our evaluation because we are using a reference translation which is a postedition of the machine-translated text, and the normal use of BLEU is for evaluating against a non-postedited reference. If we used BLEU it would give artifically high scores.

[12]That is, the word is unknown to the system, but the same in Indonesian and Malaysian. Typical free-rides include names and special terminology.

5.3 Comparative

We compared our system to another MT system for Indonesian to Malaysian and Malaysian to Indonesian, Google Translate, a web-based statistical machine translation system. The evaluation was performed the same way: the test data was translated with Google Translate, then postedited.

We notice from Table 4 that Google outperforms the Apertium system in both translation directions. For Malaysian to Indonesian, the error rate is reduced by almost a half. It is also interesting that both systems perform almost as worse for Indonesian to Malaysian, perhaps due to the fact that translating from Indonesian to Malaysian is more ambiguous than translating to Indonesian. Google seems to have a greater vocabulary coverage than Apertium, as exemplified in the first example in Table 5. The Malaysian word *mencuba* ('try') is unknown to the Apertium system (denoted by the asterisk), whereas it is correctly translated by Google as *mencoba*.

Moreover, in many cases, Google seems to be performing better in picking the most natural translations. In the second example, it translates the noun phrase *kuasa ketenteraan* ('military power') to *kekuatan militer*, which sounds much more natural than *kuasa ketentaraan*.

Source	Para saintis **mencuba** menjawab pertanyaan tersebut.
Apertium	Para ilmuwan ***mencuba** menjawab pertanyaan tersebut.
Google	Para ilmuwan **mencuba** menjawab pertanyaan tersebut.
Reference	Para ilmuwan **mencoba** menjawab pertanyaan tersebut.
	'Scientists are trying to answer that question.'
Source	Sebuah **kuasa ketenteraan** yang disegani.
Apertium	Sebuah **kuasa ketentaraan** yang disegani.
Google	Sebuah **kekuatan militer** yang disegani.
Reference	Sebuah **kekuatan militer** yang disegani.
	'A respectable military power.'

Table 5: Example translations from Malaysian to Indonesian.

Conclusion and future work

We have presented a bidirectional rule-based machine translation system between Indonesian and Malaysian, two closely-related Malay languages. The system is available as free/open-source software under the GNU GPL and the whole system may be downloaded from SVN.[13]

The resulting system provides comparable results with a leading corpus-based machine translation system, and we are looking forward to improving the translation quality of our system in the future. The long-term plan is to integrate the data created to make transfer systems with more distantly related languages such as Indonesian-English and Malaysian-English.

Acknowledgments

Development of the system was funded as part of the Google Summer of Code[14], an annual program sponsored by Google, Inc. to promote students' participation in open-source software projects.

[13] `https://apertium.svn.sourceforge.net/svnroot/apertium/trunk/apertium-id-ms`
[14] `http://code.google.com/soc/`

References

Baldwin, T. (2006). Open source corpus analysis tools for Malay. In *In Proc. of the 5th International Conference on Language Resources and Evaluation*.

Caseli, H. M., Nunes, M. D., and Forcada, M. L. (2006). Automatic induction of bilingual resources from aligned parallel corpora: application to shallow-transfer machine translation. *Machine Translation*, 20(4):227–245.

Forcada, M. L., Ginestí-Rosell, M., Nordfalk, J., O'Regan, J., Ortiz-Rojas, S., Pérez-Ortiz, J. A., Sánchez-Martínez, F., Ramírez-Sánchez, G., and Tyers, F. M. (2011). Apertium: a free/open-source platform for rule-based machine translation. *Machine Translation*, 25(2):127–144.

Karlsson, F. (1990). Constraint grammar as a framework for parsing running text. In *Proceedings of the 13th Conference on Computational Linguistics - Volume 3*, COLING '90, pages 168–173.

Larasati, S. and Kubon, V. (2010). A study of Indonesian-to-Malaysian MT system. In *Proceedings of the 4th International MALINDO Workshop, Depok*, pages 16–22.

Larasati, S., Kuboň, V., and Zeman, D. (2011). Indonesian Morphology Tool (MorphInd): Towards an Indonesian Corpus. *Systems and Frameworks for Computational Morphology*, pages 119–129.

Levenshtein, V. I. (1966). Binary codes capable of correcting deletions, insertions, and reversals. *Soviet Physics—Doklady 10, 707–710. Translated from Doklady Akademii Nauk SSSR*, pages 845–848.

Lewis, M. P. e. (2009). *Ethnologue: Languages of the World, Sixteenth edition*. Dallas, Tex.: SIL International.

Och, F. J. and Ney, H. (2003). A systematic comparison of various statistical alignment models. *Comput. Linguist.*, 29(1):19–51.

Papineni, K., Roukos, S., Ward, T., and Zhu, W.-J. (2002). BLEU: a method for automatic evaluation of machine translation. In *Proceedings of the 40th Annual Meeting on Association for Computational Linguistics*, ACL '02, pages 311–318.

Toral, A., Ginestí, M., and Tyers, F. M. (2011). An Italian to Catalan RBMT system reusing data from existing language pairs. In *Proceedings of the Second Workshop on Free/Open-Source Rule-Based Machine Translation*.

Tyers, F. M. and Nordfalk, J. (2009). Shallow-transfer rule-based machine translation for Swedish to Danish. In *Proceedings of the First Workshop on Free/Open-Source Rule-Based Machine Translation*.

Building Multilingual Search Index using open source framework

Arjun Atreya V[1] *Swapnil Chaudhari*[1] *Pushpak Bhattacharyya*[1] *Ganesh Ramakrishnan*[1]

(1) Deptartment of CSE, IIT Bombay
{arjun, swapnil, pb, ganesh}@cse.iitb.ac.in

ABSTRACT

This paper presents a comparison of open source search engine development frameworks in the context of their malleability for constructing multilingual search index. The comparison study reveals that none of these frameworks are designed for this task. This paper elicits the challenges involved in building a multilingual index. We also discuss policy decisions and the implementation changes made to an open source framework for building such an index. As a main contribution of this work, we propose an architecture that can be used for building multilingual index. It also lists some of the open research challenges involved.

KEYWORDS: Inverted Index, Multilingual Index, Search Engine Framework

1. Introduction

There are lots of open source frameworks available to build a search engine. These open source frameworks provide multiple features to build an inverted index of web documents used for information retrieval. Some features like Scalability, term storage, document posting list storage *etc*, are common across these frameworks. These frameworks facilitate customization of building index to make it compatible for the desired application.

To retain the structure of a document in an inverted index, *field based* indexing is used. Instead of viewing a document as a collection of terms, the document is viewed as a collection of fields and the field as a collection of terms. Each document that needs to be indexed is parsed and terms in the document are grouped into fields prior to indexing. The conceptual view of field based inverted index is shown in the figure 1. Figure 1(a) shows two documents as is. Figure 1(b) shows a view of inverted index built for these documents.

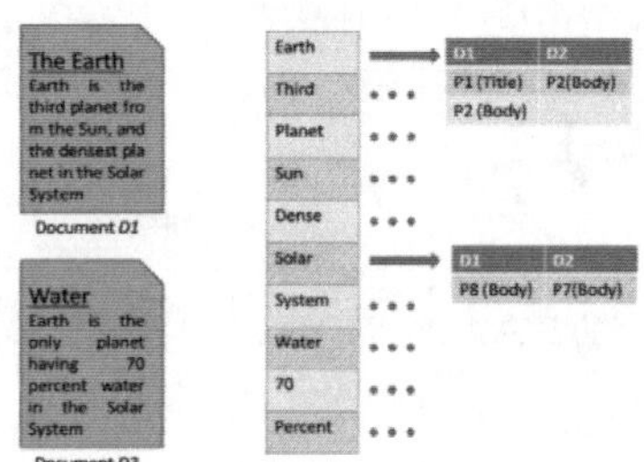

1(a) 1(b)

FIGURE 1 - Conceptual view of an inverted index

All terms in the document are indexed, and a document posting list is created for each indexed term. For every document containing an indexed term, there is a posting list. This posting list contains position information of the indexed term and the field in which this indexed term is present in the document. Field information helps in prioritizing the document for a given search.

2 Overview of open source search frameworks

There are lots of works on building the inverted index using an open source framework. The most popular indexing library is Apache Lucene (Apache Lucene, 2011). Lucene is not a complete search engine framework, but an indexing library used to generate inverted index from crawled documents. Lucene needs to be plugged in with a crawler in order to index web documents. Apache Lucene provides facilities for customizing the library and makes it easily pluggable with the crawler that is being used.

Apache Solr (Apache Solr, 2012) is an enterprise indexing solution built on top of Lucene. Along with indexing, Solr provides features to add, delete and modify documents in an index. Solr also provides basic search facilities that include faceted search, highlighting *etc*. One of the advantages of Solr is to seamlessly add documents to the index, hence reducing the down time of the application.

Apache Nutch (Apache Nutch, 2005) is an open source crawler is built using Java. This project was initiated as a part of Apache Lucene project. Nutch is a scalable crawler framework used for crawling web documents. Heritrix (Heritrix, 2012) is also a web based crawler built using Java. Heritrix provides almost all features of Nutch along with good scalability. The comparison study between the two suggests that Heritrix is better for Multimedia retrieval, whereas Nutch with Hadoop (Apache Hadoop, 2012) is best suited for distributed text retrieval.

Two most popular search frameworks used in research are Terrier (Terrier, 2011) and Lemur (Lemur, 2012). Both of these projects do not include crawler and are not designed for web based search. However, these frameworks are highly scalable and best suited for crawling local file system, TREC Collection, CLEF collection, FIRE collection *etc.*

Other open source search engines built on top of Lucene include Compass (Compass, 2010), Oxyus (Oxyus, 2010), Lius (Lius, 2010), Regain (Regain, 2004). All these search engines have similar features with different capabilities. Compass and Oxyus are designed for crawling web documents, whereas Regain is designed for local system crawl. YaCy (YaCy, 2007) is a decentralized web search framework. This project deals with the usage of networked systems to store a shared index. YaCy provides consistent retrieval for all users without censoring data from the shared index. A small scale search engine Swish-e (Swish-e, 2007), is designed for crawling web pages but for a scale of less than a million documents. MG4J (MG4J, 2005) is a scalable full text search engine built using Java. This framework uses quasi-succinct index for searching. It supports large document collection and indexes large TREC collection without much effort. Google also provides an open source search engine framework called Hounder (Hounder, 2010). Hounder is built on top of Lucene for web retrieval.

Many of the open source search engine frameworks mentioned above are compared for their efficiency in (M. Khabsa *et. al.*, 2012). Each of these frameworks provides certain good qualities. Comparison study in (M. Khabsa *et. al.*, 2012) shows that Lucene takes more time for indexing but storage size of the index is minimized. Similarly MG4J takes lesser time to index. However, these comparison studies are done for certain parameters. There is no such comparison study that considers all parameters of a web crawler.

Keeping in mind the humongous growth of the web and also the need for common solution to search multiple language documents in the web, it is important to evaluate parameters pertaining to multilingual documents while building index. These parameters include language tagging of the document in an index, retrieval efficiency for a specific language and so on.

These frameworks are designed for generating monolingual index. None of the before mentioned frameworks provides all features for generating multilingual index. Frameworks demand changes in the architecture to handle language information of the document while indexing them. Changes in the architecture for one of these open source frameworks called Solr is proposed in this work.

This work details the importance of these parameters. Section 3 describes features of a web crawler that are required to build an index for text retrieval. Features discussed in this section indicate development of web crawlers in the recent past. Our proposed architecture to build multilingual index is introduced in section 4. Section 5 lists several research problems to be addressed in the area of building multilingual index.

3. Features of Web based Crawler/Indexer

A crawler should possess certain features to build a web text retrieval engine. The crawler must be able to process different document formats like HTML, XML, doc, pdf, rtf, *etc*. These documents are fetched from the Internet and parsed individually to get the clean content. With the growth of commercial online advertisement industry, cleaning the HTML content is becoming more challenging. Obtaining the clean text helps us in indexing documents efficiently (Apache Tika, 2012).

There are several components involved in the crawler, *viz.*, fetcher, parser and indexer. Each of these components is customized to enhance the capabilities of a search engine. In this section we discuss several features of the web crawler that are necessary for a good web search engine. The challenges involved in building multilingual index with respect to each of these features are discussed.

3.1 Incremental crawl/index

Crawling is a continuous process of fetching new web documents from the Internet. This is because, all search engines try to achieve a near real time search by making the latest information available to the user . To achieve this, it is important to seamlessly add documents to the index as and when they are fetched. This process of seamlessly adding documents to an existing index is called incremental crawling.

A process need to be in place that adds latest crawled documents to the index while crawling of other pages is still going on. A crawler process that is continuously running and seamlessly adding documents to the index is essential for a near real time search. The open source framework chosen for this task should possess these qualities. There should not be considerable downtime of the index while updating. This downtime would restrict the user from searching documents in the web.

Another aspect of the incremental crawl is re-crawling of already fetched documents. Re-crawling involves identifying changes in fetched documents and indexing them again. This involves deleting a previous version of the document and adding new one to the index.

3.2 RSS Feeds

There are various categories of data in the web that need to be crawled. One such categorization is with respect to the format of a document like HTML, XML, pdf, doc, *etc*. Another categorization is with respect to the modification frequency of the website. There are several websites that remain unchanged for a longer period of time like tourism information sites. Whereas, there are several other sites that change very frequently and these changes need to be tracked in order to crawl them continuously.

As discussed earlier, all search engines try to be real-time or near real-time search engines. To achieve this, crawler should provide a facility to keep track of changes happening in a website. In recent times many websites are being developed as search engine friendly and maintain a record of all changes happening in that site. Websites log all changes in the form of RSS feeds at a single location. This helps the crawler to monitor a particular or small set of RSS feed documents to know if there are any changes in that site.

RSS feeds are generally in XML format containing links to changes done in that site along with metadata information. Crawler need to handle these pages in a special way *i.e.*, after fetching RSS feeds, crawler need to parse the page for changes. If changes exist in the RSS feed page then all out links in the RSS feed document are fetched and indexed. Currently there are many open source crawlers like Nutch which support this feature but older versions of these crawlers do not support crawling of RSS feeds.

3.3 Web graph

Crawling of web pages is driven by links present in the document. While parsing the fetched document all out-links of the document are recorded for crawling in the next depth. This process continues till the specified depth is reached. Hence link information in all documents is a vital part of the information for crawling. This link information is processed to build a web graph of crawled pages. The web graph thus built can then be used for scoring the document or for ranking retrieved results.

Several algorithms use the web graph generated while crawling. These algorithms include the following.

- Recognizing hub pages: This process involves categorizing the page as a hub page (main page or home page of a site). The number of in-links and out-links of a page is used to do this task.
- Ranking algorithm: There are several ranking algorithms designed based on the link graph among crawled pages. Google's Page Rank algorithm (Arasu *et. al.*, 2002) is one of the famous ranking principles built based on the web graph of crawled pages.
- Document scoring: While indexing, each document is given certain boosting so as to indicate the importance of a document over other crawled documents. The intuitive methodology is to use the ratio of in-link to out-link score to identify the boosting factor of the document.

Apart from the above mentioned applications, web graphs are also used to find the relation between crawled documents, clustering of related documents in the crawl, *etc.*

4. Our proposed architecture

Based on the popularity of open source search frameworks and their method of implementation, we chose tools for building a multilingual search index. The latest version of Nutch with Hadoop was chosen as a crawler and Apache Solr for building the index of crawled documents. Both Nutch and Solr support customization of modules to make them adaptable to a desired application. The desired application for which these tools are used is to develop monolingual web search engine for 9 Indian languages, *viz.*, *Assamese, Bengali, Gujarati, Hindi, Marathi, Odiya, Tamil* and *Telugu.*

During the development process, several implementation challenges were encountered. Some of these challenges were handled by developing new modules like language identifier. These were additional functionality requirements. A few other problems were addressed by building resources for modules to handle different language phenomenon. The named entity list and multiword list for each of these 9 Indian languages are examples of building resources. But there exists some implementation challenges that require a policy decision or an architectural change. In this section we discuss these policy decisions and architectural changes of Solr to make it suitable for the desired application.

Before discussing changes in the architecture of a system, it is important to detail the infrastructure that is being used for the application. Changes in policy decisions should also consider the infrastructure of a search system. The crawling process is distributed across 12 systems and the generated single multilingual index is stored in a high end search server that hosts web application.

The experience of crawling around 6 million documents possesses a few implementation challenges. One of them being re-crawling of documents already crawled. Building a mechanism to re-crawl documents that are already crawled require some insight into types of documents that are being crawled. There were documents from different domains like news sites, blogs, general sites and encyclopedia sites. We observed that frequency of updation in these sites vary enormously. News sites update on hourly basis, while blogs gets updated at a frequency of few days. General web sites change more slowly and encyclopedia sites hardly change at all. These differences make it impossible to have same re-crawl period for all documents in the crawl.

A policy decision was made to have different re-crawl periods for different kinds of sites. Nutch framework provides a facility for adaptive fetching. This method of fetching monitors a document to be crawled and adapts the re-crawl period based on whether the document has changed between two successive crawls. This algorithm reduces/increases the re-crawl period of the document by a fixed interval if the document has changed/not changed respectively from the previous crawl. Policy decisions involve bootstrapping the re-crawl period and also to decide upon the interval for different types of documents.

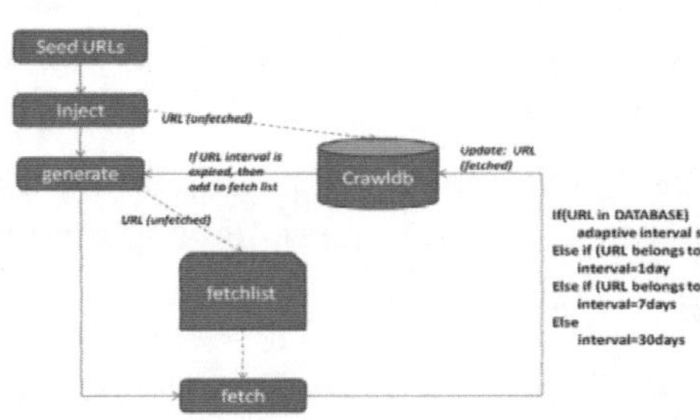

FIGURE 2 - Architecture depicting the re-crawl periods of a document

Figure 2 depicts decisions taken on re-crawl periods for different types of documents to be crawled. The bootstrapping values are used for initial fetching and then adaptive fetching is run for each of these documents. The challenge of categorizing documents is done at the level of domain name. List of sites belonging to news and blogs are built. These lists are used to fix the bootstrapping re-crawl period for a crawled document. Also, this list is prepared separately for each language.

Another important issue involves building multilingual index using Solr. Solr doesnot support use of single multilingual index, hence, architecture of Solr need to be modified. In Solr, all language analysis filters are listed in a configuration file called *schema.xml*. This file lists all filters to be called over a token stream of the document in an order. Token stream is a list of tokens that need to be indexed for a particular document. Architecture of the Solr system applies all the filters listed in *schema.xml* on the given token stream.

In the context of multilingual index, the language analyzer corresponding to the language of a document should be invoked while indexing. This demands a change in the architecture of Solr so that along with the token stream object, a language tag corresponding to the document is also passed in each module's API. Further the *schema.xml* file was changed to accommodate the language tag with each of these filters. Each filter listed in the configuration file has an associated language tag for which the filter is applicable. Figure 3 shows the differences in the *schema.xml* file before and after the architectural change in Solr. The filters listed in the *schema.xml* after changes indicate that only those filters whose language tag matches with the document's language tag are invoked while indexing.

```
<analyzer type="index">
  <tokenizer class="solr.StandardTokenizerFactory"/>
  <filter class="solr.StopFilterFactory" ignoreCase="true" words="stopwords.txt
PositionIncrements="true" />
  <!-- in this example, we will only use synonyms at query time
  <filter class="solr.SynonymFilterFactory" synonyms="index_synonyms.txt" ignor
="false"/>
  -->
  <filter class="solr.LowerCaseFilterFactory"/>
</analyzer>
<analyzer type="query">
  <tokenizer class="solr.StandardTokenizerFactory"/>
  <filter class="solr.StopFilterFactory" ignoreCase="true" words="stopwords.txt
PositionIncrements="true" />
  <filter class="solr.SynonymFilterFactory" synonyms="synonyms.txt" ignoreCase=
  <filter class="solr.LowerCaseFilterFactory"/>
</analyzer>
```

```
<analyzer>
    <tokenizer class="solr.WhitespaceTokenizerFactory"/>
    <filter class="solr.StopFilterFactory"
        lang="mr" ignoreCase="true" words="marathi-lib/stopwords_mr.txt"/>
    <filter class="solr.StopFilterFactory"
        lang="hi" ignoreCase="true" words="hindi-lib/stopwords_hi.txt"/>
    <filter class="solr.StopFilterFactory"
        lang="te" ignoreCase="true" words="telugu-lib/stopwords_te.txt"/>
    <filter class="solr.StopFilterFactory"
        lang="bn" ignoreCase="true" words="bengali-lib/stopwords_bn.txt"/>
    <filter class="solr.StopFilterFactory"
        lang="ta" ignoreCase="true" words="tamil-lib/stopwords_ta.txt"/>
    <filter class="solr.mr.MarathiStemFilterFactory"
                lang="mr" StemmerConfig = "                    apache-solr
/conf/marathi-lib/marathiConfig" MarathiStemmerBasedir="                ap
/solr/conf/marathi-lib"/>  -->
    <filter class="solr.hi.HindiStemFilterFactory"
                lang="hi" HindiStemmerConfig = "                    apache
```

FIGURE 3 - Snapshot of *schema.xml* (left) without change (right) with change

It is important to note that none of the open source frameworks discussed in the initial sections of this paper deal with building a multilingual index. To build a multilingual index, change in the architecture is must. This is irrespective of the framework chosen. In this direction, change in the architecture of open source indexing framework like Solr is an important step.

5. Research challenges in building multilingual index

The ranking algorithm drives the issues listed in this section. This is because, the impact of these issues is studied with respect to the ranking of retrieved documents. Most of the ranking algorithms used in text retrieval systems are based on variations of the tf (term frequency)-idf (inverse document frequency) based scoring. Tf–idf values are calculated based on the number of documents and terms in the document while building index.

In case of the multilingual index, it is possible to have the same indexed term that appears in multiple languages. For example, the term "दुर्गा" *{Durgaa; name of Indian Goddess}* is common for languages like *Marathi, Hindi, Konkani* and *Nepali*. This is because prior mentioned languages share the same script. This phenomenon will have an impact in evaluating idf value of the term. During creation of the multilingual index, every term is indexed with a list of documents in which the term is present. The list includes documents from all languages for the term that is same across languages. If the goal of a retrieval system is to retrieve documents for a query irrespective of languages then this phenomenon will not have any negative impact but, in case of cross lingual search or monolingual search, this kind of index would mislead. The idf value captured by this term is inclusive of all language documents, this is not desired for monolingual search of a particular language.

The intuitive solution to this problem is to tag the language for each document that has been indexed. Even though this methodology helps in identifying the language of a document while retrieving, this would not be a complete solution because of misleading idf score of the term. The idf scores are not altered during index building as only language tagging is done to the document posting list. Conceptually a term and its corresponding posting list should be present in the index as many times as that of the number of languages in which the term is present.

One of the solutions to this problem involves having language based multiple indices. This however solves the problem of recognizing a document's language as well as having precise idf score. On the other hand, this solution demands a change in the infrastructure and brings in performance issues. Variation in the number of documents of each language is so large in the web that few languages dominate the web content hence language based indexing is not prescribed. Another solution to this problem is to change the structure of the conventional inverted index and force the index to store multiple entries of the same term for each language in which it is present. This still stands as an open issue in building a single multilingual index.

Conclusion and perspectives

This paper dealt with building a multilingual index using an open source framework. We proposed an architecture by customizing an open source framework called Solr to build a multilingual index. Policy decisions taken and implementation challenges faced in this process are explained in detail. A wide range of open source search engine frameworks were discussed with their benefits and limitations. A comparative study based on several parameters of these search engines were done to get better perspective with respect to building an index.

Several features of the crawler were detailed for web based text retrieval system. These features were discussed so as to indicate the importance of the continuous crawling process and seamless modifications that need to be done to the index. The proposed architecture is already been implemented and the evaluation process of the search engine is in progress.

Few research challenges involved in building multilingual index were introduced. Having an indexed term sharing the script in multiple languages poses a challenge of getting wrong document frequency. This leads to an idea of having separate index for every language and also demands a change in infrastructure. These issues are yet to be addressed to build an efficient multilingual index.

Acknowledgments

Thanks to AAI Group, CDAC Pune for providing the crawling infrastructure for this application.

References

Apache Lucene (2011) *http://lucene.apache.org/*

Apache Solr (2011) *http://lucene.apache.org/solr/*

Apache Nutch (2005) *http://nutch.apache.org/*

Heritrix (2012) *https://webarchive.jira.com/wiki/display/Heritrix/Heritrix*

Apache Hadoop (2012) *http://hadoop.apache.org/*

Terrier (2011) *http://terrier.org/*

Lemur (2012) *http://www.lemurproject.org/*

Compass (2010) *http://compass-project.org/*

Oxyus (2010) *http://sourceforge.net/projects/oxyus/*

Lius (2010) *http://sourceforge.net/projects/lius/*

Regain (2004) *http://regain.sourceforge.net/*

YaCy (2007) *http://yacy.de/*

Swish-e (2007) *http://swish-e.org/*

MG4J (2005) *http://mg4j.di.unimi.it/*

Hounder (2010) *http://code.google.com/p/hounder/*

M. Khabsa, Stephen Carman, S. R. Choudhury and C. L. Giles (2012)A Framework for Bridging the Gap Between Open Source Search Tools, *In proceedings of the SIGIR 2012 Workshop on Open Source Information Retrieval*

Arasu, A. and Novak, J. and Tomkins, A. and Tomlin, J. (2002). "PageRank computation and the structure of the web: Experiments and algorithms". *Proceedings of the Eleventh International World Wide Web Conference, Poster Track*. Brisbane, Australia. pp. 107–117.

Apache Tika - The Parser interface (2012) *https://tika.apache.org/1.2/parser.html*

Automatic Searching for English-Vietnamese Documents on the Internet

Quoc Hung Ngo[1], *Dinh Dien*[2], *Werner Winiwarter*[3]
(1) Faculty of Computer Science, University of Information Technology, HoChiMinh City, Vietnam
(2) Faculty of Information Technology, University of Natural Sciences, HoChiMinh City, Vietnam
(3) University of Vienna, Research Group Data Analytics and Computing, Vienna, Austria
hungnq@uit.edu.vn, ddien@fit.hcmus.edu.vn,
werner.winiwarter@univie.ac.at

ABSTRACT

Bilingual corpora together with machine learning technology can be used to solve problems in natural language processing. In addition, bilingual corpora are useful for mapping linguistic tags of less popular languages, such as Vietnamese, and for studying comparative linguistics. However, Vietnamese corpora still have some shortcomings, especially English–Vietnamese bilingual corpora. This paper focuses on a searching method for bilingual Internet materials to support establishing an English–Vietnamese bilingual corpus. Based on the benefit of natural language processing toolkits, the system concentrates on using them as a solution for the problem of searching any Internet English–Vietnamese bilingual document without the need for any rules. We propose a method for extracting the main content of webpages without the need for frame of website or source of website before processing. Several other natural language processing tools included in our system are English-Vietnamese machine translation, extracting Vietnamese keywords, search engines, and comparing similar documents. Our experiments show several valuable auto-searching results for the US Embassy and Australian Embassy websites.

ABSTRACT (L_2)

Sự kết hợp giữa ngữ liệu song ngữ và máy học có thể giúp giải quyết nhiều vấn đề trong xử lý ngôn ngữ tự nhiên. Hơn nữa, các ngữ liệu song ngữ còn giúp ích rất nhiều trong việc ánh xạ nhãn ngôn ngữ cho các ngôn ngữ ít phổ biến như tiếng Việt và các nghiên cứu trong ngôn ngữ học so sánh. Tuy nhiên, ngữ liệu tiếng Việt vẫn còn có ít và hạn chế, đặc biệt là ngữ liệu song ngữ Anh-Việt. Bài báo này tập trung vào việc đưa ra một phương pháp tìm kiếm các tài liệu song ngữ từ nguồn dữ liệu Internet nhằm hỗ trợ cho việc xây dựng bộ ngữ liệu song ngữ Anh-Việt. Dựa trên những công cụ xử lý ngôn ngữ tự nhiên hiện có, hệ thống tập trung vào sử dụng chúng như là một giải pháp để giải quyết vấn đề tìm kiếm tài liệu song ngữ bất kỳ từ Internet mà không cần các quy tắc định trước. Chúng tôi cũng đề xuất một phương pháp để rút trích nội dung chính trang web mà không phải phụ thuộc vào thiết kế cũng như nguồn gốc của trang web đó. Một số công cụ xử lý ngôn ngữ tự nhiên khác sử dụng trong hệ thống của chúng tôi gồm có dịch máy tự động Anh-Việt, rút trích từ khóa tiếng Việt, tìm kiếm tài liệu từ Internet, và so sánh độ tương đồng văn bản. Bài báo cũng đưa ra một số thử nghiệm với các kết quả có giá trị trong quá trình tìm kiếm tự động các tài liệu song ngữ từ nguồn là trang web của Đại sứ quán Hoa Kỳ và Đại sứ quán Úc.

Keywords: Building Corpus, English-Vietnamese Bilingual Corpus, Search Engines
Keywords (L_2): Xây dựng Ngữ liệu, Ngữ liệu Song ngữ Anh-Việt, Công cụ Tìm kiếm

1 Introduction

Nowadays, corpus-based NLP research has been developing rapidly. There are many corpus-based studies and tools in machine translation (Koehn, 2005), information retrieval (Chen, 2000; Hawking, 1996; Oard, 1998), bitext alignment (Burkett, 2010), etc. These tools are built flexibly to work on many languages with an input corpus. For example, YAMCHA toolkit[1] was built for classifying tasks, such as POS tagging, Named Entity Recognition, and Text Chunking. It works effectively on English partly because of the quality of English corpora. However, its result on Vietnamese is not as good as on English because of the low quality and quantity of Vietnamese corpora. Moreover, bilingual corpora are also used to map linguistic tags from English to other languages (Dien, 2003). Hence, building monolingual and bilingual corpora is still valuable for many languages.

With the vast resources from the Internet, many researchers have studied to mine them to build bilingual corpora, such as Yang, C.C. and co-authors (Yang, 2003) and Zhang, Y. and co-authors (Zhang, 2006) for the English-Chinese pair; and Van, D.B. and Quoc, H.B. (Van, 2007) and Vu, P.D.M. (Vu, 2007) for the English-Vietnamese pair. However, their bilingual corpus building systems work on the supposition that these documents and their translations come from the same origin. It means that their URL addresses have the same domain or at least related domains. For the English-Vietnamese pair, authors used a bilingual dictionary to look up the meaning of words in the English documents, then search translation documents from a specific domain which cover these word meanings.

This project points out a system to search English-Vietnamese bilingual documents on the Internet by combining several NLP modules: extracting keywords, machine translation, search engine, and comparing similar documents. The system is based on a framework-free web content extraction module and search engines, therefore, it leads to our system being independent from the domains in which it searches the candidates of translation documents.

2 Related work

2.1 WPDE system

The WPDE system of Zhang and co-authors has three main stages: choosing candidate websites and extracting web contents; extracting parallel bilingual document pairs; and analyzing translation pairs (Zhang, 2006). Features which are used for choosing bilingual document pairs are domains in URLs, addresses and filename. The system determines such words, phrases such as "e", "en", "eng", "english" for English and "c", "ch", "chi", "cn" or "zh" for Chinese. Moreover, the system also uses the similarity in the html structure to detect translation candidate pairs. Analyzing the translation pairs is based on mechanical features, such as file size between two files, structures of html pages, etc. Finally, the WPDE's model uses the k-nearest neighbor approach to classify candidate pairs.

2.2 PTMiner System

PTMiner system of Chen, J., Nie, J.J. searches and identifies English–Chinese bilingual sites automatically (Chen, 2000). The system works in a similar way as Resnik's system (Resnik,

[1] http://chasen.org/~taku/software/yamcha/

1998). However, the authors used several features for filtering and detecting bilingual websites after downloading and used an approach based on web content and content alignment:

+ Filtering based on length of web pages,
+ Filtering based on structures,
+ Filtering based on content alignment.

2.3 English-Vietnamese Alignment System

The system of Van D.B. and Quoc H.B. (Van, 2007) and the system of Vu P.D.M. (Vu, 2007) download web pages from specific addresses or domains (such as www.voanews.com). In the same way as other systems, they remove HTML tags and get the main content as the raw document of the process. Then, they use several heuristics to detect parallel bilingual pairs. These candidates are analysed by a two-step filter:

+ Sentence length filtering
+ Lexicon-based sentence alignment

To reduce the dictionary size and increase precision, the authors used the Porter algorithm to stem English words before looking them up in the dictionary (Van, 2007). The authors applied their approach on the VOANews website, and the precision was 90% with about 8,500 bilingual sentence pairs. However, the limitation of the approach is using heuristics to create candidate pairs.

3 Research framework

The system uses an English–Vietnamese translation system, a keyword extraction tool based on Vietnamese words, and a document similarity comparison tool to find translated documents of English pages. Translated pages are found on the Internet by using the Google Search engine and NLP toolkits. Our searching system includes three main phases: (1) download webpages and get web content; (2) translate and search candidates; and (3) compare similarities between translated document and candidates (see Figure 1).

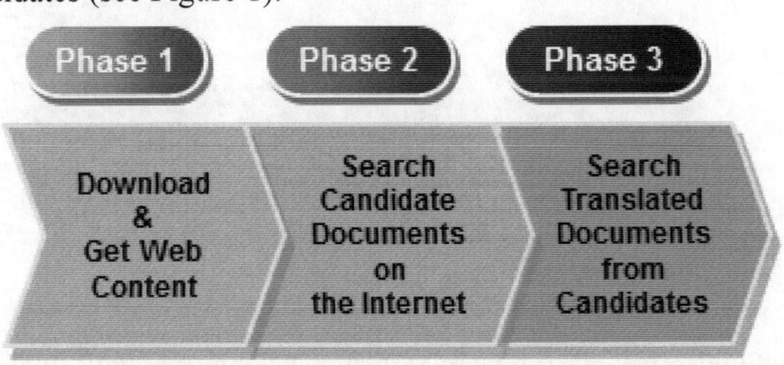

FIGURE 1 – Architure of the system for searching English-Vietnamese documents automatically

In general, Phase 1 includes downloading webpages, parsing the HTML files into the HTML trees, and then choosing the main content from the tree. Phase 2 includes translating main content of webpages into Vietnamese text by using Google Translate[2], extracting keywords from Vietnamese text, and searching Vietnamese documents on the Internet by extracted keywords

[2] http://translate.google.com/

and saving them as candidate documents. Finally, Phase 3 is simply comparing similarity between the translated Vietnamese document and candidate documents.

3.1 Get web content

Because results of the searching system can be from any resource domain, the first task of the system is detecting the main content of web pages of any domain which can be unknown in advance. These web pages are in English or Vietnamese. Unlike the framework-based approaches (Vu, 2007), our approach for this task is parsing web pages into HTML trees, identifying the content node in these trees, and then analysing their contents (see Figure 2 and Figure 3).

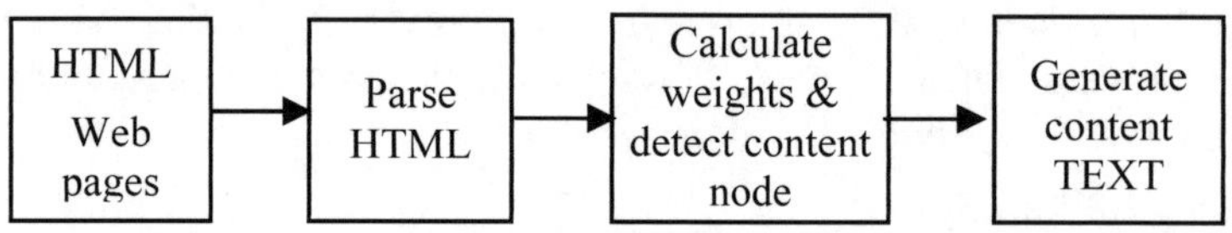

FIGURE 2 – Model of extracting web content

Parsing the web page into an HTML tree is based on the Majestic12 project[3] . Next, the process of extracting the main content includes two steps: analysing and giving marks to HTML nodes and then detecting the content node in the HTML tree. Giving marks to HTML nodes is based on counting content sentences for these nodes. Rules for calculating weights for nodes in HTML trees are (see an illustration in Figure 3):

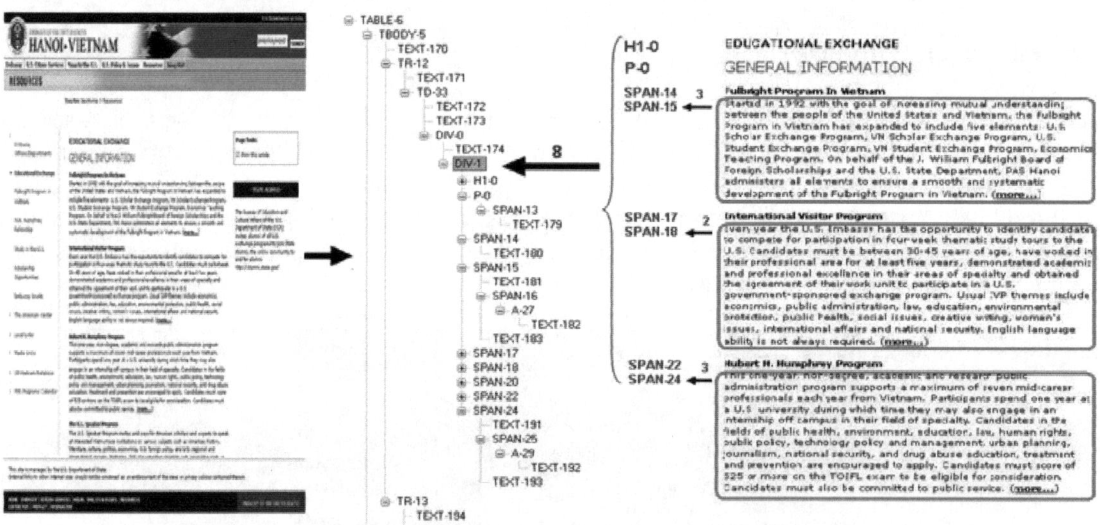

FIGURE 3 – Illustration of extracting web content for an US Embassy web page.

+ Only weighing nodes with TEXT tags because these nodes contain real content.
+ Weights of TEXT nodes are based on the number of their sentences. The more sentences nodes have, the higher weights are.
+ Nodes contain at least one paragraph.
+ Weights of parent nodes are calculated by summing all weights of children.

[3] http://www.majestic12.co.uk/projects/html_parser.php

Finally, the content node is the deepest node with the highest weight in the HTML tree. This approach can detect the content node and extract the main content of webpages without the need for frame of website as well as source of website before processing.

For example, node DIV-1 in Figure 3 contains node H1-0, P-0, SPAN-14, SPAN-15, SPAN-17, SPAN-18, SPAN-20, SPAN-22, and SPAN-24. Weight of node SPAN-15, SPAN-18, and SPAN-24 are 3, 2, and 3, respectively, while weight of other nodes is zero because they contain phrases instead of complete sentences. Hence, weight of node DIV-1 is 8 (= 3+2+3).

3.2 Get keywords for searching

Unlike English, Vietnamese words can be a group of several tokens, therefore, extracting Vietnamese keywords has to consider to extract words instead of tokens. Firstly, word segmentation is implemented by ensuring that extracted keywords have meaning and are real words. Steps for extracting Vietnamese keywords include:

+ Segment Vietnamese words,

+ Remove Stopwords,

+ Estimate term frequencies.

Calculating and extracting keywords has two sub-steps (Matsuo, 2004):

+ Calculate the co-occurrence frequency of word *w* and word *g* by *freq(w,g)*

+ Calculate co-occurrence with the $\chi 2$ estimate.

Keywords are words which have highest $\chi 2$ weights in the document. In our experiment, the system only extracts 3 first keywords for next searching step (based on our experiment shown in Section 4.2).

3.3 Using search engines for searching candidates

Keywords are provided for the searching system by generating an address which includes these keywords. Searching result is search engines' response file which is acquired by this address. For example, keywords "***building parallel corpus***" generate URL addresses for searching systems:

Google: http://www.google.com.vn/search?hl=vi&q=building+parallel+corpus

Yahoo: http://search.yahoo.com/search?p=building+parallel+corpus

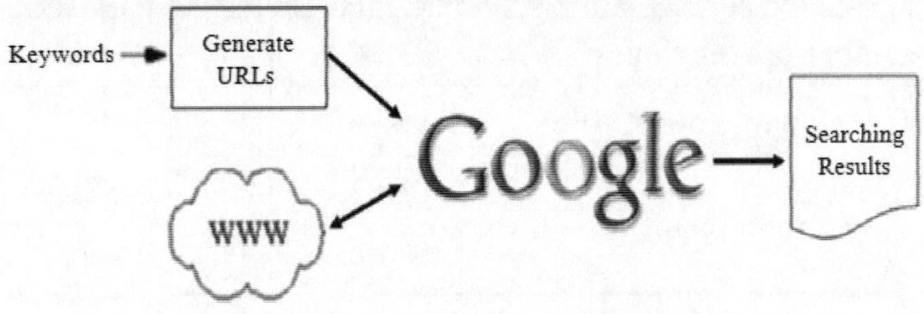

FIGURE 4 – Searching process by Google system

By acquiring web page of these addresses, the system gains searching results from Google or Yahoo (as shown in Figure 4). Google and Yahoo also support searching results which come from any domain, a specific domain or except a specific domain. This option allows our auto-searching system to be able to direct its searching results. It can be implemented by adding following parameters:

– Search in specific domain: ***site:<domain>***

– Search in except domain: -***site:<domain>***

For example, the URL address for searching "*building parallel corpus*" from site www.aclweb.org is "site:aclweb.org building parallel corpus". It means that every result of the search engine will come from aclweb.org.

From Google's results, the system continues to download candidate documents from the result addresses and extracts main content to store them as candidates for evaluating translation pairs at phase 3, comparing similarity between the automatic translation document and candidates.

3.4 Document comparison for Vietnamese

In general, the comparison module includes two steps: mechanical filter and content-based similarity comparison. The mechanical filter uses several features to remove less suitable candidates, such as rate of file size between two documents, the differences in number of paragraphs or sentences. The content-based similarity comparison step calculates documents as vectors. Words which are chosen for representation in the vector are the top 30% frequent words in the document. Comparing two documents becomes calculating the distance between two vectors by measuring the Euclidean distance between two document vectors (Guo, 2008).

4 Experiments and results

4.1 Get web content

In general, getting web content works effectively on embassy websites and result webpages of the searching process. Table 1 shows the result of getting web content from the US Embassy website and searching results from the Internet (from unanticipated domains).

For news expresses, the number of articles is very huge and there is additional information, such as title, abstract, category, publish date, authors, etc. This information is very useful for other natural language processing tasks which are based on this corpus. Hence, the system builds several specific definitions to identify content nodes for these websites. These definitions help the system to be able to extract effectively and get more information fields.

	USEmbassy	**Other Domains**[4]
Number of web pages	2,054	3,973
Number of main content files	1,870	3,035
Correct result	1,853	2,885
	99%	95%

TABLE 1 – Result of extracting main content

4.2 Keywords for search engines

Results of search engines depend on the provided keywords. To know how many keywords are

[4] Statistics based on 3,973 return records of the search engine from out of the US. Embassy website.

good for the bilingual document searching system, this project implements an experiment on the data from the Australian embassy website with 86 parallel document pairs. Tests acquire 30 returns from the Google search engine. The test has a different number of keywords to calculate the precision of returns of the search engine for our system. The result is shown in Table 2.

Number of keywords	2	3	4	5	6
Results of Google search	1,652	1,419	1,393	1,174	1,118
Result in parallel pairs	37	45	35	22	13

TABLE 2 – Results of Google search with several different numbers of keywords

Our experiments show that the accuracy of the searching module is highest when looking for 3 keywords for each document (see Table 2). In this test, correct results of search engines are addresses in the parallel pairs. In fact, the Google's response for 3 keywords has 1,419 results with 45 correct results, while it has 1,652 results with 37 correct results for 2 keywords. Similarly, the Google search just acquires 35, 22 and 13 correct results when searching with 4, 5, and 6 keywords, respectively.

4.3 Searching results on embassy websites

In our first experiment, the system carries out several tests on the US Embassy and Australian Embassy websites with totally 2,500 web pages in which there are 440 parallel English–Vietnamese document pairs (see Table 3).

Website	URL	Content pages	Data size
USEmbassy: English site	896	832	2.4 MB
USEmbassy: Vietnamese site	1,150	1,076	12.8 MB
AUEmbassy: English site	207	178	2.4 MB
AUEmbassy: Vietnamese site	158	128	12.8 MB

TABLE 3 – Characteristics of data from embassy websites

Table 4 shows the result of bilingual website of the US Embassy and Australian Embassy with the similarity threshold of 0.7 .

Website	Parallel pairs	Results	Precision (%)	Recall (%)
USEmbassy	354	197	92%	51%
AUEmbassy	86	45	93%	49%

TABLE 4 – Result of the bilingual document searching system on the US Embassy and Australian embassy pages after Phase 1

Table 5 shows the results of whole system when applying it to the US Embassy and Australian Embassy bilingual websites.

Website	Parallel pairs	Results	Precision (%)	Recall (%)
USEmbassy	354	350	90%	89%
AUEmbassy	86	84	92%	90%

TABLE 5 – Result of the searching bilingual document system on the US Embassy and Australian Embassy pages after Phase 2

In our experiments, recall parameter is only evaluated on the webpages of the US Embassy and Australian Embassy instead of on the global Internet because the resources from the Internet are enormous and, maybe, there are some correct pages from other domains which our system does not discover.

4.4 Searching result on other websites

Result of searching translation documents depends on the content of web pages. Translation documents come from any domain in the Internet. However, the original documents which are translated and then posted on other domains as well as re-published as translation versions on other locations mainly come from the Press Releases division of the Embassy website.

Another experiment is focused on news announcements of the US Embassy. It has 354 English news articles in the Press Releases section of the US Embassy website while only some articles are translated into Vietnamese and posted on the Embassy website (see Table 6).

Website	English pages (Press Releases)	Vietnamese documents in searching results
USEmbassy	354	52

TABLE 6 – Result of searching parallel documents from embassy websites

In 52 found results, there are ten results for which there are no translations on the US Embassy website. These articles are news announcements which were published in English by the US Embassy before 2004 (without in Vietnamese) and which were translated and published on News expresses.

5 Conclusions

The project has pointed out a process to search English—Vietnamese bilingual documents on the Internet. The approach allows to look for translation documents from any resource instead of from a specific domain. We also demonstrated the process by building an application to search bilingual documents automatically, the result on the US Embassy and Australian Embassy websites are very promising. Moreover, the project also has produced several valuable tools, such as getting web content, extracting Vietnamese keywords, comparing similar documents. Particularly, for getting main content, we presented a method to calculate content nodes in the HTML tree and extract the main content from the HTML parser result. This tool can be used for NLP projects which are based on web contents.

6 References

Burkett, D., Petrov, P., Blitzer, J., and Klein, D. (2010). Learning Better Monolingual Models with Unannotated Bilingual Text. Proceedings of CoNLL 2010, pp. 46-54.

Chen J., and Nie, J. (2000). Parallel Web Text Mining for Cross-Language IR. Proceedings of RIAO-2000: Content-Based Multimedia Information Access. College de France, Paris, France, pp. 188-192.

Dien, D., and Kiem, H. (2003). POS-tagger for English-Vietnamese bilingual corpus, Proceedings of HLT-NAACL, Workshop on Building and Using Parallel Texts, pp. 88-95.

Guo, Q. (2008). The Similarity Computing of Documents Based on VSM, 32nd Annual IEEE International Computer Software and Applications Conference, pp. 585-586.

Koehn, Ph. (2005). Europarl: A Parallel Corpus for Statistical Machine Translation, In Proceedings of the 10th Machine Translation Summit, Phuket, Thailand, pp. 79-86.

Hawking, D., Bailey, P., and Campbell, D. (1996). A Parallel Document Retrieval Server for the World Wide Web. Proceedings of the Australian Document Computing Symposium (ADCS), Melbourne, pp. 73-78.

Matsuo, Y., and Ishizuka, M. (2004). Keyword Extraction From A Single Document Using Word Co-Occurrence Statistical Information, International Journal on Artificial Intelligence Tools, Vol. 13, No. 1, pp. 157-169.

Oard, D. W., and Diekema, A. R. (1998). Cross-Language Information Retrieval. Annual Review of Information Science and Technology (ARIST), Volume 33, pp. 223-256.

Resnik, P. (1998). Parallel Stands: A preliminary investigation into mining the web for bilingual text. Proceedings of AMTA'98, pp. 72-82.

Van, D.B., and Quoc, H.B. (2007). Automatic Construction of English-Vietnamese Parallel Corpus through Web Mining, In Proceedings of 5th IEEE International Conference on Computer Science - Research, Innovation and Vision of the Future (RIVF'2007), Hanoi, Vietnam, pp. 261-266.

Vu, P.D.M. (2007). Building bilingual corpus by mining data from Internet, Master thesis in Computer Science, University of Natural Science, HoChiMinh City, Vietnam, 2007 (in Vietnamese).

Yang, C.C., and Li, K.W. (2003). Automatic Construction of English/Chinese. Parallel Corpora, Journal of the American Society for Information Science and Technology, pp. 730-742.

Zhang, Y., Wu, K., Gao, J., and Vines, P. (2006). Automatic Acquisition of Chinese–English Parallel Corpus from the Web. Advances in Information Retrieval, Volume 3936/2006, pp. 420-431.

Error tracking in search engine development

Swapnil Chaudhari[1] *Arjun Atreya V*[1] *Pushpak Bhattacharyya*[1] *Ganesh Ramakrishnan*[1]
(1) Department of CSE, IIT Bombay
{swapnil, arjun, pb, ganesh}@cse.iitb.ac.in

ABSTRACT

In this paper, we describe a tool that allows one to track the output of every module of a search engine. The tool provides the ability to perform pseudo error-correction by allowing the user to modify these outputs or tune parameters of the modules to check for improvement of results. Often it is important to see if certain surface level changes can help in the improvement of the result quality. This is crucial since it saves the immediate need to make changes in the system in terms of resource updation or development efforts. We describe query processing pipeline in sufficient detail and then show the efficacy of our tool for an example in Marathi along with giving a thorough error analysis for the example considered. We believe this paper will establish that such a tool is of significant importance for instant detection and correction of errors along with giving the readers an idea on how to develop the same.

KEYWORDS: INFORMATION RETRIEVAL, TRACKER, ERROR TRACKING, ERROR ANALYSIS TOOL

1 Introduction

Information retrieval refers to searching relevant documents satisfying the user information need. User information need is typically captured in the form of a query. A search system consists of two parts viz. offline processing and online processing.

Offline processing mainly consists of two parts – crawling and indexing. In crawling, documents from the web are fetched and stored. These documents have to be parsed and stored in optimal way in terms of both storage space and search time. For efficient retrieval of documents, an inverted index of terms in the documents is created.

Online processing consists of converting the user's information need in a format which facilitates the matching of query terms with terms in documents. Query expansion using feedback or thesaurus, semantic search, *etc.* are different ways of capturing user information need. A naive way to capture information need is to consider query terms as representative of user information need. These terms in the query have to be processed before they can be used to search documents. Processing of terms involves stop word removal, stemming and query formulation. Some of the search engines also do named entity recognition, multi word recognition or word sense disambiguation to enhance query processing. This processing is done in the form of a pipeline where output of one stage is fed as input to the next stage.

Most of these modules need language based resources and processing. For example, named entity recognition requires applying machine learning techniques on a large corpus and extracting named entities out of it. The output of named entity recognition engine is used as dictionary for searching named entities in the query. All such modules cannot generate an exhaustive resource list and are vulnerable to errors. Errors in each module degrade the overall performance of the system. Evaluation forums like TREC (TREC, 1992), CLEF (CLEF, 2000), NTCIR (NTCIR, 1999) and FIRE (FIRE, 2008) provide platform to evaluate the system performance in terms of precision, recall, MAP value, *etc.* However, these measures indicate end to end performance of the system and do not evaluate performance of individual module in the system. Since the architecture is pipelined, the error propagates and multiplies. In such architecture, tracking the root cause of error is important. To facilitate this *tracker* was developed.

Tracker is a tool which captures the input and output information of each stage of the pipeline and displays it to the assessor. This helps in identifying the root cause of the error. A relevance judgement tool is integrated in tracker to aid storing relevance judgments for each query.

The roadmap of the paper is as follows. We describe query processing pipeline in the next section with an example case of Marathi. In section 3, we look at different types of errors that can occur in a search engine. Then we discuss at different functionalities in Tracker in section 4 followed by implementation details in section 5. Tracker was used by more than 100 developers and assessors across the country. Section 6 covers these user experiences about tracker.

2 Query processing pipeline

Figure 1 illustrates query processing pipeline. A query given in Marathi is

मुंबईमधील किंवा रायगडमधील सुंदर राष्ट्रीय उद्यान

mumbaimadhil kiva raaygadmadhil sundar raashtriya udyaan

in Mumbai or in Raigad beautiful national park

beautiful national park in Mumbai or Raigad

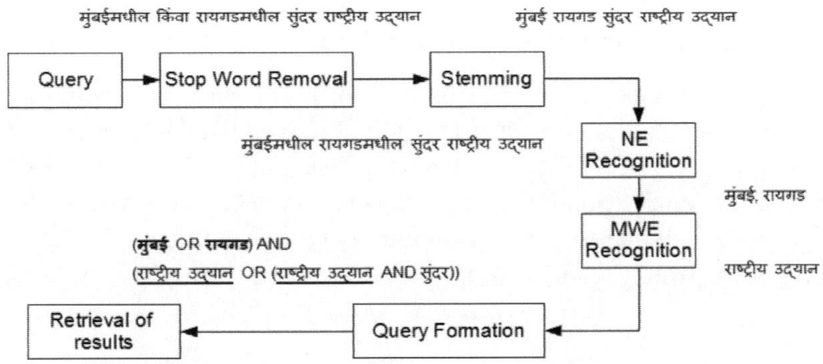

FIGURE 1- Query Processing illustrated with Marathi

The stop word removal module removes stop words by doing a dictionary look up. In this query किंवा (*kiva*) (*or*) is a stop word in Marathi which gets removed in this stage. The resultant query after removing stop word is मुंबईमधील रायगडमधील सुंदर राष्ट्रीय उद्यान (*mumbaimadhil raaygadmadhil sundar raashtriya udyaan*). This is given as an input to the stemmer.

The Marathi stemmer (Bapat *et. al*, 2010) is implemented as a Finite State Transducer in which we specify a word as a sequence of legal morphemes. Each morpheme corresponding to the root word is called the stem and this stem possesses features which are extracted by the means of a morphological parser. In this case, the suffix मधील (*madhil*) (*in*) is attached to words मुंबई (*mumbai*) (*Mumbai*) and रायगड (*raajgad*) (*Raigad*). This suffix is removed by the stemmer and the words मुंबईमधील (*mumbaimadhil*) (*in Mumbai*) and रायगडमधील (*raaygadmadhil*) (*in Raigad*) are reduced to their root forms मुंबई (*mumbai*) (*Mumbai*) and रायगड (*raaygad*) (*Raigad*) respectively. The resultant query is मुंबई रायगड सुंदर राष्ट्रीय उद्यान (*Mumbai raaygad sundar raashtriya udyaan*). The Marathi stemmer stems the words with an accuracy of 95 percent. These stemmed words are used by the named entity recognition module to detect named entities in the query.

The named entity recognition module detects named entities by searching through a dictionary of named entities. This dictionary is pre-computed from a large corpus. In this query, मुंबई (*mumbai*) (*Mumbai*) and रायगड (*raaygad*) (*Raigad*) are two named entities. After detecting named entities, multi-words in the query are detected.

The multi-word detection module takes an n-gram window to match the query terms against a dictionary of multi-words. This dictionary is precompiled from a large corpus. In this query, राष्ट्रीय उद्यान (*raashtriya udyaan*) (*national park*) is a multiword. After detecting the important terms in the query like named entities and multi-words, we form a Boolean query. The terms in the query are given appropriate boosts based on their importance. The results retrieved are then presented to the user. The quality of these set of results is a function of the accuracy of individual modules. Diagnostics of each module is called for at this stage.

3 Error analysis

Each module can contribute to error and affect the overall performance of the system. The following section describes the different kinds of errors that can occur in each stage of pipeline.

3.1.1 Types of errors and their impact on performance

In the stop word removal stage, errors can be due to a stop word not being detected by the module. This can boost non-relevant results to the top of ranked list because of high count of stop word content in it. Another possible error is wrongly detecting an important word as stop word and removing it from the query. Stemming involves two kinds of errors viz. Wrong stem and no stem. A wrong stem may be due to over-stemming or under stemming. Wrong stem results in change in meaning of the word used in the query. This can cause topic drift in results.

E.g. Consider the query

गुजरातचे लोक

gujaraatche loka

of Gujarat people

People of Gujarat

In this case, over stemming गुजरातचे (gujaraatche) (of Gujarat) will give root गुजर (gujar) (Gujar) instead of correct root गुजरात (gujarat) (Gujarat). गुजर (gujar) (Gujar) is a caste while गुजरात (gujarat) (Gujarat) is a state name. The query formed after stemming is (gujar people) (Gujar people). Instead of getting information about people of Gujarat, the user will get results related to people belonging to Gujar caste.

If the stemmer is not able to stem the word, it may return the original query term. In both cases, the error in stemming gets propagated to further stages. An error in stemming may cause error in detecting named entities and multi-words. In the above example, if गुजरातचे (gujaraatche) (of Gujarat) is not stemmed, then named entity गुजरात (gujarat) (Gujarat) will not be recognized. If a named entity is not recognized, we may lose the information about importance of that word. Similarly, if a multiword is not recognized, then information about importance as well as proximity of those query terms is lost. For example, consider the multi-word query राष्ट्रीय उद्यान (*raashtriya udyaan*) (*national park*). In this, if multi-word identification fails, then राष्ट्रीय (*raashtriya*) (*national*) and उद्यान (*udyaan*) (*park*) will be searched as two different entities. The word राष्ट्रीय (*raashtriya*) (*national*) can match with documents containing terms like राष्ट्रीय सीमा (*raashtriya seema*) (*national border*), राष्ट्रीय संस्था (*raashtriya sansthaa*) (*national institute*), राष्ट्रीय संग्रहालय (*raashtriya sangrahaalay*) (*national museum*), *etc.* and retrieve irrelevant results.

An error in a module may be corrected by adding resources or might require re-engineering to solve the issue. Changing the module for each error and retesting the system after change is quite time consuming. One way to analyze this problem is pseudo error correction. This involves correcting the output of a particular module temporarily without making a change in the module for detecting errors in further modules. To facilitate monitoring the outputs of individual modules and pseudo error correction, *tracker* was developed. As per our knowledge, no such tool for a search engine exists.

4 Tracker

Tracker is an error analysis tool developed to assist developers and assessors to analyze each module of a search engine for errors and tune the system parameter to find the best parameters that suit the system. Tracker captures input and output of each module for a query and displays them to the assessor. The assessor can then manually judge the outputs as correct or incorrect. This helps in detecting errors in modules.

For example, while processing the query मुंबईमधील किंवा रायगडमधील सुंदर राष्ट्रीय उद्यान (*mumbaimadhil kiva raaygadmadhil sundar raashtriya udyaan*), let us assume that stemmer is not able to remove the suffix मधील (*madhil*) (*in*) from words मुंबईमधील (*mumbaimadhil*) (*in Mumbai*) and रायगडमधील (*raaygadmadhil*) (*in Raigad*). As a result, the named entity module will not be able to detect मुंबई (*mumbai*) (*Mumbai*) and रायगड (*raaygad*) (*Raigad*) as named entities. By looking at the output of stemming stage, the assessor can conclude that stemmer should be further improved. However, even if we correct the stemmer, we are not sure whether named entity module will detect मुंबई (*mumbai*) (*Mumbai*) and रायगड (*raaygad*) (*Raigad*) as named entities.

To avoid delay in the detection of errors in subsequent modules, *Tracker allows assessor to replace the output of a particular module with the correct output without actually modifying the module*. Once the assessor submits the query again after modifying the stemmer output, the new corrected output will override the existing output and will be fed as input to next stage. This can be done incrementally to detect errors in all the modules. While doing this, tracker stores information about past changes and masks all the outputs of the modules which assessor wish to change. This information is stored till the assessor wish to clear it for that query. Let us see some additional capabilities in tracker which makes development and bug detection faster.

4.1.1 Capabilities of Tracker

A relevance judgement tool[1] is integrated with the tracker which allows the user to perform relevance judgement on a query. These judgements are stored in a database for future reference. The relevance judgements are pre-populated on the interface for subsequent firing of the same query. The result set for a query may change because of change in a module's output. The assessor has to perform relevance judgements only for those URLs whose relevance judgement was not stored earlier. This saves time of re-judging the same page for a query. The tracker automatically calculates precision values at rank 5 and 10 using these judgements. These figures help the assessor in analyzing the effect of current change in module outputs on the precision values of the result set.

Tracker also maintains a revision history for each query fired by the assessor. This history captures the changes done in different modules and corresponding precision values. This helps in summarizing what kind of changes can help to improve the system as a whole. Consider a scenario where the system was tested for around 100 queries. Out of these queries, 60% of the queries showed improvement after changing the output of stemmer. 20-30% showed improvement after modifying named entity recognition output and the rest didn't show a significant change in results after modifying any output. In this case, stemmer and named entity

[1] A relevance judgement tool is an interface to help an assessor mark a retrieved URL as relevant, partially relevant, link-relevant, irrelevant and error

recognition modules should be improved. Such data can help prioritize tasks for development and help improve the system faster.

5 Implementation Details

Tracker is developed in Java. Tracker has a web interface which is linked to the results page of the search engine. The system maintains login information of the assessors to store relevance judgement of each assessor separately in a database. Relevance judgment is stored in a table with primary key as combination of the username of assessor, query and URL of the search result. When a query is fired, the input and output of each module is stored in an object. This object persists till expiry of session. The values captured in the object are displayed to the assessors on the tracker web interface. The assessor is allowed to modify the output of any module. The modified output is stored back in the object and used for overriding the output of the stages for which modification is done. The object stores change information till either session expires or user fires a different query. In the latter case, the object is used for storing information about new query. A separate table is created in database for maintaining revision history of the changes done for each query.

Figure 2 shows a screen of the tracker interface used for tracking output. The first column specifies the level in module hierarchy, second denotes module name and the last column shows the output of the corresponding output. Since it is pipeline architecture, the output of one module directly forms input of other module and hence inputs are not explicitly shown. The assessors are allowed to edit one level at a time which enables tracking incremental changes.

Level	Field Name	Field Value
0	Query	मुंबईमधील किंवा रायगडमधील सुंदर राष्ट्रीय उद्यान
1	StopWord Output :	मुंबईमधील रायगडमधील सुंद
2	Stemmer Output :	मुंबईमधील रायगडमधील सुंद
3	NERs identified (';' separated) :	
3	NER Boost :	12.0
4	MWEs identified (';' separated) :	राष्ट्रीय उद्यान
4	MWE Boost (Content) :	12.0
	Query Boost :	
5	Anchor Boost :	1.0
5	Content Boost :	10.0
5	Title Boost :	3.0
5	Host Boost :	2.0
5	Phrase Boost :	1.0
5	URL Boost :	3.0
5	Domain Boost :	1.0
	Lucene Query	
	+lang:mr domain:tourism +(MWE:"राष्ट्रीय उद्यान"^12.0 content:"राष्ट्रीय उद्यान"^12.0 title:"राष्ट्रीय उद्यान"^12.0) (url:मुंबईमधील^3.0 anchor:मुंबईमधील content:मुंबईमधील^10.0 title:मुंबईमधील^3.0 host:मुंबईमधील^2.0) (url:रायगडमधील^3.0 anchor:रायगडमधील content:रायगडमधील^10.0 title:रायगडमधील^3.0 host:रायगडमधील^2.0) (url:सुंदर^3.0 anchor:सुंदर content:सुंदर^10.0 title:सुंदर^3.0 host:सुंदर^2.0) (url:राष्ट्रीय^3.0 anchor:राष्ट्रीय content:राष्ट्रीय^10.0 title:राष्ट्रीय^3.0 host:राष्ट्रीय^2.0) (url:उद्यान^3.0 anchor:उद्यान content:उद्यान^10.0 title:उद्यान^3.0 host:उद्यान^2.0) url:"मुंबईमधील रायगडमधील सुंदर राष्ट्रीय उद्यान"~2147483647^3.0 anchor:"मुंबईमधील रायगडमधील सुंदर राष्ट्रीय उद्यान"~4 content:"मुंबईमधील रायगडमधील सुंदर राष्ट्रीय उद्यान"~2147483647^10.0 title:"मुंबईमधील रायगडमधील सुंदर राष्ट्रीय उद्यान"~2147483647^3.0 host:"मुंबईमधील रायगडमधील सुंदर राष्ट्रीय उद्यान"~2147483647^2.0	
	Editing Level (1-5)	*
	Precision At 5	0.15
	Precision At 10	0.275
	Submit	

FIGURE 2- Tracker Web Interface

Figure 3 shows how a revision history for each query is maintained. The boost values used for named entity, multi-word, title, content, *etc.* are part of system parameters which can be tuned using tracker. In this case change in stemmer, which is second module in the pipeline, causes significant rise in precision values. The third row in figure shows the effect of reducing named entity boost during query formulation. The fourth row depicts that change in title boost have no effect on precision values for this query.

मुंबईमधील किंवा रायगडमधील सुंदर राष्ट्रीय उद्यान

Revision Date	Module No	Precision At 5	Precision At 10	Stop Word Output	Stemmer Output	NERs Identified	NER Boost Value	MWEs Identified	MWE Boost Value	Query Anchor Boost	Query Content Boost	Query Title Boost	Query Host Boost	Query Phrase Boost	Query URL Boost	Query Domain Boost
2012-10-19 10:36:24.0	0	0.15	0.275	मुंबईमधील रायगडमधील सुंदर राष्ट्रीय उद्यान	मुंबईमधील रायगडमधील सुंदर राष्ट्रीय उद्यान		12.0	राष्ट्रीय उद्यान	12.0	1.0	10.0	3.0	2.0	1.0	3.0	1.0
2012-10-19 23:22:38.0	2	0.8	0.475	मुंबईमधील रायगडमधील सुंदर राष्ट्रीय उद्यान	मुंबई रायगड सुंदर राष्ट्रीय उद्यान	मुंबई;रायगड	12.0	राष्ट्रीय उद्यान	12.0	1.0	10.0	3.0	2.0	1.0	3.0	1.0
2012-11-18 14:38:44.0	3	0.8	0.45	मुंबईमधील रायगडमधील सुंदर राष्ट्रीय उद्यान	मुंबई रायगड सुंदर राष्ट्रीय उद्यान	मुंबई;रायगड	5.0	राष्ट्रीय उद्यान	12.0	1.0	10.0	3.0	2.0	1.0	3.0	1.0
2012-11-18 14:39:44.0	5	0.8	0.45	मुंबईमधील रायगडमधील सुंदर राष्ट्रीय उद्यान	मुंबई रायगड सुंदर राष्ट्रीय उद्यान	मुंबई;रायगड	5.0	राष्ट्रीय उद्यान	12.0	1.0	10.0	8.0	2.0	1.0	3.0	1.0

FIGURE 3- Revision History

6 User experiences of Tracker

Tracker was used by more than 100 developers and assessors all over India for tracing errors in multiple languages. A sample of overall feedback obtained is as follows:

- Positive points:
  - Useful tool to track query processing
  - Easy to evaluate and check the system's performance on varying boosts factors.
  - Revision History helps in comparing results.
- Improvements Suggested:
  - Should be extended to calculate precision values up to 25 results.
  - Should be extended to support dynamic resource updation while tracking changes.

Conclusion and perspectives

In this paper, we have highlighted the importance of having an error analysis tool like tracker to track individual modules of a large scale system. Tracker facilitates detection of errors in different modules of the search engine. Pseudo error correction of outputs helps discovering further errors in the system without making a change in the module. With an example of Marathi retrieval system, we have shown the use of tracker and its effectiveness in error analysis and analyzing performance of the system for various system parameters. Tracker is independent of the language of search and portable across search systems. This idea can be extended for making error analysis tools for any large scale system based on pipelined architecture.

Acknowledgments

Thanks to DAIICT, Gujarat for their contribution in developing a relevance judgement tool that is integrated with the tracker.

References

Text REtrieval Conference (TREC) Home Page (1992). *http://trec.nist.gov/*

The CLEF Initiative (Conference and Labs of the Evaluation Forum) – Homepage (2000). *http://www.clef-initiative.eu/*

NTCIR HOME (1999). *http://research.nii.ac.jp/ntcir/index-en.html*

FIRE - Forum for Information Retrieval Evaluation (2008). *http://www.isical.ac.in/~clia/*

Mugdha Bapat, Harshada Gune, Pushpak Bhattacharyya (2010). A Paradigm-Based Finite State Morphological Analyzer for Marathi. *Proceedings of the 1st Workshop on South and Southeast Asian Natural Language Processing (WSSANLP)*, pages 26–34, the 23rd International Conference on Computational Linguistics (COLING), Beijing, August 2010.

An Efficient Database Design for IndoWordNet Development Using Hybrid Approach

Venkatesh Prabhu[2] *Shilpa Desai*[1] *Hanumant Redkar*[1]
Neha Prabhugaonkar[1] *Apurva Nagvenkar*[1] *Ramdas Karmali*[1]
(1) GOA UNIVERSITY, Taleigao - Goa
(2) THYWAY CREATIONS, Mapusa - Goa
venkateshprabhu@thywayindia.com, sndesai@gmail.com, hanumantredkar@gmail.com, nehapgaonkar.1920@gmail.com, apurv.nagvenkar@gmail.com, rnk@unigoa.ac.in

ABSTRACT
WordNet is a crucial resource that aids in Natural Language Processing (NLP) tasks such as Machine Translation, Information Retrieval, Word Sense Disambiguation, Multi-lingual Dictionary creation, etc. The IndoWordNet is a multilingual WordNet which links WordNets of different Indian languages on a common identification number given to each concept. WordNet is designed to capture the vocabulary of a language and can be considered as a dictionary cum thesaurus and much more. WordNets for some Indian Languages are being developed using expansion approach.

In this paper we have discussed the details and our experiences during the evolution of this database design while working on the Indradhanush WordNet Project. The Indradhanush WordNet Project is working on the development of WordNets for seven Indian languages. Our database design gives an efficient plan for storage of WordNet data for all languages. In addition it extends the design to hold specific concepts for a language.

KEYWORDS: WordNet, IndoWordNet, synset, database design, expansion approach, semantic relation, lexical relation.

---

1 Introduction

1.1 WordNet and its storage methods

WordNet (Miller, 1993) maintains the concepts in a language, relations between concepts and their ontological details. The concept in a language is captured as a Synonym set called synset. The IndoWordNet is a multilingual WordNet which links WordNets of different Indian languages on a common identification number called as synset Id. A synset represents a unique concept in a language. Synset is composed of a Gloss describing the concept, example sentences and a set of synonym words that are used for the concept. Besides synset data, WordNet maintains many lexical and semantic relations. Lexical relations (Fellbaum, 1998) like antonymy, gradation are between words in a language whereas semantic relations like hypernymy, hyponymy are between concepts in a language. Ontology details for a synset are also maintained in a WordNet.

WordNet contains information about nouns, verbs, adjectives and adverbs and is organized around the notion of a synset. Earlier the WordNet data was stored in flat text files. This storage method was found insufficient for developing multi-lingual WordNet applications requiring random access to synsets or its constituents. This was the motivation for storage of data in a relational database. The design of the database was for a single language WordNet. The approach used to build the WordNet had an impact on how the data should be ideally stored. The various WordNet development approaches are discussed next.

1.2 WordNet development Approaches and its impact on the storage structure

Various approaches are followed in the construction of WordNets across the languages of the world. WordNets are constructed by following either the merge approach or the expansion approach (Vossen, 1998). The merge approach is also referred to as WordNet construction from *first principles* (Bhattacharyya, 2010). Here exhaustive sense repository of each word is first recorded. Then the lexicographers constructs a synset for each sense, obeying the three principles namely principle of minimality, coverage and replacebility (Bhattacharyya, 2010).

For many Indian languages, WordNets are constructed using the expansion model where Hindi WordNet synsets are taken as a source. The concepts provided along with the Hindi synsets are first conceived and appropriate concepts in target language are manually provided by the language experts. The target language synsets are then built based on the concepts created keeping in view the three principles mentioned above. The expansion approach gives rise to a multi-WordNet where a concept is given an id called synset-id and is present in all target language WordNets. One of our contributions is the storage structure of such a multi-WordNet. We maintain the data common to all languages in a central shared database for the multi-WordNet and the data which changes as per the language in separate databases for each language. The issues regarding the approach which affect the storage structure are discussed next.

1.3 Advantages and disadvantages of each approach

Both the merge and expansion approaches have their advantages and disadvantages. The advantages of using merge approach are: There is no distracting influence of another language, which happens when the lexicographer encounters culture and region specific concepts of the source language. The quality of the WordNet is good but the process is typically slow. The advantages of using expansion approach are: Using this approach, instead of creating the synset from the scratch, synsets are created by referring to existing WordNet of the related language. WordNet development process becomes faster as the gloss and synset of the source language is already available as reference. Also it has the advantage of being able to borrow the semantic relations of the given WordNet. That leads in saving an enormous amount of time.

The WordNets developed using expansion approach is very much influenced by the source language and may not reflect the richness of the target language. Therefore there was a need for Hybrid Approach to achieve perfection with respect to WordNet development time and quality. In order to overcome this disadvantage the IndoWordNet Community classified the synsets in the source language as Universal, Pan Indian, In family, language-specific, etc. Each language initially developed the synsets for Universal and Pan Indian synsets and then proceeded to develop synsets which were specific to their respective language viz. language-specific synsets.

Another contribution is that our storage structure also provides the flexibility to include concepts specific to a language or group of language. We also provide for a mechanism in our storage structure whereby the concept can be accepted by all languages or a group of languages.

The rest of the paper is organized as follows – section 2 introduces the IndoWordNet, section 3 presents tools for IndoWordNet Development and limitations of the existing tool. The details of IndoWordNet Database design and its strengths are presented in section 4. Section 5 presents the future perspectives and conclusions.

2 IndoWordNet

The IndoWordNet is a linked structure of WordNets of major Indian languages from Indo-Aryan, Dravidian and Sino-Tibetan families. These WordNets have been created by following the expansion approach from Hindi WordNet which was made available free for research in 2006. Since then a number of Indian languages have been creating their language WordNets (Pushpak Bhattacharyya, 2010). The issues faced while using the expansion approach which affect the storage structure are discussed next.

2.1 Challenges faced while using Expansion Approach

The challenges faced while using the Expansion Approach are:

1. *Linking of contextual words:* Using the expansion approach, certain synsets may totally get omitted because of the variety of shades of meaning of different words.
2. *Linking a concept which is not present in the source language.*
3. *Coining of words:* Another issue that remains to be resolved is how far the lexicographer can be given the liberty to coin new words.
4. *Coverage of synsets:* Though the meaning of many words are known to the people and are not found in common literature, but one may find some of the words possibly in poetry. Whether we have to cover them is also a question (Walawalikar et al., 2010).

Some of the challenges were addressed in the following ways:

1. The first and second challenge was addressed by creating language specific synsets and validating with experts before finalization.
2. The third challenge was addressed by following two approaches: first was by adapting the source language word and second approach was coining of new words.

3. The fourth challenge was addressed by adding such words towards the end of the synonymous set.

3 Tools for IndoWordNet Development

During the development of IndoWordNet we felt the need of various tools developed which drove us to reconsider the storage strategy used to store the IndoWordNet.

3.1 Existing tools

1. For the synset creation, we use the offline tool, Synset Creation Tool provided by IIT Bombay along with Hindi WordNet sysnets. This standalone interface allows users to view the Hindi synsets, concepts, example sentences on one side and simultaneously keying the target language synsets, concepts and example sentence. The tool also has the Princeton WordNet English synsets interlinked. The generated target language synset files which are stored in a flat text files have extension as .syns.
2. English-Hindi Linkage Tool is a heuristic based tool to link Hindi-English synsets.
3. Synset Categorization Tool is used to chose common linkable synsets across all languages by classifying them as Universal, Pan Indian, In family, language-specific, Rare, Synthesized and Core.
4. The Sense Marking Tool is used to find the synset coverage of a WordNet.

3.2 Limitations of existing tools with respect to the storage structure

The tools used for the development of WordNets using the Expansion approach were mostly based on flat files. Flat files have their own advantages but there are several disadvantages too. Some of the problems faced while working on the above tools were as follows:

1. Synset counting with respect to different criteria such as getting the synset count belonging to a specific grammatical category or range.
2. Merging synset files, finding common set of synsets
3. Security and Data integrity
4. Status of synsets – to know whether the synset is validated or not.
5. Additional data about synsets (meta data – source, useful links, video, audio, domain, images which gives additional information about the synset, etc).
6. Also it is difficult to store lexical and semantic relations between words and synsets in a flat file.

The major contribution presented in this paper is the storage design we implemented for IndoWordNet in form of solutions to the above problems. This design related solutions to the above problems are:

1. The data is stored in a systematic and classified manner.
2. Meta data feature - to store additional information about the synset.
3. Language-dependent information such as synset entries in the target language, lexical relations, etc. is maintained in the individual WordNets.
4. Language-independent information such as semantic relation, ontological details of a concept, etc. is stored only once and is made available to all the language-specific modules via the inter-lingual relations.
5. Centrally controlled system for issuing Ids in case of language specific synsets.

In order to provide support for a systematic and rapid expansion approach for development of good quality WordNets for languages, it was felt essential to have the data stored in databases in a systematic manner using normalised database design.

4 Database Design Details

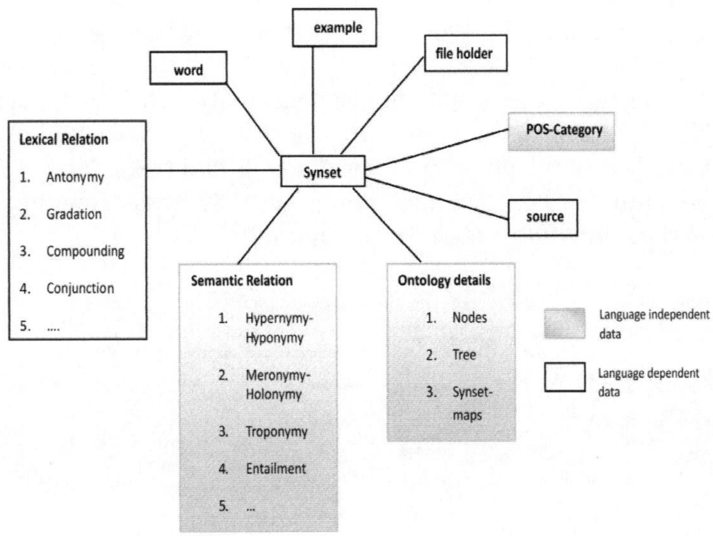

Figure 1: Database design depicting language dependent data and language independent data using colour coding.

The IndoWordNet database is designed to maintain the data for a WordNet in two databases. The common data such as semantic relations and ontology details for all languages are maintained in a common database called wordnet-master. The wordnet master maintains the data shared by all the languages. This database will keep tables which borrow the relations from the source WordNet (Hindi WordNet). The wordnet-master includes tables for semantic relations. It will include all ontology related tables in English.

The synset data for a language is maintained in a separate database for each language called wordnet-<respective-language>. Here respective-language is to be replaced by the actual language name for e.g. wordnet-konkani, wordnet-hindi, wordnet-marathi for Konkani, Hindi and Marathi languages respectively. Figure 1 shows the language dependent and language independent data represented in colour coding.

WordNet classifies word meanings into four basic lexical categories: nouns, verbs, adjectives and adverbs. Each synset in the WordNet is linked with other synsets through the well-known lexical and semantic relations. Semantic relations are between synsets and lexical relations are between words. These relations serve to organize the lexical knowledge base.

4.1 Salient features of using IndoWordNet Database design

Some of the salient features of using IndoWordNet Database design for storing synset data are as follows:

- Centralized database for common concepts and language databases for language concepts.

- Incorporates both merge-approach and expansion approach data
- Design provides for developing a centrally controlled system for issuing Ids in case of concepts specific to a language or language group.
- Open, scalable, normalized and modular design.
- Maintains language-specific relations in the WordNets.
- Achieves maximal compatibility across the different resources.
- Can be used for building the WordNets relatively independently (re)-using existing resources.
- Supports development of online and offline applications such as dictionary, synset creation tool, multilingual information retrieval, etc. Speeds up retrieval and processing time;
- Stores semantic, lexical relations,ontological details and Meta-data;

  All the above features make it a flexible design. The Entity-Relationship diagram for IndoWordNet database design is shown in Figure 2.

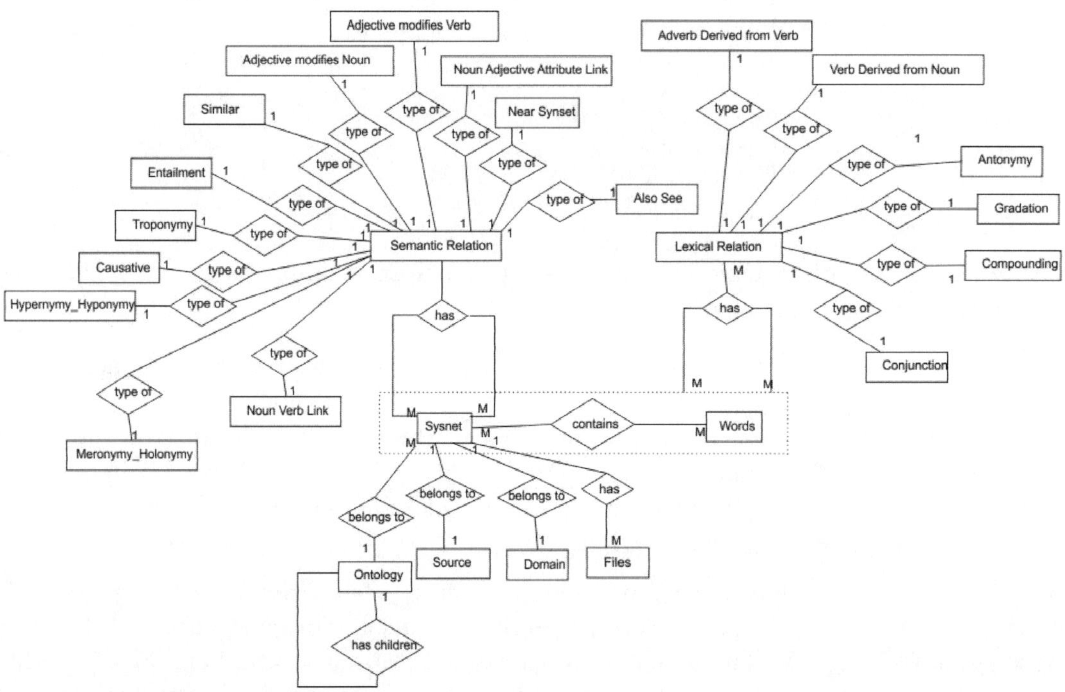

Figure 2: Entity Relationship diagram for IndoWordNet Database Design.

Conclusion and perspectives

The advantages of the IndoWordNet Database design are: Different WordNets can be compared and checked cross-linguistically which will make them more compatible. It will be possible to use the database for multilingual information retrieval, by expanding words in one language to related words in another language. The IndoWordNet Database design can be used for development of online and offline applications such as Multi-lingual Dictionary, WordNet for public use, etc. The IndoWordNet Application Programming Interfaces developed by Goa University which helps the developer to access and modify the IndoWordNet database is developed using IndoWordNet database schema.

References

George A. Miller, Richard Beckwith, Christiane Fellbaum, Derek Gross, and Katherine Miller (Revised August 1993). *Introduction to WordNet: An On-line Lexical Database.*

George A. Miller 1995. *WordNet: A Lexical Database for English.*

Fellbaum, C. (ed.). 1998. *WordNet: An Electronic Lexical Database, MIT Press.*

Pushpak Bhattacharyya, Christiane Fellbaum, Piek Vossen 2010. *Principles, Construction and Application of Multilingual WordNets, Proceedings of the 5th Global Word Net Conference (Mumbai-India), 2010.*

Pushpak Bhattacharyya, *IndoWordNet, Lexical Resources Engineering Conference 2010 (LREC2010), Malta, May, 2010.*

Shantaram Walawalikar, Shilpa Desai, Ramdas Karmali, Sushant Naik, Damodar Ghanekar, Chandralekha D'souza and Jyoti Pawar. *Experiences in Building the Konkani Word Net using the expansion Approach.* In Proceedings of the 5th Global WordNet Conference on Principles, Construction and Application of Multilingual WordNets (Mumbai-India), 2010.

Vossen P. (ed.). 1998. *EuroWordNet: A Multilingual Database with Lexical Semantic Networks.* Kluwer Academic Publishers, Dordrecht.

IndoWordNet Application Programming Interfaces

Neha R Prabhugaonkar[1] *Apurva S Nagvenkar*[1] *Ramdas N Karmali*[1]
(1) GOA UNIVERSITY, Taleigao - Goa
nehapgaonkar.1920@gmail.com, apurv.nagvenkar@gmail.com, rnk@unigoa.ac.in

ABSTRACT
Work is currently under way to develop WordNet for various Indian languages. The IndoWordNet Consortium consists of member institutions developing their own language WordNet using the expansion approach. Many tools and utilities have been developed by various institutes to help in this process. In this paper, we discuss an object oriented Application Programming Interface (API) that we have implemented to facilitate easy and rapid development of tools and other software resources that require WordNet access and manipulation functionality. The main objective of IndoWordNet Application Programming Interface (IWAPI) is to provide access to the WordNet resource independent of the underlying storage technology. The current implementation manipulates data stored in a relational database. Furthermore the IWAPI also supports parallel access and manipulation of WordNets in multiple languages.

In this paper, we discuss functional requirements, design and the implementation of IndoWordNet API and its uses.

KEYWORDS: WordNet, Application Programming Interface (API), WordNet CMS, IndoWordNet, IndoWordNet Database, WordNet Website.

1 Introduction

An Application Programming Interfaces (API) is defined as a set of commands, functions and protocols which developer can use when building software. It allows the developer to use predefined functions to interact with systems, instead of writing them from scratch. APIs are specially crafted to expose only chosen functionality and/or data while safeguarding other parts of the application which provides the interface. The characteristics of good API (Joshua Bloch, 2007) are as follows:

- Easy to learn and use, hard to misuse.
- Easy to read and maintain code that uses it.
- It is programming language neutral.
- Sufficiently powerful to support all computational requirements.

The IndoWordNet API provides a simple and easy way to access and manipulate the WordNet resource independent of the underlying storage technology. The functionality is exposed through a set of well defined objects that developer can create and manipulate as per his/her processing requirement. Although the current implementation expects the data to be available in a relational database, a two layered architecture separates functionality offered to the user from the data access functionality. This allows for future enhancements to support any data storage technology and design without changing the API provided to the developer.

The IndoWordNet API allows parallel access and updates to single or multiple language WordNets. A new design using relational database has been implemented for this purpose. This database design (IndoWordNet database) supports storage of multiple language WordNets. An effort has been made to optimize the design to reduce redundancy. Certain data common across all languages i.e. ontology information, semantic relationships, etc are stored in a separate master database and data specific to a language i.e. synsets, lexical relationships, etc are stored separately for each language in the database of respective language. The rest of the paper is organised as follows – section 2 discusses functional requirements of IWAPI, section 3 presents the architecture and design of IWAPI. The implementation details of IWAPI are presented in section 4. Section 5 presents the conclusion.

2 Functional Requirements

Users often have to rely on others to perform functions that he/she may not be able or permitted to do by themselves. Similarly, virtually all software has to request other software to do some things for it. To accomplish this, the asking program uses a set of standardized requests, called application programming interfaces that have been defined for the program being called upon. Developer can make requests by including calls in the code of their applications. The syntax is described in the documentation of the application being called. By providing a means for requesting program services, an API is said to grant access to or open an application.

Following information needs to be maintained for any WordNet resource. The synsets of the langauge which includes concept definition, usage examples and a set of synonym words (Miller, 1993). Each synset also belongs to a specific lexical class, namely noun, adjective, verbs and adverbs. There is also an ontology maintained and every synset maps to a specific ontology node in this hierarchy. The synsets are related through semantic relations and words are related through lexical relations. IWAPI should allow developer to access and manipulate above information. Besides the above requirement it was also felt that it should be possible to maintain additional information about the synsets i.e. an image describing a concept, pronunciations of words in the synsets, links to websites and other resources, etc. The IWAPI should also support storage and access to such additional information. The developer based on his application requirement may also require accessing multiple language WordNets simultaneously. The IWAPI should also support this feature.

3 Architecture and Design

The IWAPI has two layered architecture. The upper layer is the Application layer and the lower layer is the Data layer. The class diagram of IndoWordNet API (Application layer) is shown below. The Application layer exposes the set of classes and methods which the developer will use to access and manipulate the WordNets as discussed in section 2. The Application layer does not directly access the data stored on the disk but uses Data layer for this purpose. The Data layer provides this service through a set of data classes and methods which it exposes to the Application layer. The Data layer understands the design and storage technology used to store the data i.e. relational database, flat text files, indexed files, XML etc. The Data layer is responsible for actual access and manipulation of data stored in files/database and is expected to reorganize the data in memory so that it can be exposed to the Application layer using the Data objects. This protects the Application layer from changes in storage technology or storage design. In the current implementation the Data layer accesses the data from relational

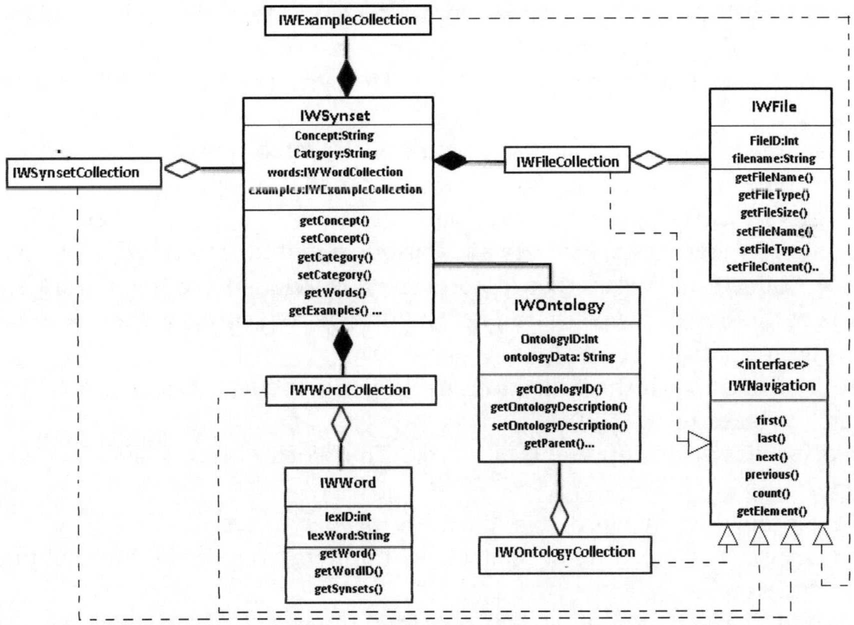

Figure 1: A simplified Class diagram of IndoWordNet API (Application Layer).

database. In future any changes in the storage method would only require a new Data layer to be implemented for that specific storage technology. Only the Application layer classes are exposed to the developer and Data layer classes are hidden so any changes will not affect the tools and software already created by the developer. The implementation maintains the classes and objects belonging to the different layers in separate libraries facilitating replacement of Data layer when desired.

Some of the important classes of Application Layer are as follows:

1. **IWAPI :** A static class that allows initialising the IndoWordNet API library for use. To use the IndoWordNet API the first thing you need to do is authenticate the user i.e. ***IWAPI.init ("username","password");***
   This class manage connectivity to language specific databases. By establishing a single connection with the master database, you can connect to multiple language specific databases using, IWAPI.getLanguageObject(IWLanguageConstants.KONKANI); where IWLanguageConstant is static class that contains all the constant names for language specific databases. It also allows developer to maintain Meta information:
   - To get/add/delete various lexical and semantic relation.
   - To get/add/delete various property values of lexical relation such as action, amount, color, direction, etc and semantic relations.
   - To manipulate domain names, grammatical categories, ontology nodes, ontology hierarchy, etc.
2. **IWLanguage:** A class that provides connection to language WordNets by using ***IWLanguage langObj = IWAPI.getLanguageObject(IWLanguageConstants.KONKANI);*** Using the langObj i.e the object of IWLanguage it allows the developer:
   - To get the total number of synsets, total number of words of a given language.
   - To get all synsets/words belonging to a domain/ category/range of Id's.
   - To create/destroy a new synset, word, domain, category, ontology, relation, etc.
   - To get words and synsets having a given semantic and lexical relations.
3. **IWSynset:** A class that represents a synset. The synset object of IWSynset class allows developer:
   - To get the concept, translated concept, transliterated concept of a given synset which is present in the database. To get usage examples of the synset.
   - To get/set the category, domain, source, concept of a given synset.
   - To add/remove examples, files and various semantic/lexical relations of a synset.
4. **IWSynsetCollection:** A class that represents a collection of synsets. It allows developer:
   - To get the size of the collection i.e. the number of synsets present in the collection, using the method, count();
   - To iterate through the collection, using getElement(); first(); next(); previous(); last(); respectively.
5. **IWWord:** A class that represents a word. The word object of IWWord class allows developer:
   - To get the id of the word, to get synsets for a given word.
   - To get various lexical relation such as antonymy relation, compounding relation, gradation relation, etc.
   - To add/remove various lexical relations for specified synset and word such as antonymy relation, compounding relation, gradation relation, etc.
6. **IWWordCollection:** A class that represents a collection of words for a synset. It allows developer:
   - To get the size of the collection i.e. the number of words present in the collection.
   - To iterate through the collection, using getElement(); first(); next(); previous(); last(); respectively.
   - It also allows deleting a word, to insert a word at a particular location, to move a word to a particular location, to change the priority of the words, etc.
7. **IWExampleCollection:** A class that represents a collection of examples for a synset. It

allows developer:

- To get the size of the collection i.e. the number of examples present in the collection.
- To iterate through the collection, using getElement(); first(); next(); previous(); last(); respectively.
- To move the current example at a specified location, to insert a new element in a collection at a specified location, to insert a new element at last position in the collection, etc.

8. **IWFile:** A class that represents files. Using the object of IWFile class it allows developer:
   - To get/set the file content, file Id, file size, file type, etc.
9. **IWOntology:** A class that represents ontology node. Each synset is mapped to an ontology node in the ontology tree. Using the object of IWOntology class the developer can
   - get/set the ontology Id, ontology data, ontology translated data, ontology transliterated data,
   - get/set the ontology description, ontology translated description, and ontology transliterated description from the database.
10. **IWOntologyCollection:** Collection of child nodes for a given onto node. Using the object of IWOntology class it allows developer:
    - To get the size of the collection i.e. the number of ontology nodes present in the collection.
    - To iterate through the collection, using getElement(); first(); next(); previous(); last(); respectively.

    Similarly we have classes such as **IWAntonymyCollection, IWGradationCollection, IWMeroHoloCollection, IWNounVerbLinkCollection,** etc.
11. **IWException:** A class that defines all the exceptions which occurs in case of error or failure.

Note: There are additional classes like IWAntonymy, IWGradation and IWMeronymyHolonymy which are the private classes used internally in the API and are hidden from the developer.

The Data layer will change depending on the storage technology but the Application layer will remain unchanged. The Data layer deals with encapsulation of the storage design. It provides a standard interface to the application layer. The Data layer supports all the operations needed to be performed on the data. Data Layer consists of the following important classes:

1. **IWDb:** A class that represents to a database/file store.
2. **IWCon:** A class that represents up an authenticated connection to a database/file store.
3. **IWStatement:** A class which contains all data manipulation functionality required by the Application layer.
4. **IWResult:** A class which returns result to the application layer i.e. synsets, collections, etc.

4 Implementation

Reference implementation of IndoWordNet API is done in JAVA and PHP. The size of JAVA jar file is 224 KB and the size of PHP API package is 452 KB. The IndoWordNet API classes are stored in 4 packages:

- **unigoa.indowordnet.api:** This package consists of important classes of Application Layer such as the IWAPI, IWLanguage, IWSynset, etc. as discussed earlier in section 3.
- **unigoa.indowordnet.constants:** This package consists of static classes which define all

the constants used by API and do not contain any methods.

- **unigoa.indowordnet.maintenance:** This package consists of a class which allows the developer to maintain master data.
- **unigoa.indowordnet.storage:** This package consists of classes of Data Layer such as the IWDb, IWCon, IWStatement and IWResult. They provide a standard interface to the application layer and their implementation will change depending on the storage technology.

```
1.  public class Synset {
2.  public static void main(String[] args) {
3.  String userName = "userName";
4.  String password = "password";
5.  int synsetID = 1;
6.  int category = IWGrammaticalCategoryConstants.NOUN;
7.  String concept = "Concept Definition";
8.  String word = "word";
9.  String exmple1 = "example1";
10. { IWAPI.init(userName, password);
11.  IWLanguage languageObject =
12.  IWAPI.getLanguageObject(IWLanguageConstants .KONKANI);
13.  IWSynset synsetObject =
14.  languageObject.createSynset(synsetID, concept,
     category);
     IWWord wordObject = null;
15.  try { wordObject = languageObject.getWord(word);
16.  } catch (IWException ex) {
17.  wordObject = languageObject.createWord(word);
18.  }
19.  synsetObject.addWord(wordObject);
20. synsetObject.addExample(exmple1);
21. String data = "";
22. data += "Synset ID: " + synsetObject.getSynsetID();
23. data += "\nConcept: " + synsetObject.getConcept();
24. data += "\nCategory: " + synsetObject.getCategory();
25. data += "\nWords: ";
26. IWWordCollection wordCollection = synsetObject.getWords();
27. do {
28. IWWord wordObject1 = wordCollection.getElement();
29. data += wordObject1.getWord() + " ";
30. } while (wordCollection.next());
31. data += "\nExamples: ";
32. IWExampleCollection exampleCollection = synsetObject.getExamples();
33. do {
34. data += exampleCollection.getElement() + " ";
35. } while (wordCollection.next());
36. System.out.print(data);
37. } catch (IWException ex) {
38.   System.err.println(ex.errorMessage());
39.   } } }
40.
```

Figure 2: Example to create a new synset using IndoWordNet API.

An example to illustrate the use of IndoWordNet API is shown above. The basic flow is as follows: Initialize the API library and authenticate the user (line no. 10). Connect to a language WordNet (Konkani WordNet line 11-12). The same method can be used repeatedly to create connections to multiple language WordNets. Each call will return an object representing connection to a language WordNet. This facilitates simultaneous access to multiple WordNets. Create a new synset using the language object (line no. 14). Add a word or an example to the new synset (line no. 19-20). Similarly, to get synset information of a given synset Id. First, create the object of the synset, and use the synset object to get synset information (line no. 22-39).

Conclusion

The IndoWordNet API can be used to facilitate easy and rapid development of tools and other WordNet related software resources with minimal effort, with enhanced features by a developer in a very short time for any language. The ease and speed at which new tools to support research community can be developed was demonstrated during the implementation of WordNet Content Management System(CMS) which used IndoWordNet API implemented in PHP. A demo paper on WordNet Content Management System has been accepted at COLING 2012. The Konkani WordNet website is deployed using WordNet CMS.

The IndoWordNet API has been successfully used by other IndoWordNet members to develop web-based tools such as bi-lingual dictionary, multi-lingual dictionary, Lexical Relation Tool to capture various lexical relations such as antonym, gradation, etc. A Synset Management System is under development to assist creation of language specific synsets and manage their linkages to other Indian language WordNets. We expect that in future the IndoWordNet API's will be used for the development of tools and software resources by IndoWordNet members.

References

George A. Miller, Richard Beckwith, Christiane Fellbaum, Derek Gross, and Katherine Miller 1993. *Introduction to WordNet: An On-line Lexical Database.*

George A. Miller 1995. *WordNet: A Lexical Database for English.*

Joshua Bloch 2007. *How to Design a Good API and Why it Matters.*

Pushpak Bhattacharyya, *IndoWordNet, Lexical Resources Engineering Conference 2010 (LREC2010), Malta, May, 2010.*

Pushpak Bhattacharyya, Christiane Fellbaum, Piek Vossen 2010. *Principles, Construction and Application of Multilingual WordNets, Proceedings of the 5th Global Word Net Conference (Mumbai-India), 2010.*

Author Index

Association for Computational Linguistics
209 N. Eighth Street
Stroudsburg, Pennsylvania 18360

CURRAN ASSOCIATES INC
proceedings
.com